DUELING

DUELING

THE CULT OF HONOR IN
FIN-DE-SIÈCLE GERMANY

Kevin McAleer

PRINCETON UNIVERSITY PRESS   PRINCETON, NEW JERSEY

Copyright © 1994 by Princeton University Press
Published by Princeton University Press, 41 William Street,
Princeton, New Jersey 08540
In the United Kingdom: Princeton University Press,
Chichester, West Sussex
All Rights Reserved.

Library of Congress Cataloging-in-Publication Data

McAleer, Kevin, 1961–
Dueling : the cult of honor in fin-de-siècle Germany /
Kevin McAleer.
p.   cm.
Includes bibliographical references and index.
ISBN 0-691-03462-1 (alk. paper)
1. Dueling—Germany—History.   I. Title.
CR4595.G3M35   1994
394'.8 0943—dc20   94-4401

This book has been composed in Adobe Palatino

Princeton University Press books are printed
on acid-free paper and meet the guidelines
for permanence and durability of the Committee
on Production Guidelines for Book Longevity
of the Council on Library Resources

Printed in the United States of America

1   3   5   7   9   10   8   6   4   2

Man has always found it easier to sacrifice
his life than to learn the multiplication table.

W. Somerset Maugham,
"Mr. Harrington's Washing"
(1927)

Contents

List of Illustrations

I would like to thank Dr. Adelheid Rasche and Eva-Maria Borgwaldt for the reproductions from the Staatliche Museen zu Berlin, Kunstbibliothek; Dr. Edith Schipper and Dr. Pointner for those from the Bayerische Staatsbibliothek, Munich; and Heidrun Klein and Dr. Karl H. Pütz for those lent by the Bildarchiv Preussischer Kulturbesitz, Berlin.

Acknowledgments

FIVE YEARS have spanned this work's gestation, and that is a good long time to be pregnant with thoughts on a single theme. It is therefore with a sweet, rondo sense of closure that I write these final words for the beginning of a book that had its start, and now its finish, in the once and future capital of a unified Germany, Berlin. It is more than a little gratifying to be able to deliver finally a work in the place where it was once so passionately conceived—and to at last get on with something else. But before I do, and in a fine academic tradition, I want to thank those people who were intimately associated with this book's production. Some were directly involved, some indirectly, and some even without their knowledge. The writing of history is a metabolic process, into it flows the entire person, not just the front of one's brain, and with that in mind, and asking the brief indulgence of the reading public. . . .

I thank first my adviser, Professor Allan Mitchell of the University of California at San Diego, for cheerful and worldly guidance from the project's inception through to his incisive reading and criticism of the manuscript's various revisions, on each occasion probably muttering to himself, in the manner of Dorothy Parker, "What fresh hell is this?" I also owe special debts to Professor Robert Nye of the University of Oklahoma and Professor István Deák of Columbia University not only for their very civilized appraisal of the manuscript, but for their constant readiness to share with me the results of their own research into the modern French and Austro-Hungarian duels, respectively. Professor John Marino, of the University of California at San Diego, also offered some very fine pointers. My Musil muse, Professor David Luft, also of U.C.S.D., was and remains a constant inspiration.

The research and writing of this book was carried out in three stages, on three continents. From 1988 to 1989 in West Berlin, the German Academic Exchange Service (DAAD) generously supported my inquiry into its nation's dueling heritage. Professor Jürgen Kocka of Berlin's Freie Universität aided in prolonging my stay so that I could be present in body if not in mind when the Wall came down—so absorbed was I in what came to be this work and so ivory-tower high above the city in my elegantly unappointed eighth-floor Fasanenstrasse flat, that I did not learn of this world-historical event until two days later, making me feel a rather exceptional fellow. Eva-Lore Jacob, Karin Lafferentz-Krueger, and the ravishing Elke née Jungkuhn of

West Berlin all valiantly suffered my typewriter's incessant clacking and kept the vicious downstairs tenants at bay. Jonathan Kalb and Julie Heffernan, fellow Americans (using the term advisedly since they are first and foremost New Yorkers), kept my precarious sanity intact. Training partners Christian Heinrich and Boris Bill kept my competitive edge stropped, allowing me to address the grinding brainwork of dissertation-writing with renewed vigor; albeit in Boris's case, with usually renewed swelling on the right side of my jaw. Dr. Manfred Zimmermann, formerly of the University of Halle, was a boon research companion in East Berlin, and well he might have been. Anja Fodor and her husband Herbert were gracious hosts during my Munich sojourn, proving that Bavarian *Gemütlichkeit* is really not all that it is cracked up to be—but more. Euriel Donval and her family were dazzling hosts in Paris during the French leg of my research and I was lucky to have gotten any work done at all. (I ask you, is it really necessary to spend four or five hours every day just dining?) In Madrid on my bullfighting junket, undertaken—I kept telling my-self—so as to gain insight into the process of modern ritual violence, Dave Ortiz was everything one could want in a maestro of ceremonies, and no fancy cape-twirling tricks either.

I was able to transform my 1990 dissertation on the German duel into a book during a postdoctoral year as a Wiener research fellow in Comparative European History at the University of Tel Aviv. I would like to thank Tel Aviv University's Institute for German History for its financial backing, and its director Professor Shulamit Volkov for not only this but her more general support as well. Ruth Sauer, Miriam Broshi, and Gila Michalowski all made my workaday routine at the Wiener Library a dream. My roommate in Tel Aviv, Michael Berkowitz of Ohio State University, assisted with my textual tinkering and, more important, provided needed comic relief from its drudgery; most notably, in our discussions of that certain monumental "sheath" of Theodor Herzl's in the basement of the Zionist Archives ... but that is another story. Ann Swersky slogged through one of the many final drafts, and, like the lovely Yiddish mama she is, mended and darned with care. Dr. Ilana Bet-El of the University of Tel Aviv, and her clan, were like a second family, and I will confess now to drinking Elijah's wine on Passover.

Home in Los Angeles I put the manuscript through its gun-lap paces. Old school chums Bart Devaney and John Costello kept my writing somewhat honest through a) their remorseless wit, and b) their complete lack of respect for what I was doing. My genius brother, Timothy, endured numerous cries for assistance with noble forbearance, enabling me to clarify and better express various of the book's ideas and one of the book's acknowledgments. My oldest sister, Jennifer Klein, permitted me illimitable use of her word processor, facilitating the manuscript's endless modifications. The little sister, Melinda, kept my spirits buoyed with chocolate chip cookies and icky-baby hugs.

Back in Berlin, at the Arbeitsstelle für Vergleichende Gesellschaftsgeschichte under the direction of Professors Jürgen Kocka and Hannes Siegrist, I was graciously afforded the leisure, facilities, intellectual environment, and splendid colleagues to feed upon with creative lust and wrap the book up in a timely fashion. Princeton University Press's own Lauren Osborne and Bill Laznovsky were superb editors, and, as goes without saying, any deficiencies in the book can never be traced to their unstinting professionalism and competence.

Most of all I wish to thank those two people who through some undeserved twist of fate were assigned the task of being my parents, Tom and Doris McAleer. Although they have always managed to contain themselves, I am sure their enthusiasm for the arcane subject of German dueling verges somewhere between their felt passion for guano farming and their curiosity about the love life of the banana slug. They have nonetheless indulged my efforts in manifold ways, and it is to them, who taught me the meaning of personal sacrifice better than a whole generation of duelists could, that with love and affection this work is humbly dedicated.

December 1993
Berlin, Germany

DUELING

Introduction

AT THE fin de siècle, most civilized countries had wiped dueling from their slate of national customs. In America, where Yankee dueling dandies had never been much in evidence, formal dueling died with the Confederacy in 1865. England had foresworn the activity in the 1840s. The Benelux and Scandinavian countries and the Swiss cantons had largely jettisoned the duel by the half-century mark as well. By the early twentieth century, Czar Nicholas II of Russia and the kings of Italy and Spain had taken the international Anti-Dueling League under their protection. The practice was also fading fast with the glories of empire in Austria-Hungary where in 1904 the Minister of War issued an unprecedented edict sanctioning the membership of all inactive and reserve officers who wished to join the Anti-Dueling League. Although the French continued to duel with a vengeance, their engagements were more gay romp than mortal combat.

At the fin de siècle, the Germans were Europe's most tenacious and serious duelists—serious, because the most striking aspect of the German duel was its deadliness. This is what makes the German duel so fascinating, compelling the historian to ask why it endured into the twentieth century with such persistence. For in order to derive the duel's essentially "German" character, it is necessary to probe the question of its *lethal* character—only then can it be vividly distinguished from other national styles still lingering at the time. Dueling viewed through this morbid lens neatly refracts certain uncommon dynamics of imperial German society, symbolized and exemplified in many respects by the practice.

One can adduce five main reasons for the German duel's singularly terminal quality. Accordingly, the book is divided into as many main chapters, each addressing one of these hallmarks:

    1. *Standesehre.* This was a term used often by duelists to describe why they dueled. It translates roughly as "caste-honor," meaning the collective honor of German society's upper strata. Its definition also denoted group solidarity over and against the lower orders, for in every "affair," or *Ehrenhandel*, the participants were representing not only their own interests but those of their class. The duel drew a strict line of division between "men of honor" (*Ehrenmänner*) and the rest of society, which enjoyed none of the psychic, social, or legal entitlements of honorable status. Among German males, in order to be considered *salonfähig*—fit for good society—it was necessary that one also be *satisfaktionsfähig*— capable of dispensing satisfaction in a duel. Highly dangerous rencontres endowed this term with the real substance of character, and so upper-class men of honor also pretended a moral supremacy that bolstered their claim to leadership of the German nation.

2. *University Dueling.* Quite a few men of honor acquired both their dueling zeal and their caste consciousness at the university. Elitist sword-dueling fraternities at German institutes of higher learning primed students for the social expectations that would await them upon graduation. These practiced duelists staffed important posts in the imperial establishment and brought severe imperatives to bear in postgraduate affairs of honor—partly in an effort to distinguish these mature duels from their juvenilian swordplay.

3. *Army.* The army exerted an enormous influence on civilian society in Wilhelmine Germany, and the duel was an integral component of the officer's code of honor. Because officers considered the duel a professional hazard of their risky vocation, the army's authority lent the practice its peculiarly somber character of a moral duty rather than an act of heroic voluntarism as was the case in France. This German ethos fostered a duel that was a notable widowmaker, the immense reserve officer corps—consisting of many former student duelists—helping to disperse the regular officer's exacting code and his perilous duel to a lay public whose idolatry of the army made adoption of military habits a spontaneous process.

4. *Pistols.* The officer's duel was so dangerous because in almost every instance he chose pistols or was commanded to choose pistols by a military court of honor. Consequently, these weapons (as opposed to comparatively innocuous sabers) became the choice of the private citizen, who—in what almost appears an attempt to outdo his role model—imposed exceedingly mortal stipulations for duels that would regularly conclude with one or even both combatants stretched in their blood.

5. *Women.* Another reason pistols were so ubiquitous in Germany was that women so often sparked the controversies emitting in a challenge. German men of honor perceived the duel as a most efficacious device by which to redeem a woman's honor, and pistols immeasurably raised the stakes. The sigh of Cupid's bow could portend a screaming bullet.

Apart from a concluding sixth chapter which compares dueling in the French Third Republic as a foil to its Rhenish rival, all of the chapters explicate individual aspects that gave the Wilhelmine duel its rare venomous bite. Johann Gottfried Herder (1744–1803) spoke of the idea of *Volksgeist*, or national character, a concept that was for him expressed most vividly in the language and letters of a nation. This notion has lately suffered at the hands of certain historiographic schools and their strained, clean-shaven treatments that do not sniff out, so much as snuff out the vital reality of a given historical situation. History will never be a science, not even a soft one—science is not even a "science"—and those histories written as if it were are usually about as edifying as a long, drawn-out, after-dinner belch—and never as satisfying. Therefore at the hazard of further stigmatization, it is my aim to recover this quasi-mystical idea of *Volksgeist* as expressed not in language and letters, but in the act of ritual violence. As the point of intersection between primordial destructive drives and civilizing impulses, ritual violence in the modern age also provides historians with a prime example of humankind's perennially ambivalent nature, thus serving to transcend universally an otherwise parochial German topic.

In an excellent work, *Blood Sport: A Social History of Spanish Bullfighting* (Philadelphia, 1991), Timothy Mitchell asserts that the stylized bull-baiting of Iberia's traditional *corrida* "is no trivial pastime, but the very mirror of Spain's social and historical traumas in the modern period."[1] A similar argument is often made for the Land of the Rising Sun, that to "understand [the code of] Bushido . . . is essential to a comprehension of the soul of Japan."[2] One hears comparable archetypal claims made for American baseball. The German duel, although its practitioners were few (the vast majority of Spaniards do not attend bullfights, most Japanese are not Samurai, and most Americans would probably have difficulty naming last year's World Series winner), likewise reflected German society at large, reproducing its best and worst qualities in that all-engulfing moment when senses swim and temples pound. In the process of describing this meeting place of dream and fantasy, I hope to challenge the conventional shibboleth of cultural anthropology that sees Mediterranean societies as far more sensitized to the *point d'honneur* than their neighbors to the north. And incidentally, as Robert Nye points out in his *Masculinity and Male Codes of Honor in Modern France* (Oxford, 1993), I am playing a little catch-up with the rapidly expanding field of women's history by submitting this specific study of German manhood.[3]

I have limited myself to an examination of the fin de siècle period, roughly from the 1880s to the First World War. It was during this long generation that dueling in Germany experienced its latest and most luxuriant flowering. It was also during the fin de siècle that the political debate surrounding the duel was most vehement. Contemporary tracts, essays, and monographs addressing the subject were excavated chiefly from the Bavarian *Staatsbibliothek*. Here also of exceptional value were the half-dozen dueling codes published after 1880, gangwaying a detailed analysis in chapter II of the manner in which duels unfolded, and dozens of French sources which formed the core of a chapter on the French duel. Material culled from the military archives of Munich, Stuttgart, and Karlsruhe facilitated a chapter on the officer duel. The Prussian Ministry of Justice records housed in Berlin's *Geheimes Staatsarchiv* were key for government documents. Stenographic minutes of Reichstag parliamentary sessions pertaining to the duel paid off handsomely in developing the political angle. These records also proved useful in comprehensive ways, providing a greater sense of the variegated issues at stake in the dueling question. Actual depictions of duels were hard to unearth, but for these a main source was the journal that the Social Democratic leader August Bebel in 1896 called the "official organ of the duelists" and that Theodor Fontane in *Effi Briest* (1896) described as "always know[ing] everything" with regard to duels—*Das Kleine Journal*, a Berlin daily of which the only extant copies for the years relevant to this study are housed in East Berlin's *Staatsbibliothek*.[4] General sources in West Berlin's *Staatsbibliothek* also proved beneficial. I made particular use of *belles lettres*, delving into the works of authors such as Alexander Pushkin, Heinrich and Thomas Mann, Theodor Fontane, Arthur Schnitzler, Guy de Maupassant, and Mark Twain for their own expert renditions on the dueling theme. If Lionel Trilling can say that "a large part of literature is properly historical, the recording and interpreting of personal, national, and cosmological events,"[5] then these writers were first-rate social historians. To gain an added visual perspective, I examined materials at the Axel Springer publishing house, as well as the Berlin *Kunstbibliothek* and *Bildarchiv*. I even witnessed the modern student duel, the *Mensur*, courtesy of several accommodating dueling corps from Berlin's Freie Universität, who shall remain nameless.

The reader will not discover tables of statistics. This is not due to any lack of interest by me in quantitative measurements. But as all historians of the duel can attest, available dueling statistics of almost any kind—criminal convictions, rates of fatality, demographic distribution, etc.—are notoriously unreliable, usually spotty, and often misleading. Rather than indecently expose readers to a recapitulation of dubious raw numbers, I have deployed them selectively in the narrative, which is appropriately footnoted.

The two most recent serious historical works on the subject of German dueling are V. G. Kiernan's *The Duel in European History: Honour and Reign of the Aristocracy* (Oxford, 1988) and Ute Frevert's *Ehrenmänner: Das Duell in der bürgerlichen Gesellschaft* (Munich, 1991). As may be surmised from their titles, these sweeping studies are conceptually antithetical to one another. Kiernan concentrates primarily on England and France in the early-modern period, but he consigns a section to the German duel, subsuming it under his overarching thesis that the European duel in modern times was the last bastion of aristocratic privilege against encroachment of mass industrialized society represented by a rising middle class. He labels dueling in the nineteenth century as "the phantom virtue of a bygone era" (p. 274). Weberian Frevert turns Marxist Kiernan on his head, arguing that the German duel in the modern era was in reality a middle-class institution, well integrated into the main currents of German bourgeois culture. Whereas Kiernan thus fails to credit the extent socially to which bourgeois participation in the Wilhelmine duel kept it flourishing until very late, Frevert misses the still essentially aristocratic character of the duel culturally in these final decades before the Great War. The implications of these facts for a reassessment of the German *Sonderweg* question will be taken up in my Conclusion.

Though grappling with these macro-issues, this study endeavours to simultaneously transcend the structuralist divisions—"feudal" or "bourgeois"—which have hitherto circumscribed discussion of the German duel, in order to explore the use of this combination ideologically in creating a type of neo-chivalry. Dueling was not the offspring of a conservative orthodoxy or the product of certain bourgeois moral-educational precepts, so much as it was a kind of attempt at recovery of an illusory German past in which men of honor righted all manner of wrong with a single stroke of the winking blade. The feudal conditions for chivalry had long faded from Imperial Germany, but as an extinguished star illuminates yet the night sky, chivalry irradiated the moral consciousness of the late-nineteenth-century duelist. The self-regard of the German duelist was that of a warrior, because the defining tenet of his masculinity was physical valor. This was also the keynote of the medieval knight, who was theoretically a saint (as standard-bearer of the Church) and a gentleman (as his Lady's loyal admirer), but was really first and last a warrior. Honor in the Middle Ages boiled down to courage, because this was the quality in greatest demand by a ruling warrior class that based its sovereign rights and dominion on military preparedness. And every time he dueled, the privileged and elitist German man of honor would figuratively close his visor, fix his lance, and tilt—at the spirit of the modern age. As I time-traveled with the duel, I began to feel a bit like the Connecticut Yankee in King Arthur's court, a foursquare American coming to grips with a Round Table mentality. Fritz Stern has written that "few societies in the modern world were so remote from reality as the Germans in the years of the empire."[6] German men of honor were even more psychologically detached from their immediate environment than the rest of their countrymen. They fancied themselves the last of a dying breed—and die they often did. It is a goal of this book to capture the texture of these psychic and emotional states through a close rendering of the duel's phenomenology: to rekindle the duel's spirit by emphasizing its objective details. I have therefore made generous use of direct quotations, listening for the duelist's unique voice and recording its sharp national and historical accents. "Just as one who has never seen it cannot properly appreciate the psychological phenomenon of war," men of honor would routinely insist, "so also is he alone equipped to assess the duel who has repeatedly experienced such things."[7] Despite such caveats—indeed, *because* of such caveats—it has been my objective to evoke a certain masculine ideal that to the modern mind must appear both extraordinary and grotesque. Yet in the higher social strata of Wilhelmine Germany this ideal was a conventional type that was realized and personified by duelists.

In shoptalk with German dueling expert Ute Frevert, I discovered that not only were our our methods dissimilar, our emphases assorted, and our theses at variance, but that our sentiments concerning the subject were diametrically opposed. Professor Frevert had begun her inquiry with open skepticism toward this institution of super-masculinity. In the course of her study, however, this reservation was transformed into grudging admiration for consequential men who saw life as fraught with purpose and who accepted accountability for the smallest action or word. I, on the other hand, having lived a very sheltered life, traipsed in wide-eyed as a marigold, undertaking my investigation with disproportionately high expectations; the cold Olympian detachment with which men blithely risked their lives seemed to me to conceal a depth of purpose. It did not. It concealed a value vacuum. Destitute of noble values by which to live, duelists embraced a set of aristocratic guidelines for which to die: a code of honor. They proved all-too-human, less modern-day knights than adolescent schoolboys in the locker room snapping towels to exhibit some simple-minded and vaguely slapstick notions of masculinity. Nevertheless, had their ritual not been so absurdly sublime—had they not run anything you could like about it firmly into the ground—had duelists not emerged as sanctimonious caricatures of themselves, I might have been more sparing in some of my judgments. But, during the progression of my study having become an apt pupil of their exigent code, I felt honor-bound to appraise them at their own rate of exchange and therefore give them the lie.

A close examination of the duel discloses a milieu circumscribed by a rigid, inequitable class structure and regulated by aggression and coercive relationships. It reveals a community marked by admiration for military force. It shows the overwhelming emphasis placed on a hard masculine approach to the detriment of womanhood. The duel exhibits a moralistic, intolerant, and tradition-bound world incapable of liberating self-irony. It suggests a society awash in romantic ideology that promoted the notion of regeneration through bloodshed, a society where liberal compromise increasingly gave way to faith in extreme and often violent solutions in the arbitration of social and political problems, a society where confrontation was taking the place of conciliation and humanistic dialogue. And, amid the collapse of enlightened values, one would at least expect a brutal honesty to surface. But no. For an analysis of the duel's accompanying code of honor sheds light on that society's hypocritical nature: its advocacy of physical courage while flaunting its moral complement; the emphasis on good breeding while encouraging a form of lawless ruffianism; the obsession with personal integrity while restricting it through the tyranny of a legalistic social tutelage; the chivalrous preoccupation with service in the cause of the "gentler sex" while claiming the lives of its loved ones.

Yet all of these attitudes were actually distortions of something fundamentally pure, worthy, and—if unable to think of a better word—honorable about the duel. Paraphrasing Scott Fitzgerald, a foul dust floated in the wake of its dream. The duel was an effort at dignity in a vulgar age, a gamble on quality. In an otherwise fear-ridden and very often drab and enervating world, the duel lent a bold dash of color. That which can succeed in intensifying our basic being-alive sense, even at the peril of total extinction, is never completely barren. And Wilhelmine society believed in manners. The duel was not only the safeguard of impeccable conduct, it personified decorum. To remain civil and sedate as someone tried to kill you pressed the limits of even the most fastidious politesse. In view of these somewhat redeeming features, it is not terribly surprising to find but scant trace of irony in lambent lines that Austrian author Arthur Schnitzler, critical of the duel throughout his life, wrote as he looked back on a never-never prewar world:

> Life was more beautiful, in any case, offered a nobler vision then— among other reasons, certainly because one had to risk it occasionally for something that in a higher or at least another sense was possibly nonexistent, or, at least according to the standards of today, was actually not worth the stake; for the honor or the virtue, for example, of a beloved wife, or for the good reputation of a sister, or more of the same emptiness. Anyway, it should be called to mind that in the course of the last decades it was necessary for one to sacrifice his life for much less and to no purpose, upon the command or wish of other people. In the duel, at

least one's own discretion had a certain say, even where it was seemingly a matter of compulsion, convention, or snobbery. That one had to reckon at all with the possibility or even the inevitability of duels within a certain circle,—that alone, believe me, gave the societal life a certain dignity, or at least a certain style, and lent the people of these circles, even the most insignificant or ridiculous, a certain bearing, indeed the appearance of a constant readiness to meet death—even if to you this phrase, used in such a connection, should appear all too resplendent.[8]

The duelist's soul was unquestionably tinged by a certain high-mindedness. But it was never sluiced thoroughly clean, and more is the pity. A little idealism, like a little knowledge, can be a dangerous thing; it can even change into its opposite. "Man is neither angel nor brute," wrote Pascal, "and the misfortune is that he who would act the angel acts the brute."[9] Perhaps I have grown cross with the German duel because, frankly, I am hopelessly smitten with what it aspired to be. Alive at the time and the situation warranting, I myself would have probably dueled, and without apology. This book, therefore, should be seen less as a lacerating critique than as a regret for what might have been, as an elegy to a romantic impulse that finally failed to beget Beauty and Goodness. Corny, but true.

CHAPTER I

The Last Imperial Knights

Sir Palomides and Sir Goneyeres entered the field, jousted,
and broke their spears. Then they both drew their swords;
with his first stroke Sir Palomides knocked his opponent to
the ground, and with his second stroke beheaded him. Then
Sir Palomides went to supper.
—Sir Thomas Malory, *Le Morte d'Arthur* (1485)[1]

THE FIRST SECTION of this initial chapter will serve as prologue
through consideration of the German duel's historical provenance. By
tracing its development across time, salient features will emerge to
distinguish it practicably and conceptually from other armed and violent clashes of the ancient and medieval eras. Although deep-fixed in
medieval chivalry, the German duel for honor seems paradoxically to
have found its most graphic, and in some ways fullest expression in
the final years of the *Kaiserreich*, a time when its inner tensions—and
those of the Empire it reproduced—became most readily visible in the
harsh glare of a brave new world of reason and progress.

Following this diachronic preamble, the chapter's second section ex-
amines Imperial Germany's penal system, judiciary, bureaucracy,
monarchy, and government, revealing the extent to which the dueling
ideology had ensconced itself within these critical institutions. Personal combat was a felony, but the Wilhelmine state apparatus was
honeycombed with personnel who retained very strong mental reservations vis-à-vis the law's dueling clauses. Governmental efforts to
contain Reichstag abolitionist bids were as tenacious as was unregen-
erate that fifth column of duelists whose uncompromising views the
ruling oligarchy represented.

The third and final section of this chapter emplaces the duel within
its social framework through a discussion of *Standesehre*, or caste
honor. Although there is difficulty in gauging the extent to which the
idea of caste honor may have been operative in other countries, it is
scarcely imaginable that any other group should have had as great a
stake in the notion of collective upper-class honor as the patriciate of
Europe's fastest industrializing nation. As Germany marched toward
the twentieth century, the beleaguered Junkers and their fellow caste

travelers became increasingly possessive of inherited prerogatives that were being steadily subject to the modern pressures of change. To counteract these erosive forces, they huddled together in the defensive circle of caste honor, with the duel serving as rallying point. As long as traditional privileges were paid for with lives, they remained well earned. In this sense, the German duel's elitist and perilous character were complementary facets. Co-extensive with Machiavelli's dictum that short of being loved a prince should be feared, the menacing duel helped invest the empire's so-called "upper ten thousand" with an aura of power and majesty that induced so much consternation among the lower classes. The German duel therefore appears the most relevant of all European types to the maintenance of an iniquitous political and social order.

ORIGINS

Whence the German duel? Wilhelmine jurists, politicians, and social observers seemed incapable of forming a comfortable attitude toward the custom without first considering its historicity. In fin-de-siècle Germany, where the issue of cultural decline was of preeminent concern and critics ceaselessly warned against the external threats to undefiled German *Kultur*, the duel assumed a symbolic national significance. To portray it, as did one *Reichspartei* conservative in 1912, as "a centuries-old, a millenia-old tradition of the Germanic race," or, as did the War Ministry in 1905, as a custom harking back to "the gray dawn of our people," was to accredit it with an honest Teutonic seal.[2] On the other hand, to assert a French, Spanish, or Italian legacy, was, in most arguments, to undermine its legitimacy entirely as an alien and, what was worse, latin import. Accordingly, abolitionists would habitually underscore the duel's supposedly latin origin, while advocates would contend a German heritage. But the one thing all Wilhelmine commentators on the duel had in common was that they were classicists at heart and would customarily inaugurate their historical litanies by citing the example of Greco-Roman society. Greeks and Romans, so went the abolitionist argument—and notwithstanding their latin claims—exhibited their personal honor in service to the state and in faithful obedience to its laws, not in an egoistic code with dueling as its awful guarantor. Exponents like Albert von Boguslawski were fond of countering that "in the Greek and Roman world individual honor paid *too much* deference to one's honor as a citizen." [my emphasis][3]

Even though the German word *Duell* derives from the Latin word *duellum* (from *bellum* and *duo*, war between two) it is hopeless to trace

the duel's ancestry back to the classical age. The Greeks included contests between sword-bearing hoplites in their Olympiads, but these
were national athletic spectacles, not personal conflict at private law.[4]
For the same reason, Roman gladiatorial bouts were not dueling either; moreover, gladiators were not of gentle birth but usually prison-
ers of war, slaves, or criminals. When the German chieftain Hermann
challenged the Roman general Marius to individual combat, Marius
rejected the call to battle on the principle that the centurion's life belonged to the Roman state and was not his to arbitrarily squander. He
commissioned a pair of gladiator stand-ins with whom Hermann was
in no mood to tangle. Even Hermann's original proposal would still
have been an engagement on behalf of a larger unit (like David and
Goliath) and not in defense of personal honor.[5] Historian of the duel
V. G. Kiernan correctly concludes that "the well-drilled Greek or
Roman was [not] the ancestor of the duelist."[6] Neo-classical defenders
of the duel were on weak ground.

The single combat for personal retribution had its beginnings as an
ancient Germanic custom whose most ardent practitioners were
pagan Scandinavians. They would stage their battles on lonely isles,
the two nude combatants strapped together at the chest. A knife
would be pressed into each of their hands. A signal would be given—
at which point they would stab each other like wild beasts. They
would flail away until one of them either succumbed or begged for
quarter. Gradually this ghoulish rite developed into a battle between
two dissidents (or their representatives) before a judge, and certain
rules of combat were observed. The Roman historian Tacitus mentions
how the belief was current that God would assist the man to victory
whose cause was just, and it is this notion that places the Nordic
knife fight a mincing step away from the medieval "ordeal," in which
the hand of God was thought to play a determining role in the outcome.[7]

God works in mysterious ways. One of the ordeal's more excruciat-
ing forms was to have the accused hold a fiery plate of iron for a period. Another was to pluck a consecrated ring from a vessel filled with
boiling water. In either instance, the victim's cooked forelimb was
then bandaged. After three days the dressing was removed and if
scalding was visible he was declared guilty. Ordealing was a disagreeable business but, in lieu of employing a callous-handed proxy, the
defendant was furnished the option of taking a solemn oath before
God as to his innocence. Understandably, the defendant frequently
availed himself of the oath, often perjuring himself in the hope that
omniscient God would empathize and not subject him to a hotter punishment than even the ordeal could devise.[8]

To save people from eternal perdition, Gundebald King of the Burgundians legally instituted the trial by battle. In Gall's *Lex Burgundiorum* of A.D. 501, the sundry Celtic, German, and Roman traditions dovetailed in a single code to regulate the practice known as judicial combat. The two litigants—or their champions if one or both were women, elderly, disabled, or clergy—would take their respective places on black-veiled seats, submit themselves to a religious ceremony, and swear an oath that they had no magical charms or potions at their disposal, presumably a primitive form of drug-testing. At the marshal's command, the challenger would fling down the *Fehdehandschuh*, or "feuding glove," before the feet of his opponent, who would then accept the challenge by snatching it up.[9]

> In the law in Northern Germany care was taken that the advantage of the sun was equally divided between the combatants; they fought on foot, with bare heads and feet, clad in tunics with sleeves reaching only to the elbow, simple gloves, and no defensive armor except a wooden target covered with hide, and bearing only an iron boss; each carried a drawn sword, but either might have as many as he pleased in his belt. Even when nobles were concerned, who fought on horseback, it was the rule that they should have no defensive armor save a leather-covered wooden shield and a glove to cover the thumb; the weapons allowed were the lance, sword, and dagger, and they fought bare-headed and clad in linen tunics.[10]

These struggles were to the bitter end. Later, it seems, commoners were restricted to fighting on foot with wooden stocks, and sword and horseplay gradually became the preserve of the nobility, whose engagements were nonetheless often as feral as those of peasants. In one account, a pair of knights dismounted from their steeds and vied with two-handed swords until exhaustion set in; they began wrestling, groping for chinks in the armor, when one had his testicles manually ripped away.[11] Those lying in submission were allowed to plead for mercy, but even if clemency was approved by the victor, the overseers of the combat, viewing defeat as a heavenly judgment and proof of guilt, would frequently string the loser up at a nearby gallows.[12] Vanquished proxies would escape with a chopped-off right hand; but their principals, kept off to one side with nooses about their necks, would be immediately attended to. Sometimes they would escape strangulation by being decapitated.[13]

At first the Church disapproved of this beguiling convention. In the early part of the ninth century Pope Stephen IV criticized judicial combat, and at the Council of Valencia in 855 its practitioners were threatened with excommunication. But by 967 the Council of Ravenna—following Gundebald's original line of reasoning almost five hundred years earlier—declared the judicial combat in its guise as holy ordeal to be an acceptable surrogate for the much-abused practice of compurgation (corroborative testimony through oaths of innocence or veracity by third parties). By the beginning of the second millenium the Church seems to have fully accorded the words of one of its theological fathers, St. Augustine, who had written: "During the combat, God awaits, the heavens open, and He defends the party who He sees is right."[14] The clerisy practiced what it preached and there are several recorded instances at this time of priests and monks engaging in the judicial combat.[15] With the Church's permissive views in effect sanctioning the practice, judicial combat spread throughout medieval Christendom.[16] By the end of the eleventh century the institution had become interwoven with the whole fabric of European jurisprudence and "the distinction between legal procedure and vindication of personal honor began to blur."[17] In German lands the judicial combat was theoretically permitted everyone and stemmed from the traditional right of freemen to bear arms.[18] Even women would now sometimes undergo the test. If their opponent was a man, he was obliged to wallow waist deep in a hole armed with a club, while she could stand at the trench's edge and batter away with a leather thong weighted by a heavy stone.[19] Such conditions were ostensibly imposed to equalize the conflict, an early manifestation of affirmative action.

The German abolitionist Carl von Rüts declared in 1903: "The parents of the duel . . . were namely the judicial combat, the ordeal, and the law of the jungle."[20] That was his version. The ordeal was at best a duel with God. Judicial combat was not dueling either. It was a component part of European law, a public event, was sanctioned by the Church as a judgment of God, open to every class of citizen, and was largely unregulated in its fighting. Conversely, the modern German duel was outlaw, private, secular (duelists were threatened with excommunication in the sixteenth century by the Council of Trent), elitist, and courtly in character, being enclosed by prim rules—so much for the "law of the jungle." The telling point, however, is that it was not "judicial" but illegal, defiant of state authority. Historians, in lieu of reliable statistics, are able to largely trace the proliferation of dueling in certain places in certain epochs through the number of edicts promulgated to suppress the activity. In 1887 Conrad Thümmel noted, "The judicial duel was merely to aid in the resolution of an uncertain legal question; the contemporary duel seeks to make this superfluous, or to evade it."[21] Check. Although it is no fiction that judicial combat helped prepare German soil for the dueling seed, this seed was a nonautochthonous transplant.

In 1896 Albert von Boguslawski asserted: "The modern duel developed independently in Germany . . . and has absolutely not been imposed on us by France,"[22] but his thinking was likely influenced by the German's condescending view of the modern French duel as being an epicene contest restricted to mama's boys and crybabies. Despite such protestations, the modern duel was indeed French, not German. Even before the duel for honor arose in France, judicial combats there had long been exploited for the carrying-out of private vendettas under protection of law.[23] However, the definitive historical point of departure for private dueling in France was a series of Draconian measures condemning judicial combat first promulgated in the reign of St. Louis (1226–70). Private dueling subsequently sprouted to supplant the forbidden judicial function. By the time of Charles VI (1380–1422), judicial combat had all but vanished from the French legal agenda, the practice having degenerated so horrendously by the year 1400 that a fight between a man and a hound was staged.[24] Jealous of its secular prerogatives, burgeoning state authority in France now began demanding conclusive "proof" for conviction of criminals, instead of judicial combat's meddlesome "divine judgment." Circumstantial evidence, interrogation of witnesses, and confessions coaxed through torture now displaced judicial combat. In Germany, by comparison, minus the firm hand of a centralizing state polity, judicial combat was more gradually eliminated through an evolution of legal theory. And because the German practice disappeared by degrees, what we know as the modern duel did not spontaneously generate—as in France—to fill the sudden ritual-battle void left by judicial combat. No other trial by arms, legal or otherwise, sprang from German soil to take its place.[25]

German chivalry owed a great deal to French knighthood, and the German concept of the knight during the High Middle Ages is, in fact, inconceivable without this French impulse.[26] The duel had its origins in the ethical conventions and procedural guidelines of French chivalrous contests—the tournament, the joust, and the *pas d'armes*.

Although the tournament's precise lineage is difficult to trace, it was born in France and, existing concurrently with judicial combat throughout the Middle Ages, did not therefore develop in response to the latter's proscription. It eventually made its way into England and Germany, where it became sensibly known as the "French combat." The first tournaments were bloody free-for-alls in which two miniature armies would engage in life-sized battle. Scores sometimes perished, but it was considered an honor to take part in these mêlée massacres, and any knights found guilty of disgraceful, unchivalrous behavior could be banned from future fighting. Gradually the number of participants was pared down to two small teams; and soon the personal component jutted to the fore with formal challenges to "joust" being issued in decorous language by independent knights.

The joust, condemned by the Church in the twelfth century for its appalling casualties, paid dividends for valor and fairness, both prominent features of the modern German duel. A concomitant code of honor developed that was informed by notions of caste fellowship,[27] akin to later German *Standesehre*, or caste honor. It was this exclusionary "code" in particular that radically demarcated the modern German duel from the medieval judicial combat, and one could only take part in these chivalrous contests upon proof of noble descent.[28] Moreover, as the joust emerged it assumed the appearance of the duel. Although a knight was expected to christen a combat with three shivered lances, "the real business was done on foot,"[29] as discovered by the unhappy Sir Gonereyes in Malory's chronicle.

But not a few high-spirited paladins were dissatisfied with the occasional joust, and the *pas d'armes* was devised by those whose fighting instinct chafed beneath the restrictions of a domesticated pageant. In the *pas d'armes*, the knight would announce his intention to "hold" a designated terrain—usually a natural passage of some sort—for a certain duration and, alone and palely loitering, wait to face all comers. By the fifteenth century, individual challenges were issued to particular knights and from "the *pas d'armes* to the duel was but a short step."[30]

Although the demonstrable number of duels in France's late-medieval period is seldom, around the middle of the fifteenth century a certain Jacques de Lalaink was accredited with eighteen contests by the age of thirty. Hence, dueling by then must taken fair root.[31] However, it did not alone fill the vacancy left by judicial combat. Although already a long-established practice, royally authorized public duels between captious noblemen formed a parallel interim step (with the *pas d'armes*) from the judicial combat to the extra-legal duel in France. The private duel, in fact, would not become truly popular until the extinction of the royally sanctioned public contests in 1547, when it would finally come in for the full share of its chivalrous inheritance. In that year the last approved combat took place in the presence of Henry II (1547–59), who witnessed the inglorious death of a court favorite (La Châtaigneraye, the reputed finest swordsman and wrestler in France) at the hands of an opponent named Jarnac who cut him down with a crippling blow to the back of the leg. The bereaved king foreswore such exhibitions in the future and the duel as legal public spectacle retired from the field for good.[32] The floodgates of the modern duel for honor were thereupon opened, the swell overflowing into Germany during the religious and political upheaval that rocked France during its next century.

The years between the Treaty of Cateau-Cambrésis (1559) and the Treaty of Westphalia (1648) saw the French duel at its virulent peak. Under the reign of Charles IX (1559–74) the nefarious Chevalier d'Andrieux gained a reputation for touchiness and toughness, weathering seventy-two rencontres as a young man.[33] Not one to crowd, d'Andrieux would invariably culminate every duel by massaging a victim's throat with the point of his sword, pledging to spare him if he would deny his Maker. No sooner, however, would the saving words be uttered, then the double-crosser would break his promise and lean on his blade, later explaining, "In this way I corrupt his soul along with his body."[34] In the short reign of Henry IV (1589–1610) over seven thousand French noblemen were killed in duels and an equal number of royal pardons were characteristically distributed by the pragmatic monarch. The situation hardly improved over the next half century, an average of five hundred aristocrats annually finding death in duels. Numerous anti-dueling edicts were issued but they were powerless to staunch the flow of superior blood.[35]

Simultaneous with the dueling explosion in France, in Germany the first recorded "duel" and the first prohibitive edict made their appearance in the last third of the 1500s. Throughout the first half of the sixteenth century, the Holy Roman Emperor Charles V had on five separate occasions clashed with his Valois antagonist Francis I, inevitably exposing his armies to the French novelty.[36] Also, the French cultural example was beginning to serve as absolute standard in all matters pretending to a certain grace and beauty in their execution, and personal combat was not exempt from its exacting criterion. The abolitionist Georg von Below, who inferred that the duel was "smuggled" into his country because of its "indifference toward life," wrote in 1896 that "the history of the duel in Germany also forms a chapter in the history of this pitiful German copying of French fashions."[37] The enthusiasm with which well-bred Germans adopted the duel does indeed suggest its alien and predominantly French extraction.

But Italian and Spanish contacts also aided in escorting the duel into Germany during the sixteenth century. Europe's first anti-dueling decrees had been issued in Iberia in 1473 when the Council of Toledo reaffirmed the Council of Valencia's decision six hundred years earlier to condemn *mano a mano* combat (in its judicial form), and in 1480 when Queen Isabella expressly forbade the duel in her province of Castile. With the election in 1519 of a Habsburg King of Spain as Emperor Charles V, Spanish etiquette and manners gained a foothold in the Viennese court and, by virtue of the sovereign's peregrinations, soon spread throughout imperial German lands. Spanish fashions such as the ruff and its accessory rapier found particular favor among German caballeros. With the advent of gunpowder quickening the pace of modern warfare, this lighter sidearm eventually replaced the unwieldy double-edged sword.[38]

The art of fencing and the rules codifying its practice were imported from Italy. In the fifteenth century, German scholars began making transalpine treks to attend such prestigious Italian universities as Padua, Bologna, and Salerno, where lessons in the cavalier science were offered, and the students brought back what they learned to the Fatherland. By the end of the sixteenth century, fencing had become an integral part of the German university curriculum.[39] Already in the middle 1500s a flood of instruction manuals—and fencing masters to explain them—began pouring across Italian frontiers inundating the rest of Europe, Germany included. Handbooks like *Trattato di scienta* (1553) by Camillo Agrippa, an architect and mathematician, described the terminology which is still used today and laid the foundation for a new style of fencing in which thrust, parry, and footwork would eventually displace the deliberate and cumbersome movements affili- ated with the traditional German long sword, wielded like an axe and unable to compete with the defter Hispano-Italian rapier.[40] A trio of theoreticians—Alciati, Muzio, and Pigna—established rules for challenges, choice of weapons, and combat, and they elaborated the general duties encompassed by "honor."[41] The Frenchman Brantôme commented about this time that Italian duelists were "a little more cool and advised in this business than we are, and somewhat more cruel," mentioning how when faced with a defenseless enemy they would seize this "glorious opportunity of showing their generosity, by maiming their fallen foe, both in his legs and arms, and moreover giving him a desperate cut across the nose and face, to remind him of their condescension and humanity." An Italian fencing master had given lessons in craft to Jarnac shortly before his duel with La Châtaigneraye.[42]

In 1617 the Holy Roman Emperor Matthias (1612–19) promulgated an anti-dueling edict, testifying to the widespread nature of dueling in German lands by this time. The comingling of Richelieu's troops with those of other continental armies during the Thirty Years' War (1618– 48) helped to further disseminate the French custom throughout Eu- rope, but particularly in Germany where the battles were taking place. Although passed on chiefly through the auspices of marauding French soldiers, the duel was still being actively embraced by German aristocrats as an ideal way to assert precedence and resolve their high-toned squabbles. France was now the ascendant power in Europe and the collective European urge to mimic her fashions was more tyrannical than ever. But in addition to Bourbon France, a nascent power to the north had freshly emerged from the struggle for continental mastery, the state of Brandenburg-Prussia.

As a result of Matthias's edict of 1617, almost all German territories by the middle of the seventeenth century had anti-dueling laws assigning rough penalties to convicted duelists. Brandenburg-Prussia was no exception.[43] At the same time that he was concentrating his power by subduing the noble Estates, the Great Elector Friedrich Wilhelm of Brandenburg (1640–88) issued Prussia's first anti-dueling law in 1652. He branded duelists common rebels who were to be summarily executed, and promised legal indemnity to all those who chose less violent ways of mending their rifts. Enforcement of the dueling laws was, however, made difficult by the fact that the courts were equivocal in their judgment of the newly criminal act—a pattern that would persist into the twentieth century. In addition, the word *satisfaktionsfähig* entered the vernacular about this time to indicate those persons worthy of carrying swords—primarily aristocrats and officers, but state officials and students, too. These considered themselves sole watchmen of their special honor and court of last appeals in its defense[44]—a mental outlook, again, that would remain unaltered over the next two and a half centuries.

In 1688, Friedrich III (after 1701, known as Friedrich I, King in Prussia) published sixteen lengthy articles addressing the duel. Friedhelm Guttandin mentions how duels about this time were being interpreted as "insults" to the state on two levels: the theft of such citizenry as officers and officials who could render it valuable service, and the rape of justice through infringement of its sovereignty in the administration of law.[45] Measured by the severity of Friedrich III's regulations, the duel was become increasingly insulting. The articles punished a challenge or its acceptance either with release of the offender from his state post or, if not serving in an official state capacity, impoundment of his income for three years. Part of the ordinance, as in that of 1652, was devoted to a positive guarantee of judicial recompense for the offended, presaging the army "honor courts" of the nineteenth century. If the injured party opted for more direct and forceful means of adjusting his dispute, partners in crime would be companions in death. In 1695, a sixty-year-old survivor of a duel and the corpse of his victim were both publicly hanged in Berlin.[46] Applications for royal pardon were consistently ignored.[47]

Friedrich Wilhelm I of Prussia, the so-called "Soldier King" (1713–40), was more forgiving, thus adumbrating the fundamental connections between dueling and militarism that would emerge full-blown by the Second Empire. Upon his succession to the throne in 1713 he lightened the penalties for a nonmortal duel to eight to ten years imprisonment, and for duels with fatal outcomes he made the sentence contingent on the severity of any wounds rendered in the encounter.[48] But Friedrich Wilhelm, like his father, enjoyed making pendular examples of his duelists, and so he decreed that the bodies of the losers, "if an officer, a nobleman, or in any other way distinguished personage," should be publicly hanged for the edification of potential duelists.[49] The belief in the display of cadavers as a deterrent continued into the nineteenth century in Germany, when it seems that for a time after 1851 survivors of duels were compelled to witness the postmortem scrutiny of their victim's corpse and "pay strict attention to the proceedings of the surgeon."[50] Friedrich Wilhelm's ordinances, however, had little obvious effect at a time when Prussia's identity as "an army with a state" was being formed and the officer's Spartan sense of honor, with the duel as its staunch confederate, was being propagated.[51]

Friedrich the Great's oft-quoted statement, "I love brave officers, but executioners are something my army does not need," was more an expression of sentiment than a view that served as the basis for an effective plan of action against the duel. Despite his rejection of the activity in principle, Friedrich tolerated dueling in his military.[52] His opinion of the duel as "this misplaced sense of honor, which has cut short the lives of so many respectable men from whom the Fatherland had expected the greatest service," was his enlightened objection to it. The more realistic statesman, however, recognized the exigencies of an entrenched class prejudice that informed the splendid battle performance of his aristocratic corps of officers.[53] Subsequent Prussian kings and kaisers were destined to experience this same divided allegiance when it came their turn to pass judgment on the duel. Honor and its machinations were condoned so long as they did not interfere with the smooth day-to-day business of harsh Prussian discipline—otherwise, the duel was a ruddy nuisance.[54]

Under Friedrich Wilhelm II (1786–96), officers became nominally subject to the law of the land. The Prussian Law Code of 1794 imposed three to six years of detention for a challenge, ten years to life as well as loss of noble title and honorable position for a duel, and the supreme penalty for sole survivors.[55] Unlike the French *code Napoléon*, which did not address the duel as a special crime, and unlike Imperial

Germany's penal code of 1871, which treated both the duel and its bodily effects as a *delictum singulare*, the Prussian Law Code (valid until 1851) offered a mixed bag, prosecuting the duel as a particular transgression of statutory law while penalizing a resultant death or injury under the general rubrics of murder and assault.[56] Additionally, by punishing insults among the higher strata of society (officers, nobility, and royal advisors) much more severely than those among the lower orders, the Prussian Law Code of 1794 imposed an elitist bias by attributing a more fully developed sense of honor to this upper crust. A double standard also existed in cases when an insult crossed formal social divisions: an insult from high to low usually incurred a fine, whereas insults directed from low to high were almost always punished with imprisonment. Similarly, armed clashes between members of the bourgeoisie were denied treatment under the dueling statutes and prosecuted under those of murder and assault, the idea being that a duel only existed where its participants were of incontestably honorific stamp, that is, were officers or noblemen—quite often the same thing. This distinction began to evaporate from German jurisprudence only in the 1820s and 1830s.[57]

Two years after the abortive political insurrections of 1848–49, the penalties that had been on the books for civilians since 1794 in Prussia were revised downward. This lax trend also applied to most of the other thirty-odd members of the German Confederation.[58] In the Prussian Code of 1851, instead of three to six years for a challenge (Prussian Law Code of 1794), a duelist was threatened with confinement of only six months, called *Festungshaft*, amounting to hardly more than a mild convalescence; instead of ten years to life for a duel, the penalty was three months to five years of more *Festungshaft*; instead of capital punishment for killing an adversary, one could receive as little as two years and, even if the duelists had arranged for conditions that helped to ensure a fatal outcome, a minimum of only three.[59] These unintimidating provisions could not but have encouraged the dueling demiurge, and would be identical to those of the new German Empire's 1871 penal code.

At the time of the *Kaiserreich*, the German duel was more robust than ever. By the end of the nineteenth century this foreign product of a preindustrial age had become an eminently modern and eminently German phenomenon. And compared to cruel precursors like the ordeal in which men could be obliged to walk barefoot and blindfolded over red-hot ploughshares,[60] it was eminently civilized, hardly the barbaric anachronism it was often accused of being. Although pro-and anti-duelists could not agree on the German duel's precise origins, there was little dissent that it was experiencing a kind of golden age at the fin de siècle. In 1896, Social Democratic leader August Bebel stood up in the Reichstag and challenged his listeners to gainsay the fact that "in the 70s and 80s . . . or even in the last decade of this century, especially since 1890, the dueling mischief has not increased."[61] For a change, in Wilhelmine Germany, no one took up the gauntlet.

THE LEGAL AND POLITICAL SETTING

With the two notable exceptions of Sweden and Austria, the dueling articles in the 1871 German penal code were perhaps as punitive as those of any other European country.[62] This is not to say the German articles were equally effective. They suffered from several inherent defects. By their very nature, penalties of any sort addressing the specific crime of dueling contained an implicit recognition of the duel's legitimacy as a delict sui generis, whose fatal or injurious results would be treated with far less severity than those of murder or assault with a similar deadly weapon. By indulging duelists in this manner, lawmakers made it easy for them to undertake lethal action without fear of excessive state reprisal. In comparison with a country like France, where a duel could not be punished but its harmful effects could, Germany had a lower dueling rate but a higher percentage and absolute number of fatalities. German legislation was betwixt and between: it extended tacit recognition to the duel and then failed to secure sufficiently worrisome penalties to discourage mortal results. Only in countries where the duel was on its last legs, like Belgium and Denmark, could such an extravagance be afforded.

The justificatory paragraph to the penal code's dueling articles admitted, in fact, to a lack of conviction where the state's own legal prerogatives were concerned:

> Because the practice, or bad habit, of the duel has always proved stronger than the law, for better or for worse the law is left no other alternative but to come to terms with the task of establishing its regulations so that they on the one hand do not conflict too sharply with the requirements of justice, and on the other, of taking into some consideration the necessities of life [und anderseits dem Bedürfnisse des Lebens ein wenigstens annäherndes Genüge leisten].[63]

The duel henceforth achieves a veritable rung on the German hierarchy of needs as one of the "necessities of life." This was hardly a means to overawe potential duelists, and the penal code's ten dueling articles carried the same equivocal, almost indifferent aftertaste left by this scarcely concealed reluctance to prosecute. Article 207 fundamentally approved the regulations set down by the dueling codes: "If a death or injury has been effected by means of an infringement of the agreed upon or traditional rules of the duel, the violator is to be punished according to the general regulations governing the crimes of murder or bodily injury." There was a considerable difference between two years of honorable internment and a lifetime in lockup, and thus a mannered, textbook kill was always preferable to other methods of homicide. At least Wilhelmine jurisprudence thought so. There was indeed a thin line between honor and murder: the articles addressing murder commenced with number 211, immediately following the duel clauses 201 to 210.

It is uncertain, however, whether duelists were at all aware of the penalties they were liable to suffer. One Reichstag deputy pretended outrage at the fact that "nine-tenths of all duelists do not even know where in the penal code dueling is discussed and what sort of penalties are imposed on it."[64] Had duelists been fully apprised of the possible legal ramifications of their actions, it is still more doubtful whether they would have greatly cared. A highly commutable two-year prison sentence was no deterrent for men stupid, gutsy, or complacent enough to stare into the round eye of a live pistol. Prison itself was a privileged sentence, sort of a bed-and-breakfast arrangement just shy of room service at the Waldorf. Detainees were treated not like crooks but as bold-spirited martyrs and were regularly allowed to amuse themselves beyond penitentiary walls. One south German low-security operation gave new meaning to the term "behind bars" when a duelist was granted permission to refresh himself in the taverns of the local village. Drinking privileges were only revoked after he got his jollies one night by shooting the warden's kitty.[65] This sort of dubious indulgence presaged the gentle treatment meted out right-wing revolutionaries under the Weimar Republic. Alan Bullock described the 1924 stay, following the aborted Beer Hall Putsch, of Adolf Hitler and some forty other National Socialists in Landsberg prison: "They had an easy and comfortable life, ate well—Hitler became quite fat in prison—had as many visitors as they wished, and spent much of their time out of doors in the garden. . . . He had a large correspondence in addition to his visitors, and as many newspapers and books as he wished." Rudolf Hess later voluntarily left his exile in Austria to savor the sweet life at Landsberg.[66]

As in Weimar, within the fortress walls of Imperial Germany's state judicial system lurked a Trojan Horse crammed with conservative public defenders, prosecuting attorneys, and other lawyers called judges who themselves were loyal followers of honor's greater glory. University-educated, many of these jurists were so-called *Alte Herren*, alumni of student dueling associations. If not bearing a conspicuous scarface, these public officials might still be members of the reserve officer corps, whose prescription for the defense of honor was every bit as painstaking as that of the scholar-knights. By virtue alone of their standing as high civil servants, judicial magistrates, when their honor fell under putative attack, were compelled to trample underfoot the law they pretended to uphold. The legal process itself could foment duels among tendentious lawyers who would occasionally send judges their seconds as the result of court cases.[67] The pressure within the legal profession to litigate one's honor in a duel was so great that one clerk at the turn of the century, shunned by his colleagues for pleading no contest to a challenge, had to eventually switch careers.[68]

Sentences for duels brought to trial were notoriously insipid. The three-month minimum was apportioned in practically every instance and the modest penalty of two years was almost always levied in fatal encounters. Judges were usually soft touches, and defendant's attorneys were shrewd enough to exploit this lenient tendency. August Bebel complained in 1903 that the most rigorous sentence he could recall was that of six years (of a possible fifteen) given an individual who first seduced a married woman and then shot her hapless husband dead.[69] In a precious example of judicial logic, a law clerk who had challenged and killed a friend at the distance of ten paces with rifled barrels was given only ten months, based on the fact that shortly before the duel he had gallantly inquired of the acting physician where it would be best to aim so as to avoid inflicting a terminal wound. Yet he then proceeded to shoot his friend straight through the midsection. Little matter. He was pardoned by a humane monarch after four months on hospitality row.[70]

Thus, if the courts did not take pity, the Kaiser would. Such far-ranging mercy did not originate with Wilhelm II (1888–1918). In a missive to the Ministry of Justice in May of 1885, Wilhelm I (1871–88) reduced a three-month stretch for pistol dueling to two weeks, noting that the appellant was a young doctor who had been practicing for less than a year and whose career would suffer irremediable damage were he to be given the raw deal of an extended incarceration.[71] The ultimate futility of repeated Reichstag attempts to restrict the duel was occasionally revealed in frustrating remarks from the refractory Right, reminding overzealous reformers of their impotence in the face of the unimpeachable power of the Imperator Rex to partition grace as he saw fit. In 1886 a Reichstag deputy facetiously protested that anti-dueling legislation was pointless, as Wilhelm I was prone to overturn most decisions anyway.[72] Capitulating to despair, abolitionists often made personal appeals to the Kaiser, entreating him to give dueling the coup de grâce by unambiguously voicing his disapproval of it, thus giving the acquiescent German subject a clear conscience in declining a challenge. In view of Wilhelm II's 1897 army decree (discussed at length in chapter III), the assumption of good German obedience was not unfounded, but such unequivocal utterances were too much to expect from an emperor who took daily fencing lessons[73] and who identified so strongly with an army whose code of honor was second to none in unyielding severity. Duelists had a nice line of protection with the supremo.

Having been forced to swallow this fact of life for so long, by the year of their landslide electoral victory in 1912, the Social Democrats were fighting mad. In an embittered parliamentary diatribe, the writer Georg Lebedour likened dueling's social construct to the grossly unjust Prussian three-class suffrage system. (Prussian voters were divided into three electoral blocs according to the amount of taxes they paid, and so roughly the wealthiest 15 percent of the population commanded two-thirds of the seats in the lower house of the state legislature. Because of Prussia's political control of the federal government, this local voting arrangement helped ensure a conservative impediment to reform at the national level too.) Lebedour described "Honor" as a three-runged stepladder consisting of a wide base formed of *unsatisfaktionsfähig* (literally, "incapable of giving satisfaction") elements, a middle rung inhabited by disciples of the gentleman's code, and a final level of royal potentates who were *hors concours* by virtue of their transcendent, autarchical honor. Topping this ladder—but bottoming another—was the judas goat himself: "However, those who stand at the very lowest level of the moral stepladder are strictly those persons who themselves would reject a duel and yet force others to duel. They stand upon the basest rung of morality. These are unfortunately those persons, among whom in the foremost rank stands the bearer of the power of supreme command. . . ." With the Kaiser coming into the line of fire, pandemonium issued, and Lebedour was called to order by the bell of the president. But Lebedour concluded his harangue by sharing the conviction that it would require a couple of princes gathered to the Lord before a cabinet order emanating from Sans Souci would fairly condemn the crime.[74] It was of course unthinkable that Wilhelm II, a gimp-armed advertisement for regicide, should have been fair game for a challenge.[75] But other royalty, too, did not as a rule duel (although one between a First Lieutenant Mattachich and Prince Philipp von Sachsen-Koburg occurred in 1898[76]), and it seemed incongruous and hypocritical to anti-duelists that something eschewed in princely circles should be de rigueur in slightly lower ones—a case of the high nobility eating their cake and having it too.[77] The opposition felt that

Wilhelm could assuage the inequity through direct action but that the will to do so was lacking, which it was.

The emperor's first obligation was not to abstract theories of social justice or to the constituted legal order, but to the historical preroga-tives of the *Ständestaat*, the corporative state. Integral to the preserva-tion of the Prussian corporate structure was the duel's function as a line of demarcation between the "two nations." A double standard prevailed that allowed upper-class untouchables to kill in the name of honor, while demanding unquestioning obedience to statute law from those of lower condition. Even though the German penal code failed to define its terms when it spoke of "duel" (*Zweikampf*) and "lethal weap-ons" (*tödlichen Waffen*) in its strictures against "*Zweikampf mit tödlichen Waffen*," different legal paragraphs came into effect when the rabble dueled after their homespun fashion with knuckles or knives.[78] In a Berlin trial of the year 1895, a man with horny hands but an honest heart was charged with promoting a brawl after disparaging remarks were made concerning his wife. He argued the case that his little tussle was an affair of honor just like those of the upper classes: "When the genteel folk are insulted, then they send out their seconds and it's off to the races with swords or pistols in the Grunewald or the Jungfern-heide. And he who earlier had the big mouth will perhaps be silenced by the other. And then the other goes to prison for a short while, and then when he returns he's a splendid fellow."[79] In 1885 a subcommittee of the Reichstag discounted a petition authored by the "Master-Tailor L. Röhr" requesting that the duel be punished more harshly. The peti-tion was rejected on basis of the poor blighter's tradesman status, which placed him "recognizably very far from those circles in which the duel is practiced, [hence] the basis and actual essence of the duel are completely alien to him."[80]

The dueling ideology was not only fully integrated into the worka-day routine of the German judiciary. It found a welcome home within the nation's bureaucracy. Consequently, the strong Prussian-German bureaucratic tradition that hindered the "parliamentarization of the constitutional system" and prevented a "full *embourgeoisement* of the culture,"[81] was doubly reinforced. The duel was regarded kindly by the German mandarinate, and its convenience in resolving the sticky *point d'honneur* was openly endorsed by no less a personage than the Prussian Minister of the Interior Robert von Puttkammer, Bismarck's loyal bureaucratic aide. Puttkammer headed the conservative house-cleaning of the Prussian civil service during the 1880s and was also instrumental in Bismarck's contemporaneous purge of the Ministry of Justice. Addressing a case in the Reichstag in 1886, in which an East Prussian panjandrum had issued a challenge in a work-related setting,

Puttkammer insisted that his officials should not be criticized but rather commended for their pugnacity in these matters, calling such attitudes "highly praiseworthy." He even approved insubordination when honor was in clear and imminent danger:

> I make still yet the reservation that there can occur situations in which the subaltern can say: this far and no farther—here ends the disciplinary subordination, and here begins the inalienable boundary for the preservation of my personal honor. Gentlemen, I go even so far as to say: I can think of a state of affairs in which even the subaltern himself rejects the direct orders of his superior because he is of the opinion that apart from him and his conscience no one presides over certain things that touch upon his personal honor and its preservation.[82]

Responding to a plea for intervention in one case of 1894, the Chancellor Leo von Caprivi stated that "in principle he did not involve himself in the affairs of honor of his subordinates."[83] As with members of the judiciary, bureaucrats could find themselves in situations whereby their very standing as imperial or Prussian civil servants forced them to profane their professional oaths through dueling—and their superiors were no obstacle.

To trace the entire political chronology of the dueling issue from its inception as a matter of serious parliamentary concern in the mid-1880s to its terminus at the hands of embattled conservativism a few months before the First World War would be a tedious and unrewarding venture. The Reichstag's powers of initiative and interpellation were so tightly corsetted by Bismarck's jury-rigged constitution and parliamentary system that, despite widespread discontent over the duel's continued vitality and general agreement among the parties as to the duel's essential reprehensibility, the legislative changes effected in almost thirty years of vigorous debate amounted to little. As a useful sounding-board for the competing ideologies and as a barometer of prevailing social tempers, the Reichstag debates serve the historian well; but as a shaping force in the imperial government's policy, the disputations were of dubious value.[84] Typical of the deputies' frustration was the 1896 comment from a representative of the German People's Party:

> Gentlemen, if one were to award a prize for that civilized land where the most is said and written against the duel, where the legislature is called upon to affect moral outrage, where the best is promised and

the least achieved, and when possible—despite everyone's promises—
the old ways still remaining in place, the prize would in any case fall to
Germany.[85]

In 1902 a National Liberal deputy expressed scarce amazement at the
fact that Reichstag consensus should be so difficult to obtain in the
sensitive dueling issue when general accord was hard enough to
achieve in matters far less emotionally charged.[86] A member of the
German Liberal People's Party in 1906 aptly depicted ten years of
Reichstag debates as "fruitlessly firing charges in the air."[87] Socialist
Bebel wearily recognized the obvious handicap to reform and the reason for the Reichstag's failure when he noted that, "The primary cause
lies in the fact that the Reichstag has no power, that our resolutions
receive no consideration from the federal government."[88]

The government's stratagem was threefold. Its principal ruse was to
fan up a rhetorical smokescreen. Governmental spokesmen stressed
the insufficient protection afforded a gentleman's honor by the law.
They would emphasize the law's inadequacy in punishing honor violations and declare that to impose greater penalties on duelists would
be to treat the symptom rather than the source of the problem, which
lay in the unattractiveness of "legal satisfaction," an oxymoron for the
dedicated man of honor. Perhaps the government half believed its
own casuistry. In a directive emanating from the Prussian Ministry of
Justice and circulated among the various district courts in 1897, Minister Schönstedt reminded his officials that the problem of the recent
increase in duels was not due to weak laws but to permissive courts,
part of Puttkammer's legacy. While urging his public prosecutors to
put the bite on duelists, he also underscored their complementary
duty to pursue cases of slander and insult—the immediate cause of
many duels—as swiftly and purposefully as possible. Whenever people acquired the conviction that affronts to honor would be efficiently
prosecuted and properly punished by the courts, said Schönstedt, it
was reasonable to expect that duels would abate and, "All the more
will it then appear justified to proceed with full severity against viola-
tors of the dueling law."[89]

Despite reams of documentation from the Justice Ministry drawing
correlations between mild penalties for insult and high dueling rates,
this assumption of Schönstedt's was a red herring. There was no real
evidence to corroborate such a relationship and, if the truth be known,
the German penal code was a vicious weapon of retribution in cases of
alleged insult, more severe than its dueling law in some ways. Almost
everything could be construed as an insult under the *Beleidigung* (insult) clause, including impoliteness and cursing. Both of these latter

transgressions could be punished with a maximum prison sentence of one and two years, respectively. In English law, for example, there was no provision for the "simple insult" (*einfache Beleidigung*). The only way such a charge could be substantiated and tried was in the case of material, that is, financial, loss as a consequence of a defamatory attack. These were rare. In general, behavior considered in Germany as sufficient grounds for a challenge and often punishable by law—sneering or cutting remarks, epithets, not to mention staring or gestures—was perceived in England as harmless and unworthy of judicial attention. And dueling was extinct in England. Perhaps mere mention of the crime of "insult" on the law books in Germany consecrated the extraordinary means a man of honor might seek to rectify a personal injury.[90] In France, on the other hand, where dueling was very alive in the last decades before the war, penalties for slander were piddling.[91] The only conclusion to be reasonably drawn from all this is that concern over inadequate penalties for insults was generally an irrelevant factor in the motivational makeup of a recusant duelist, who cared nothing for the discomfiture of an antagonist if he was to be denied a direct and personal role in it.

An *Ehrenmann* never placed his honor in the hands of a third party because he was supposedly not subject to the same standards as the great herd of men, and appeal to a court of law was interpreted as a groveling confession of assailability and weakness. Even the German Anti-Dueling League lent unwitting support to the government's deception through its dismissal of plain suppression of the duel in favor of surrogates by which to render it superfluous; namely, the dodge of higher penalties for insult and slander, and adjudication of affairs by subordination of litigants to civilian courts of honor.[92] These proposed courts of honor were a dead letter from the start. Since they would have been erected specifically to intercept duels, only those men determined to elude personal imperilment in the first place would have presented themselves before such tribunals. The suspicion of meekness and irresolution would not have endeared them to watchful peers whose criterion for honorable satisfaction was risking one's skin. "Since an insult is almost always of a morally harmful nature," wrote the duel codifier Gustav Ristow, "the satisfaction must also be a moral one."[93] A court process, therefore, was morally reprehensible: men of honor preferred the supreme justiciar of death to mediate their disputes with finality. All told, the dynamic counterpoint of the duel to the dank and musty juristic route helped to create the *illusion* of legal insufficiency—at least to men who felt that "there is only one way to abolish the duel: abolish the feeling of honor."[94]

Auxiliary to this diversionary ploy of the government were some clever delaying tactics, which postponed dueling amendments until completion of the penal code's general revision, a process during the final decade preceding the Great War. The government's standpoint was that because the dueling question was integrally bound up with a reassessment of the laws governing slander, insult, and libel, the issue should be treated holistically and deferred as part of the penal code's more comprehensive, protracted facelift—in other words, placed on ice until the government was good and ready to confront it. This view had been represented to the Reichstag in January of 1906.[95] By 1914 there had still been no results, and the government reiterated that "remedial action can only be achieved through the simultaneous reform of the regulations concerning the duel and the regulations concerning insults, and that this reform is to be left to the penal code's general revision."[96] Any anti-dueling agitation was handily deflected by governmental representatives with reference to the *Gesamtrevision*, or total revision enterprise. Consistent with the government's prevarication and evasiveness in other areas of policy, the Reichstag was repeatedly rebuffed with this unmistakeable stall.

If all this were not enough, the third feature of government strategy was to pretend stupefaction at the Reichstag's demands. It played dumb. In its own defense, the government would point to the nominally tough dueling laws, to the Kaiser's decree of 1897 discouraging the duel among officers, to the general decrease in rates since that order, to the government's agreement in principle as to the duel's deplorable nature, and to its patient consideration of all recommendations from parliament. However, whether taken seriously or not, parliamentary proposals would be ultimately dismissed as impracticable. Typical of the comments accompanying rejection were those made in 1913 by Chancellor von Bethmann-Hollweg, who summarized governmental views by saying that because no set of laws was perfect or able to prevent all of the duels all of the time, the Reichstag was being unrealistic and already had everything it demanded.[97]

Despite these protests of innocence, there were actually two very concrete demands that the imperial government refused outright to countenance. The first was the desire, chiefly represented by the Catholic Center Party, that the government bolster and enforce the existing laws as they stood. This demand, of course, entailed the notion that the courts should prosecute to the law's full extent (a five-year maximum sentence for the duel itself, and fifteen years for the sole survivor of a duel), and that the Kaiser should be more grudging when pro forma pleas for imperial leniency were entered. The curtailment of a divine right prerogative implicit in this demand did not make it altogether welcome to the government. Besides, five years for a harmless duel seemed a very long time to spend in confinement, even if of a limited variety. No, the government would not commit itself to unstinting enforcement.

A second unacceptable proposal was one most often forwarded by the Social Democrats, who proved themselves intolerant of anything less than complete absorption of the penal code's dueling clauses into the general articles pertaining to homicide and assault, thus depriving the duel of its status as a privileged form of murder. Had the Social Democrats obtained their desiderata, the duel would have ceased to exist, and the first step on the slippery slope of social equality would have been trod, a horrifying apparition to high-bred men of honor. Such an uncompromising view was difficult to accept on three other counts. By revoking the penalty for dueling where the combat had benignly run its course, the Social Democrats would also have eliminated the punitive consequences of a simple challenge. It was important to retain the penalty against a challenge (up to six months' imprisonment) because a rejected challenge was regarded in the highest circles as a social demerit. A challenge could be and sometimes was an empty bluff to ruin someone of pacifistic nature by leaving their reputation in tatters. There had to remain a vestige of punishment meted out for challenges, as well as duels, so as to discourage such random means of character defamation. By most standards, except those of the doctrinaire Social Democrats, this was a reasonable objection to placing the duel's urbane ceremony on a par with a dock worker's brawl. In such an event, conservative opponents unironically insisted, manslaughter and premeditated murder would then assume the place of the duel. Another consideration was that juries might have shown themselves even more reluctant to convict a duelist if a fatality was made a capital crime, the case in early-nineteenth-century England and contemporary France.[98]

The last objection by the government to this SPD program was the widespread notion that the socialists were not being terribly candid with their proposals. It was not the duel per se that the Social Democrats opposed, but the *Ständestaat* and its feudal patronage. The overt agenda of socialist anti-dueling agitation was a declaration of war against the German hierarchy of status, and so the duel was assailed as a symptom of superannuated privilege and the upper-class feelings of superiority that accompanied it.[99] "If the gentlemen from the so-called upper classes want to bash in each other's heads or shoot each other down with pistols," once chortled August Bebel, "fundamentally we can have very little objection to it. The more they practice the business of self-obliteration, the better for us."[100] Socialists thought that the upper-class sense of honor, like capitalism, contained the seeds of its own destruction, and so there was always an ambivalent quality to their condemnation of the cannibalistic duel. They felt it their moral duty to unconditionally reproach the institution, but still held it their ideological responsibility to permit the bourgeois cum-feudal sore to fester. This can account for the categorical attitude ("Either murder or nothing!") among socialists when it came to the duel. The SPD was continuously beseeching the government and the Reichstag to take a "fundamental stance" (*grundsätzliche Stellungnahme*) against the practice. As far as they were concerned such a stance was never forthcoming in all the "trivial little bills" (*kleine Gesetzentwürfchen*) attempting to engage the duel on its own terms by uncritically encompassing the question of honor and how best to defend it.[101]

The Social Democrats never accepted the ground rules of the debate: namely, that such a restricted classification as "man of honor" did indeed exist, and that personal honor could be impugned by another. Any party that so much as qualifiedly accepted these premises—and that was most—was suspect in socialist eyes not only of Junker sycophancy but of an implicit recognition of the duel's theoretical legitimacy in repatriating nicked pride. Because the Social Democrats scorned conventional notions of honor, they also scorned parties that subscribed to such notions. For this reason compromise was repugnant, and on more than one occasion the SPD was accused by other Reichstag parties of sabotaging parliamentary attempts at a consensus for the sake of political goals.[102] In 1896, Rudolf von Bennigsen of the National Liberals pleaded for the immediate cessation of dueling, because it offered "a very effective agitation device for those parties that subvert the status quo."[103] Similar concerns were echoed in the upper chamber of the conservative Prussian Landtag by the Graf Praschma in 1907 when he posed the rhetorical question: "Is it not furthermore an irrefutable duty to deprive Social Democratic agitation . . . of such a weapon?"[104] By 1912 the SPD was conceding its motives: "For us the ethical and religious elements take a back seat. For us the duel is firstly a purely political question. We primarily perceive the duel not as a means for the preservation of Junker class honor but as a symbol of Junker class rule, and even more: a device for the maintenance of this class rule."[105]

If the German Social Democrats had evolved into a tame revisionist party by the turn of the century, the dueling plank of their ideological platform remained exceedingly hardline. Practically speaking, however, it was a failure, for this hardline only succeeded in splitting the Reichstag and in provoking a defensive posture from the government, which took its "fundamental stance" not against the duel but against the socialists. The chances of ever achieving a common understanding between pro- and anti-duelists were, in any case, unusually slim. As one analyst wrote, "friends of the duel and its enemies proceed more often than not from two directly opposed life philosophies. They operate, so to speak, with two thoroughly dissimilar conceptual lexicons."[106]

With the outbreak of war in the summer of 1914, the dueling question was shelved. Maybe the duel survived briefly as "dogfight," with ace Baron von Richthofen and other aerial knights of the realm bearing the chivalrous ethos aloft one last time in their canvas coffins. But by the end of the war that too had gone down in flames. Although a few duels occurred in the Weimar Republic, the duel as a social institution died in the trenches alongside its faithful. The relevancy of heroic individual action emerged as a fatuous delusion in the wake of Verdun and the Somme, where men were butchered like cattle. The concussive blows of modern warfare succeeded in finally knocking out what thirty years of parliamentary shadowboxing had failed to lay a real glove on.

THE SOCIAL DIMENSION

In the last part of 1893 the satirical magazine *Kladderadatsch* published an article attacking the political division of the German Foreign Ministry accusing it of insidious influence on the Kaiser.[107] The magazine's venom was notably directed at Friedrich von Holstein, éminence grise behind the haphazard course of German diplomacy in those years, and his assistant Alfred von Kiderlen-Wächter. On behalf of the Wilhelmstrasse, and in order to vindicate his own good name, Kiderlen challenged the *Kladderadatsch* editor Wilhelm Polstorff to a duel. The summit took place in Berlin's Grunewald in April of 1894 with rifled pistols at fifteen paces. At the third exchange (of a possible five) Polstorff took a ball in his right armpit. It penetrated to the lung and required a convalescence of two months. In the subsequent trial, the prosecuting attorney applied for sentences of four months for Kiderlen and six months for Polstorff. He argued that the primary guilt lay with Polstorff for having forced Kiderlen's hand: Kiderlen's high office and the prevailing views of his social milieu made the challenge unavoidable and a duel inevitable. Despite the probable truth of *Kladderadatsch's* assertions (the government did not relish a process in which charges could be substantiated through sworn witnesses), and notwithstanding the fact that Kiderlen had not only issued the challenge but had imposed its harrowing conditions and seriously wounded his opponent, the presiding judge conceded the public prosecutor's arguments. In consideration of the peer pressure attendant to the case, the judge slapped their wrists and gave them each four months.[108] The affair did Kiderlen's career no harm, for he went on to become Secretary of State and display as much truculence in his hamhanded provocation of the Bosnian and Agadir crises as he had in his duel with Polstorff. Traits that made an exemplary duelist were liabilities for a diplomat, who should never place himself in a position from which he cannot if necessary withdraw tactfully. The imperial foreign service was fairly bulging with men of honor—the profession itself bestowed the title—and German diplomacy from 1890 to 1914 was, in fact, pretty wretched.[109]

Probably the most significant psycho-social fact about the medieval knight was that he was "a member of a caste with a strong sense of solidarity," finding his identity in "a community of similar life style and similar ideals."[110] This chivalrous legacy had not been abnegated by German men of honor—an aristocracy of the spirit—centuries later. The upholding of "caste-honor," or *Standesehre*, was undoubtedly a pivotal factor in motivating a great many upper- and middle-class men to take sunrise target practice. For the *Ehrenmann*, personal and caste honor were so intimately related as to be quite indistinguishable. The duel served a split-level function: "The individual parties are not only rehabilitated. The entire social order . . . is thereby sustained and ensured."[111] Duels were undertaken out of a feeling of co-responsibility for the collective reputation of Germany's social elite, out of a sort of tribal egotism, and not from a selfish amour propre:

> The duel is for the sake of the individual only insofar as he is a member of an entire caste, his honor being identified with caste honor, with that of the caste. . . . For this reason, it testifies to egoism if someone, despite acknowledgment of the aforementioned, says: "What do I gain if I am insulted and on top of everything, if I am killed for it," because he places the "ego" in this case higher than the totality, for whose welfare he is unconditionally pledged to work.[112]

According to contemporary reckoning, only about 5 percent of German society was *satisfaktionsfähig*,[113] directly corresponding to the estimated percentage of the population included in the first voting bracket of the Prussian three-class suffrage system.[114] This 5 percent was composed mostly of well-to-do professionals from the upper-middle class, that is, the middle class in its narrowest social sense.[115] In recent years there has been much discussion among German historians, utilizing various Marxist models and Weberian typologies, about who belonged to the upper-middle class, whether or not one can indeed wad *Besitz* together with *Bildung*, where to situate petty officials and artists, etc. For example, should one divide the classes according to income, profession, standard of living, or political allegiance? Or, to what extent are these categories consistent with the social reality of the time and not just analytical constructs of later historians? The German upper-middle class is admittedly a somewhat amorphous grouping that may best be described in negative terms. Its constituents belonged to neither the rural nor the urban lower classes, to neither the peasantry nor the priesthood, to neither the proletariat nor the petty bourgeoisie nor the nobility of birth. Because all of these groups (excepting the aristocracy, and leaving aside temporarily the singular category of officer) were *not* capable of giving satisfaction and were pigeonholed from this standpoint by those that could, what "upper-middle class" meant in the most positive and definitive sense was the competence to duel. Those who possessed and generally employed this competence were doctors, judges, engineers, architects, lawyers, civil servants, academics—men who had been to the university, the so-called *Bildungsbürgertum*—and wealthy businessmen, industrialists, bankers, entrepreneurs, the so-called *Besitzbürgertum*. Suffice it to say that the social stratum represented by these men was one whose boundaries, though hardly impermeable and sometimes blurring along lines of orthodox class division, were clearly drawn in the abstract by a cohort united in its readiness to tempt death in a certain way for the sake of shared attitudes that were distinctly elitist in character. Elitist in the sense that what elevated one above the crowd was not so much one's station in life as the character that this station implied. And dueling was the tautological proof of such character. By risking physical extinction for the sake of the ineffable, one was thought to exhibit the ultimate in moral rectitude and personal autonomy. The defense of one's honor with one's life, in the knowledge that the "ideational personality has more worth than one's physical personality," had, in fact, something "poetic" about it.[116] Both Goethe and Heine once mongered verse with blood for ink.[117]

The self-sacrifice entailed in the duel's heroic couplet was properly acknowledged by communal peers. At the funeral in April 1896 of the Freiherr Carl von Schrader—victim of a duel fomented by Hohenzollern court intrigues—all of Berlin high society turned out, each of them arriving "because he had a social obligation to fulfill, and drove away again after he had faultlessly performed it."[118] The defiant pastor who delivered the elegy did not fail to mention that "the man who here rests is a victim of caste prejudice."[119] Because honor in war had

once been equated with noble honor, the martial duel served as a traditional affidavit of good breeding. Moreover, according to the German historian Heinrich von Treitschke (1834–1896), it represented political power, which "is particularly an effect of the right to wield
arms, and [which] more often than not dwindles to a few externals
where the nobility has lost this [right]."[120] Men of honor were determined to preserve their power and influence by keeping inviolate
their duel, which distinguished them from the average man in the
street. Although the German duelist bore an uncanny resemblance to
the average soldier in the field. His forlorn courage was not of the rare,
inborn kind. It was borrowed from a cause, an army, its officers. The
cause was his inextricable predicament as defined by the code; the
officers were the attending seconds; and the army, which swept him
forward into battle, consisted of his tony societal counterparts and
their *bien pensant* opinions. If the first great thing to learn about life is
to refrain from doing what you really do not want to do, then duelists
were to be pitied more than anything else. They lacked the courage not
to be brave; like a young woman today lacking the self-confidence to
be unapologetically overweight in body-beautiful Southern California—although no one for a moment is pretending that duelists were
subject to pressures quite so extreme.

A more provident illustration comes to mind: In *The Gulag Archipelago*, Alexander Solzhenitsyn relates the story of a Communist
Party conference that took place at the height of the Stalinist purges in
which a tribute to the Leader was called for. During the ensuing ova-
tion, all present rose to their feet and applauded with mechanical
vigor. The disingenuous acclaim lasted five, six, seven minutes. Each
in the audience feared being the first to resume his seat and induce
Party censure. After eleven minutes of ringing salvos, the noise had
lowered not a decibel. Solzhenitsyn: "Insanity! To the last man! With
make-believe enthusiasm on their faces, looking at each other with
faint hope, the district leaders were just going on and on till they fell
where they stood, till they were carried out of the hall on stretch-
ers!"[121] Likewise, it seems, duelists did not partake in their devotions
out of any genuine adoration. Although Russian party leaders risked
their honor to save their necks, whereas duelists risked their necks to
save their honor, both cultivated a finely tuned toadyism that payed
anxious homage to a brutal totalitarian overlord and his cult.

The term *Standesehre* echoes the German word *Gemeinschaft*, or a
sense of community, but with the prime difference that *Standesehre*
encompassed only a privileged male few in the upper echelons of society, and also implied an "us against them" attitude vis-à-vis the

masses. The duel was the historical symbol of caste solidarity and it was also the guardian of class differences. A challenge was like a secret fraternal handshake, bizarre on the surface but possessing a logical subtext that banished incogniscenti. The anthropologist Pierre Bordieu describes how

> for a challenge to be made, the challenger must consider whoever he challenges to be worthy of it—to be, that is to say, in a position to riposte. . . . Because it presupposes recognition of equality in honour, offence is opposed to disdain which is essentially a refusal of the dialogue, because it excludes the possibility of riposte. To disdain, in effect, is to refuse to give one's opponent a chance; it is to enclose him within a fate that is imposed upon him; to refuse dialogue with him is to deny symbolically that he is equal in humanity. Humiliation corresponds to disdain, and is the situation of the individual confined by his nature to an inferior position, to whom one denies the dignity of being a man to the extent of refusing to enter into a dialogue with him even by an insult.[122]

In this sense, over 90 percent of Germany's male population were not only not men of honor—they were not even real men. *Untermenschen* is probably too strong a word. Racial overtones were, however, frequently in evidence—for example, in the assessment of popular philosopher Eduard von Hartmann (1842–1906) when he inveighed against first allegedly Japanese, then Italian methods of violent recourse: "Opposed to all these types of reaction the orderly duel constitutes an unmistakable advance toward civilization. . . . The calmer temperament of the Nordic peoples . . . achieves this degree of self-mastery more easily than the Mediterranean type."[123] Similar eugenic asides were dispensed by Bavarian Lieutenant Hans Hell. Among the prates of Hell was to bewail the duel's possible extirpation as "the first symptom of miscegenation. But we are still not 'Europeans'; can the German really wish such a thing?"[124]

As a mark of class distinction and claims to rule, the duel is thus an explicable phenomenon. It was a form of tribute paid in lives for the privileges naturally obtaining to the exalted sectors of German society. In the autobiography of her childhood, Marion Gräfin Dönhoff portrays Prussian honor before the First World War as the negative complement to privilege. Privilege represented the Dos; honor, the Don'ts. The rules of honor were "a shield against all kinds of temptations, a security railing, so to speak, along which one could feel one's way."[125] A shield and a security railing but also a cage—a cold and heartless cage, whose confines German men of honor suffered in uncomplaining silence. Although it was jealously guarded by its loyal minions, the duel itself was no privilege. And even so, it was hardly one to be coveted. In contrast to the French duel, whose benign aspect made its appeal more universal, the German duel's menacing countenance seems to have generated greater public dismay than envy. There was plenty of resentment of upper-class arrogations, but never was remorse expressed over the duel's exclusionary clause.

The German code of honor formed what anthropologists call "a nexus between the ideals of a society and their reproduction in the individual through his aspiration to personify them";[126] what the German moral philosopher Friedrich Paulsen (1846–1908) termed "an enduring reflection of the individual essence in a collective conscience."[127] A contemporary critic employed the more demotic locution: the duelist's honor existed "in the heads of strangers."[128] One might speak of Wilhelmine Germany as a "shame society," whose members did not necessarily internalize their societal values but avoided violating them "out of concern about the opinions and reactions of fellow group members."[129] Another author summed up the conflicting feelings involved: " 'I alone am in possession of my honor, no one except myself can destroy it.' Very true, but as is known, the world in which we live sees things only as they manifest themselves."[130] A generation later, in 1912, the Prussian Minister of War von Heeringen echoed this note of resignation when he told the Reichstag that "no one can rob me of the honor residing in my heart. But one can never see into another's heart, and howsoever noble and pure may be the motives behind a refusal to duel, they are not for everyone outwardly visible."[131]

Herein lies the essential and singular meaning of Wilhelmine *Standesehre*: personal feelings of guilt or conscience played only an abbreviated role in the determination to duel, whereas caste convention carried the day. This is the only clear explanation for those not infrequent occasions when men dueled against their real convictions and better judgment. The rural antebellum South, with its teeming understratum of black slaves and its wealthy planter class, placed a similar importance on honor/shame to the detriment of conscience/guilt, this latter a supposed specialty of the industrial North.[132] Yet the capitalistic infusion of *Besitzbürgertum* into the German dueling cult at mid-century also helps to clarify that certain feeling one gets from Wilhelmine men of honor that their duel was simply an elaborate marketing ploy to advertise their bravery; that they were selling it, not experiencing it. But perhaps the most useful comparison to draw would be to an execution, in which the cooperative and poised duelist performed "the final and awful socialized act, for the condemned man smoothes out the social situation, supporting the most evanescent part of our social life—its social occasions—just at a time when he can very little longer share in what he is supporting."[133] The German upper classes relied on reputation to regulate social relations, and the duel provided an opportunity to show strong character and uphold or generate status. It looked good on the résumé.

The insidious counterpoint to the duelist's vaunted courage was his subcutaneous fear of social censure. Manful virtue was sure to grow in the fecund soil of shame. Bismarck's bold words, "The Germans fear God and no one else!" disguised the banal fact that the duelist's nerve was steeled through concern for his public standing. The panic of dueling was nothing compared with the terrors of nonconformity. His swagger and dash, as is often the case, were fueled by a wealth of insecurities. Although dueling abolitionists were generally poor amateur psychologists, one critic, Professor Karl Binding, had the right idea when he described "the eternal *Angst* of the German that his honor might be robbed of him by any frivolous fellow, his trembling worry that perhaps already through an upturned nose or a derisive word his whole world has gone up in smoke."[134] What Binding termed *"Ehren-nervosität"* was a chronic nervous affliction of the carriage trade, usually characterized by acute and persistent hallucinations that someone was trying to trespass their personal integrity by belittling them. Before assembled doubters in the Reichstag in 1914, General Erich von Falkenhayn carefully explained that the duelist "places himself opposite his opponent, openly and under the same conditions of weaponry, [believing] himself capable of expunging the befallen ignominy, of being able to regain *the respect of his social peers, which he fears has been shaken."* [my emphasis][135]

Viennese playwright Arthur Schnitzler's (1862–1931) *Freiwild (Fair Game)* is a lively pastiche of contemporary honor motifs, and gives an illustrative account of the exogenous pressures to duel. *Freiwild* had its premiere in Berlin at the Deutsches Theater in 1896 and, because of its great initial success, enjoyed a second run at the Schiller Theater in 1901.[136] It tells the story of the earnest young intellectual Paul Rönning, and First Lieutenant of the Cavalry Karinski. In the first act, Karinski makes unwanted advances to Paul's good friend and possible love interest, the prissy Anna Riedel. Frustrated, Karinski provokes Paul, who reacts by striking the officer in the face; whereupon Paul's friends Wellner and Poldi volunteer their expertise, rightly anticipating a challenge from Karinski. The question is whether Paul wants their help.

When Wellner and Poldi arrive early the next morning at Paul's lodgings in order to receive Karinski's seconds, they discover that Paul has already spurned the envoys and rejected the challenge. Wellner and Poldi are aghast at this momentous blunder. They ask if he is jesting, he assures them he is not, and what follows is a classic defense of the gentleman's code of honor from the standpoint of its social function. Poldi leads off:

> I really don't understand how we can dispute for so long over such a clear case. As the doctor said, we live in a certain stratum, and so on; thank heavens we're not people who go around beating each other up like common thugs. We have a code, thank God, that covers every eventuality. Yesterday, according to the code, you behaved incorrectly.

Wellner makes Paul aware of the public consequences of not playing the game:

> What's important for you, Paul, is only one thing: if you are firmly set in your refusal to give satisfaction . . . . [y]ou abdicate all rights within the circle in which you've heretofore lived. . . . Anyone can insult you without you ever daring to demand chivalrous satisfaction.

Poldi pronounces the death sentence: "In plain German: you are *unsatisfaktionsfähig.*"

But before closing their case, Poldi and Wellner assume another tack designed to shock any man worth the name out of his dogmatic slumber. They attempt to persuade Paul of the necessity of defending his reputation against charges of cowardice:

> WELLNER: But consider that until now you've never had the opportunity in some way to prove your courage[. . . .] We are men, after all, my friend: and that's why we have to vouch with our blood for what we say and do. What would happen if everyone behaved like you?
>
> PAUL: If everyone behaved like me, pretty soon no one would be forced to it anymore! But the comedy of virile courage and contempt for life has to play itself out.
>
> WELLNER: Comedy . . . Courage!? . . .
>
> PAUL: That's right; and a very despicable courage it is. Who puts his life at risk so long as he has reason to love it? Nobody. If you then risk your life without loving it, then where's the courage?
>
> WELLNER: Ridiculous sophistry. You'll never be able to banish heroism from the world with this impoverished wisdom—and only we will be regarded as men who are capable of doing that very thing you so little value: risking your life.

Duelists' standards were mostly scruples, their principles usually expedience, and their hackneyed arguments the only fitting ones for a hackneyed institution. The compulsion to duel was the oldest trick in the book: a form of blackmail extorting blood money to virile notions of character. As Wellner warns the apostate Paul: "People will think that you are very attached to your life!"[137] This was the greatest infamy in a world where the essence of manhood was affectation of a serene scorn for one's own puny existence.

CHAPTER II

Cowards Die a Thousand Times

I look forward to it like a spectacle. I can see it now: not
batting an eyelash, the barrel of the pistol trained at him,
possibly falling dead, . . . By God, wouldn't it be wonderful
to be a fellow like you! But I fear it would be forced with me.
My friend, let us speak frankly: one must be somewhat
limited to stare death so calmly in the face.
—A second reproving his pistol-dueling client.
From Arthur Schnitzler, *Ritterlichkeit*
(a posthumous play fragment).[1]

IN 1907 the Prussian Minister of Justice Maximilian Beseler lectured
delegates to the Prussian parliament's upper chamber:

> It is not to be mistaken that our duel rests not only on injured honor but
> also indirectly on the fact that the *masculinity* of the injured is attacked
> and that the offended seeks restoration of his questioned *masculinity* in
> the duel. It is impossible to find punishment wherein it would be ex-
> pressed that the impugned *masculinity* is once again recognized. [my em-
> phases][2]

As the sole method by which, at certain pivotal moments, one's "masculinity" could be "expressed" and "restored," the act of dueling articulated certain upper-class German conceptions of manhood. For clues
to these conceptions, the thing to do is look at turn-of-the-century dueling codes. By examining them we discover an ethos of spurious
heroism that fell considerably short of its extravagant claim to being
the masculine apotheosis.

The alpha and omega of German masculinity was physical courage.
A critical inquiry into possible revision of the dueling law in 1912
made amply clear that "the German people sees in bravery, thank
God, the highest purpose of the man."[3] Even the abolitionist Graf Keyserling granted that "courage is an essential prerequisite of honor.
Cowardice is as little compatible these days with the concept of honor
as earlier."[4] In Thomas Mann's *Der Zauberberg* (*The Magic Mountain*,
1924), set before the First World War and in which a duel takes place,
the novel's engineer main figure Hans Castorp at one point reminisces

1. "Pistol duel." Wood engraving from a drawing by G. Tetzel, ca. 1860. (Bildarchiv Preussischer Kulturbesitz, Berlin)

that "at school, whenever in the book it read *'virtus,'* we always just said 'bravery' [*Tapferkeit*]."[5] This in contrast to the transatlantic experience of the American educator and literary critic, Lionel Trilling (1905–75), who remembered "that in my own undergraduate days we used specifically to exclude physical courage from among the virtues."[6] Neither birth, position, education, taste, or intelligence (although these played a role) were the most necessary endowments of the *Ehrenmann*. A bedrock of guts was the single attribute the most cultivated and accomplished gent could hardly forego, and not only did its pedigree compensate for other deficiencies of character, it was an excuse for them. Such hard-boiled standards are not unexpected in a working-class pub in Belfast, but they are somewhat startling when found in the upper flights of imperial German society. Then again, because the imperative of unqualified bravery has had its adherents in all countries, in all classes, across time—even the "Renaissance Man" Baldesar Castiglione was a disciple—maybe this is no shocking revelation after all. What may be interesting, however, is that German duelists took this imperative so seriously that they conceived of an insult— any insult, whether impinging on their family, caste, or personal honor—as testament to the secret opinion of the offender that one was powerless to retaliate; that he could injure with impunity because the object of his affront would not fight back. Thus, *every* insult implied the *supreme* insult among men of honor: imputation of physical cowardice—an imputation tied to notions of effeminacy. The duel was, therefore, an ostensible measure of courage, a litmus test of manhood that pretended to overturn the implicit emasculation entailed in every indignity.

But it is doubtful whether the German duel fulfilled the criteria it set for itself, because there was precious little about it that qualified as a virile readout. By the end of the nineteenth century, the ritual had become overly refined and excessively formalized, indicating a shrinking, a withdrawal. The self-conscious obsession with technique and protocol was a symptom of decadence. But the rot had set in much earlier. While the Italians, French, and Austro-Hungarians were roused by the zip and pace of tensile swordplay, increasingly in the first half of the nineteenth century Germans were drawn to the more flaccid demands of marksmanship. Spaniards and Russians appear to have been avid pistoleros, but probably not to the same quantitative or lethal degree of the Germans. As will be shortly explained, in the world inhabited by men of honor in which physical bravery was coin of the realm, firepower deflated the currency and at the fin de siècle, despite vociferous assertions among German duelists to the exact contrary (and at the expense of the reputation of other national styles), the German institution of dueling was bankrupt. Its battle cry of physical courage—the male sine qua non—was no longer valid. Modern weaponry was primarily to blame. The First World War, which spelled dueling's demise, was the poetic end of a static engagement in which bravery was mediated by machines and gauged indirectly across an open space. If you needed a dress rehearsal for Armageddon, this was it.

CODES, INSULTS, AND CHALLENGES

The Austrian novelist and essayist Robert Musil (1880–1942) once remarked that the German does not know whether he wants heaven or hell, he only knows he wants to organize it. Whether divine or unspeakable, the German duel was a well-organized affair. Its recondite rules were meticulously exposited in the dueling codes published in Central Europe toward the end of the nineteenth century. Prior to this period, however, there were so many contradictory guidelines, written and unwritten, that duelists were often themselves unsure of just how to go about the matter of bringing off a duel.[7] Since the invention of the printing press, over five thousand works on dueling had appeared worldwide, and before the 1880s men of honor were either vague on the subject's finer procedural points or were confidently following archaic practice.[8] By the end of the century, however, when dueling in Germany surged, a series of authoritative handbooks had been published which dispelled the confusion and, in tandem with fate, stage-managed the whole drama from insult to post-mortem.[9] These categorical manuals also succeeded in canonizing a custom that had long stood in direct opposition to statute law but had hitherto never been officially codified in German lands. As one of the new codes announced—perhaps not disinterestedly—it was now every gentleman's duty "to instruct himself thoroughly in the procedures that have been generally approved for the execution of affairs of honor and duels."[10] There is in fact every indication that the average *Ehrenmann* was a superb study who at least knew better when he exceeded the code's strict limits to make a duel more dangerous, which, in ways to be discussed, was not infrequently. This dualistic penchant for codifying all and then playing fast and loose with the rules betrayed the schoolbook fussiness of a doctorate-producing bourgeois class, followed closely by its parvenue affectation of aristocratic contempt for details and the void.

Apart from minor points, the dueling codes of honor published in Vienna, Budapest, and the German Empire in the last decades before the First World War were very alike. This resemblance stemmed from the fact—which the codes themselves dutifully acknowledged—that they shared a common ancestor in the Paris Jockey Club's Comte de Chatauvillard and his 1836 *Essai sur le duel*,[11] the most comprehensive codification of dueling ways and means to appear on the continent in the early nineteenth century, and which quickly became the universally accepted handbook of duelists across Europe. In 1881, Franz von Bolgar could remark that Chatauvillard was "even today still fully valid."[12] French codes also traced their heritage to Chatauvillard, and a French commentator in 1894 expressed surprise that his countrymen and the Germans, widely divergent in so many other respects and especially in consideration of their cultural and political antagonisms, should possess so very similar guidelines in settling the *point d'honneur*.[13] The only real difference, for example, between the German-language codes and the French dueling manuals is the more uncompromising tone assumed by the former, and any discrepancies between the Austro-Hungarian and German codes were chiefly the result of soft Danubian trills on the Chatauvillard theme. The effective difference, however, between Germany and the rest of Europe lay in the tough way German men of honor implemented their rules and then sometimes burst their confines in an effort to make the combat as treacherous as they could stand. The average German duel was not a cynical affair where men went through the motions of combat, firing over each other's heads or ending sword bouts with token first blood. In the German codes, duelists were enjoined to maintain "the serious-ness of the situation" lest the institution degenerate into a vapid cha-rade. The injunction read: "The duel should be serious, or it shall not be at all."[14]

A duel was only possible where there had been an insult, of which there were three broad categories. The first classification was the sim-ple slight (*einfache Beleidigung*), constituted by impoliteness or incon-siderate behavior. The second level of insult was cursing or attribution of shameful qualities, examples of which might be calling someone an *Esel* (jackass) or a *Schwachkopf* (imbecile). A tertiary offense was grav-est and was rendered through a blow or a slap, the spectacular gaunt-let-in-the-face falling under this heading, although they were rarely that hammy. To merely touch another's person qualified as a third-level offense, and if at a masked ball you were goosed by a tipsy sol-dier demanding a beer, the pinch that the Königsberg lawyer Ernst Borchert found himself in in 1896, a twenty-pace pistol duel with five exchanges was hardly an overreaction, though the rascal was dead by four.[15] The violation of another's physical integrity was considered so reprehensible that even a threatened blow was regarded as an ex-treme offense, and so gentlemen would spare themselves the exertion by stating simply: "Consider yourself slapped!"[16] The seduction or lewd touching of one's wife, daughter, sister or other female depen-dent, could constitute a "blow," and similar actions or words that jeopardized one's entire moral being (as the phrase usually went) were also aggravated third-level insults, amenable only through bloodshed.

The common assumption that the challenged was awarded choice of weaponry is an erroneous one. It was irrelevant who was the chal-lenger and who the challenged. This ascription was important only to legal investigation of the crime of dueling and played no formal role in planning a combat. The challenged choosing weapons—a Spanish tradition—was German only insofar as in the twelfth century the Em-peror Friedrich Barbarossa had permitted the challenged party in judi-cial duels to select the site, hour, and weapons.[17] Such an arrangement in modern times might have swung open the door for ruffians with strong arms and practiced eyes to go around intentionally picking fights. For this reason the classification of insults was crucial because it determined the extent to which a duel could be designed specifically for the benefit of the insulted party. At the first level, the offended had the choice of weapons; at the second level, a choice of weaponry and style of combat; and in cases of third-level injury, the choice of arms, style, and distance.[18] (German-language codes recommended that all third-level insults be settled with pistols.)

There were certain exceptions to the rules. Gustav Hergsell cites the hypothetical situation of a masher who makes indecent advances to a married woman, is upbraided by the husband and advised to leave, but who persists and is then cursed and threatened with a blow. Technicalities aside, the distraught husband is the aggrieved party.[19] The dialectical variables were endless, like two mirrors aface one another, receding into eternity. The spirit of the codes took precedence over their letter and the psychology of a quarrel was more nuanced than a simple eight-step escalation from retort courteous to lie direct. In the final analysis, honor was devoid of clearly conceived ethical content, defying Enlightenment notions of a human behavioral alphabet founded on systematic theory.[20] One commentator described honor as a sort of "aesthetic sense."[21] Insults were a "matter of feeling" (*Gefühlsache*) in which, "Every word, every writing, intention or gesture which injures the self-esteem or sensibility of another is for this person an insult."[22] The result was an oversensitivity among men of honor to any conduct of a questionable ilk. Because of the manifold variety and indefinite nature of insult in Germany, and because it was not only the right but the duty of every man of honor to demand satisfaction for an affront, the "offense" was very often an intuitive judgment which, in order to allay all suspicion of cowardice, might ultimately issue in the verdict: when in doubt, challenge.[23]

Challenges were rarely delivered on the spot. Principals exchanged their names and addresses by swapping calling cards with a promise to be in touch soon. One or both parties would notify two trustees of their honor—seconds—who would then demand satisfaction on behalf of their client. The acceptance of a challenge was not a recognition of culpability. Similarly, the demand for satisfaction was neither a recrimination nor an actual challenge in the legal sense, but a proposal to choose deputies and have the foursome see if it could not defuse the dispute.

Selection of these sidekicks transformed the most trivial incident into a courtly ceremony of grandiose proportions. Contemporaries believed that the presence of seconds made the encounter chivalrous, every knight requiring at least one faithful squire: "For in the moment when seconds intervene in an affair of honor, one has chosen the chivalrous route—to differentiate from the judicial—in its adjudication. Whether or not the seconds are able to peaceably dispose of the matter, or whether they permit it to be settled with weapons, it has always been managed in a chivalrous fashion."[24] For special legal validation of the encounter as a "duel" and not as the felony of attempted murder, seconds were also a necessary prerequisite.[25] Their selection was to be undertaken with obvious care, since "one sets his entire trust in these; the fate of his life and honor is laid in their hands."[26]

What were the attributes of the ideal second? Blood relatives need not apply (although this clause was often violated), he was to be *satisfaktionsfähig*, and he was definitely not Zaretsky's "rowdy sheik" as portrayed in Alexander Pushkin's *Eugene Onegin*.[27] Chatauvillard's "Father Confessor" was more the type.[28] Young hotheads were always objectionable picks because a phlegmatic temperament was indispensable to the negotiation of a mutually acceptable arrangement. Irish, for example, were expressly precluded from consideration in eighteenth-century England because, according to one expert, "nine out of ten Irishmen have such an innate love of fighting they cannot bring an affair to an amicable adjustment."[29] Judicious men of experience and authority were preferable so long as they were not too elderly, otherwise the requisite spryness pertaining to the moderation of such high-tempered mise-en-scènes would be lacking. He was naturally to be "cold-blooded" and the possessor of a "sharp eye," always on the lookout for breaches of the honor code during battle. It was also desirable that he have more than just a passing acquaintance with side-arms, and possess a thorough knowledge of the dueling code. He was brave, seasoned, and had impeccable social credentials—in ascending order of importance.[30] All these attributes in one man would theoretically avert a serious combat, or one with mortal stipulations attached. Albert von Boguslawski, who never met a duelist he didn't like, attested to his own pacifistic nature by citing some fifty *Ehrenhändel* in which he had brought his solemn counsel to bear, only five of which spiraled into duels and only two of those taking place under parlous conditions.[31] But full-timers like him were rare. It was not always the simplest task to commandeer a fellow both suitable and willing to break the law, a fact emphasized by the commentator to an 1888 German translation of Chatauvillard.[32]

Before fulfilling their duty as squires, seconds were first commissioned as pages (*Kartellträger*) to deliver up the complaint of their client and his accompanying demand for satisfaction. Having ascertained the *Satisfaktionsfähigkeit* of their charge's antagonist, these all-purpose factotums would pay him a visit, usually on the morrow, preserving a cordial yet reticent mien, avoiding all behavior that might be construed as inflammatory, and purveying the message, written or spoken, with as much tact as they could muster. Incidents were possible. In Paris in 1870, to cite a famous example, the emperor's skittish cousin, Prince Pierre Bonaparte, shot and killed his challenger's plenipotentiary in a crazed fit of panic.[33]

On the chance that no one was home, messengers would leave their calling cards and return later that day. Persisted their quarry unflushed, they would post their conditions with a servant or landlady. If within twenty-four hours the challenged had failed to summon himself, a protocol was drawn up legitimizing the challenger's failure to receive adequate satisfaction, and was especially crucial when the initial insult had been sustained before witnesses or had excited reaction in the newspapers. Press publication of the protocol could be used both to clear one's name and to rebuke an antagonist. In 1892 the editor of Berlin's conservative *Kreuzzeitung* employed this alternative:

> As I ascertained in the *Kreuzzeitung*, on the sixth day of this month in a handling of the jury court, Herr Mosse, attorney-at-law in Berlin, permitted himself to make insulting remarks against me. As a result, I have commissioned two friends to inquire of him whether he is ready to publicly retract his statements accompanied by an expression of regret, or else to represent his personal insults with his person, as is usual among men of honor. Herr Mosse rejected both. I confine myself to the simple confirmation of this fact.[34]

The restraint of it is fatal. The direct or indirect rejection of a challenge was never a blot on the challenger's honor, for the protocol had "the exact same worth as if he had stood face to face with his opponent, weapon in hand."[35]

If the demand for satisfaction was not spurned by the challenged (always at his social hazard), it was his responsibility to choose seconds of his own, whose duty it then was to arrange a meeting with their opposite numbers. The seconds' initial priority, unless bearing special instructions from the side of their client to choreograph an affair at all costs, was an attempt at reconciliation. If the peaceful solution was not forthcoming, then the seconds would address themselves to the task of negotiating a *pactum pugnandi* as guideline for the upcoming combat.

After the provocation, one had just twenty-four hours to challenge, and the actual duel was to take place within forty-eight hours of that. This may have been a way for procrastinators to get a wiggle on, and an implicit effort at reducing potential practice time. The underlying idea was that an insult could hardly be considered aggravated if patiently endured for any longer period. If a challenge was forwarded after the twenty-four-hour expiration, there was no obligation to accept it. The only exception to this rule involved seduction, where many months or even years might elapse before irrefragable evidence could come to light permitting the matter to be taken out of mothballs. Knowledge of a tacit, so-called *Verjährungstheorie* (statute of limitations) among duelists probably prompted Professor Medem in his 1902 "Petition to the Reichstag concerning the Duel" to include the following sub-clause to Article 209 of the penal code exempting seconds from punishment if they had done their level best to reconcile antagonists: "Impunity ceases to apply if the duel is fought out earlier than three months after the challenge. The efforts of the *Kartellträger* pass for serious only if they had been repeated upon several occasions within these three months."[36] Although duelists could give the appearance of glacial calm under fire, challenges were often issued in the heat of the moment when it was ulikely that cooler heads would prevail, as Medem realized. In *Der Zauberberg*, on the eve of a duel in which two days and three nights will have elapsed between insult and combat, Hans Castorp hopes that,

> Tomorrow morning, gun in hand, neither of the litigants would be the man he was the evening of the strife. At most, they would simply go through the motions to satisfy the demands of honor, not fighting according to their own free will of the moment, as, out of desire and conviction, they would have fought that same evening; and such a denial of their actual selves in favor of those they once were must somehow be prevented![37]

One imagines that many duels were underpinned by such inauthentic motives, for the most stubborn courage is rarely proof against lengthy contemplation unrelieved by action.

These time limits may have played a greater role in promoting harmless affairs into apocalyptic struggles than the most flagrant insult, whose burning effects were likely to simmer and cool with the gradual passage of time. The twenty-four/forty-eight-hour clause rode with spur and rein over doubts and made caution a luxury even the most prudent man of honor could ill afford. In one Berlin episode of 1902, the imbroglio was laid to rest with characteristic German energy at one a.m. of a Sunday morning when a quickie duel with sabers replaced tongues to determine a political dicker earlier that evening.[38] Pistols by moonlight? A dicier affair, but an exchange of words one evening in Berlin's Friedrichstrasse could be settled early the next morning at ten paces crosstown in the Grunewald.[39] Officers tended to dispatch these matters with even greater alacrity.[40] Twelve hours was officially the earliest that a duel could be fought after a challenge—probably to ensure regularity in its execution and to leave suitable time for the ordering of one's affairs—but the above examples are in-

dicative of the impatient haste with which duels were generally prosecuted, since an overstepping of the deadline without sufficient good
reason could irreparably damage one's reputation as an honorable
man of decision. Although forebearance in every other way was the
hallmark of the German *Ehrenmann*'s creed, it was thought better to
precipitate a premature action than to gain the ascription of a weak
and vacillating character by dawdling.

There were myriad restrictions inhibiting challenges and their acceptance. Although honor was fundamentally a matter of feeling, its
satisfaction was a highly proscriptive business. For example, one
forfeited the right to chivalrous satisfaction by instigating a judicial
process against one's antagonist, even if the complaint was later with-
drawn. Since the legal nostroms of the *Rechtsstaat* were clearly incompatible with the dictates of unconditional honor, which demanded
lightning-swift, self-wrought justice, one could reject the challenge of
anyone who had ever sustained an action against someone on the
grounds of insult (*Beleidigung*). Minors under twenty-one years of age
were 4-F, although those pursuing a course of study at a university
were removed from this ban. A younger man could only duel with one
over sixty if he had been insulted at the third level, in which case the
elder gentleman probably had enough fire in him to withstand same.
Those with a sole arm or leg were allowed to reject sword challenges,
but only if they had not offended at the third level, the principle being
that "the hand which deals the blow must also wield the weapon."[41]
Pistol duels could only be rejected by men with one good eye if they
had not offended at the second or third levels. Fathers could not fight
sons, and brothers had to settle their filial spats without benefit of
sword or pistol.

In short, the qualifications were endless. The dueling codes were
freighted with plenty of exploitable loopholes for clever, legalistic seconds serving as proxy for a mollycoddle warrior. Franz von Bolgar
lamented that too many seconds were overly eager to put their lambs
through the meatgrinder—like Schnitzler's Wellner and Poldi—and
felt sure that if in every instance competent assistants were chosen,
more than half of all encounters would never take place.[42] Many serious German duels were the result of passionate affairs of the heart in
which there was no hope for compromise, but quite a number were
the consequence of trivial squabbles generated at cards or in late-night
taverns. Only acute third-level insults led unavoidably to general mo-
bilization. Bagatelles were negotiable, normally through agreement as
to the insult's unintentional character, and with regret expressed—but
apology rarely given—by the offender's seconds for the misunderstanding. Granted, the true sources of conflict for first- and second-

level insults may have resided much deeper than the visible and immediate ones. But all things considered, a great many men in Germany were sacrificing their health and very lives without sufficiently compelling reason. In this respect, the saying, "It's neither pistol ball nor blade which kills—it's the second," had special significance in a country whose rate of dueling mortality was second to none.[43]

PRELIMINARY EVENTS

Undoubtedly the prospect of a duel was likely to "call forth a certain excitement" the night before.[44] In his short story "*Un Lâche*" ("A Coward," 1884), Guy de Maupassant, a knowing duelist himself, described the distress of a young man on the eve of a rare French pistol duel at twenty paces. Overcome by a premonition of unholy dread at the site, "he imagined the dishonor, the whispering in the clubs, the laughing in the salons, the scorn of the women, the innuendo of the journals, the insults of cowards." He cannot sleep and has a parching thirst. He reads Chatauvillard and imbibes a decanter of rum to deaden his nerves. Nothing helps. When day breaks, he deadens himself with a bullet.[45]

There were surely as many different strategies for diversion preparatory to a duel as there were duelists, but the ever-dwindling hours would ordinarily be spent in the lugubrious business of writing letters of farewell to loved ones, communicating last wishes to friends, drawing up a will, and generally ordering one's affairs so that no one could be compromised by posthumous papers and documents—especially if the duel impinged on a third party. A bath was suggested to set one up tingly fresh for the next morning and probably as a calming influence, but was also reminiscent of a candidate for knighthood who would undergo a rare wash as a symbol of spiritual purification. It was strongly advised to refrain from food or drink that might in any way spawn an embarrassing scene at the site of battle.

To appear for the duel with an untidy toilet was tantamount to a third-level insult. Although some combatants showed up decked out in tails or full evening dress, a humble black frock coat, furnished with wide lapel to flip up and obscure a highly visible starched white shirt collar when pistol-dueling, was more than adequate in meeting the needs of propriety. Beneath the dark coat was a white undergarment of plain silk or linen, preferably with detachable sleeves for saber duels to avoid the ill-bred habit of rolling them up. Woolen tricots were disallowed because of their ability to absorb superficial saber slashes, but, if of lighter material, shirts were usually kept on so that incidental cuts would not be readily apparent, thus preventing a premature stoppage of "first blood" contests. Headdress was ordinarily doffed, but no one objected if a duelist exchanged rounds in his top hat. Footgear was irrelevant in pistol duels, but recommended for bladework were light boots with broad heels whose soles gained better traction through an application of rosin.[46] This was the battle array.

Pistol duels generally took place at sunup; although it was bruited about whether rosy-fingered dawn was expeditious for sabers.[47] A famous fictional example is Arthur Schnitzler's *"Leutnant Gustl"* (1900), who fights his saber duel at four o'clock in the afternoon. First blood at first light was more than most could stand, for sabers demanded a performance level above that required of pistols, where grogginess verging on somnambulism was probably an advantage as you assumed your position: nervous energy was a detriment when it came to that rock-steady aim. During the week, professionals had to be at work later on, it was surely a relief to have the ordeal over with as soon as possible, and the early morning hours also afforded a privacy unavailable in the later part of the day.

To guard against prying eyes, the most popular dueling haunts were sylvan. Glades, glens, canopied meadows or any other dim, dustless locale (often scouted and prepared the day before by efficient seconds acting as groundskeepers) where duelists could engage each other free from interference, were favored points of rendezvous. Some spots were more popular than others. In Berlin, for example, most duels took place in the Grunewald or the Tegeler Forest abutting the affluent western half of the city, where men could expire peacefully far from the urban tumult. During the first days of October 1896, there were three reported engagements in the Grunewald, two of these duels on account of women,[48] thus making it a normal week in the *Reichshauptstadt*. In 1907 a group of duelists was found occupying an apparently well-known venue in Berlin's Tegeler Forest; but it was a good day to die and the septet moved their duel to Pankow where one of their number could.[49] If a gendarme or forest warden happened to run afoul of the proceedings, the contingent was enjoined by the codes to snap it up and transfer the combat to another site.[50] In 1883 the Berlin police learned of a duel in the city's outlying Hasenhaide, but the intrepid group anticipated the ambush and hastened downtown to the Tiergarten.[51] In such situations when the authorities were tipped off to a forthcoming affair, it was likely that either a well-meaning second or a faint-hearted duelist had leaked the information, an ugly violation of the gentleman's hallowed code, but one that could seldom be proven. It was suspicious timing indeed in 1883 when in Reinickendorf on the outskirts of Berlin a gendarme interrupted a duel between a jurist and a doctor with loaded pistols at the ready; he may have been delaying to catch them red-handed, but a duel was not official until shots had been fired.[52] It was advisable to post lookouts. In an 1898 saber duel in Berlin's Hasenhaide, the fathers of the two young duelists orchestrated a tough-love intervention by bursting forth from surrounding bushes when the command *"Los!"* was pronounced to give them a thrashing with malacca canes.[53] All this hide-and-seek and cabalistic planning could not but have heightened the duel's romantic allure, more glamorous for its clandestine illegality.

The German duel was not necessarily a seasonal affair. By contrast, the Italian dueling aficionado Jacopo Gelli was able to assert that his compatriots were most febrile in spring, while the French got frisky in winter.[54] The ever-stolid German was less beholden to the humor of climatic flux, and naturally the twenty-four/forty-eight-hour clause would not abide delays. In Berlin in 1896 two aristocrats arose early Easter Sunday not to attend morning services but to wage ritual battle, death kindly taking the holiday.[55] Four years earlier, a Graf Armin-Wimpen was seriously injured in a duel by a Baron Duka during the latter's honeymoon in Zurich with his June bride.[56] In the autumn of 1901, at the garrison town of Insterburg, a young lieutenant of the artillery had his marriage annulled by a pistol duel, the result of a drunken altercation the night of his bachelor party. He was drilled through the kidney, his spinal cord was shattered, and his wedding day was celebrated with a graveside eulogy.[57] Instead of rice, they tossed earth.

With the time clause to speed them along, duelists showed rare concern for meteorological conditions, although excessive precipitation could drive an alfresco saber bout indoors and in pistol duels special care would be taken to keep the powder dry. After a snowfall, it was advisable to shed one's coat and spoil an opponent's aim by making the outline of white shirtsleeves indistinct against a pallid backdrop. It was hoped one's chattering teeth would not be mistaken for undue anxiety.

It is natural that Prussian territory (constituting two-thirds of German land and population) should have witnessed more duels than any other region in Germany, and within Prussia the capital city of Berlin and the administrative district of Cologne had the heaviest concentrations, with those of Stettin and Celle close behind.[58] Demographically then, most duels were occurring in the population belt stretching west-east across the middle of Prussia from the Rhineland to Pomerania, an overwhelmingly Protestant distribution.[59] German trains were most reliable, so geographically undesirable opponents could not gain release from their obligations. In such cases, it was suggested that a duelist sit to the left of his seconds in the compartment's backward-facing seats[60]—perhaps to savor one last lingering look at the landscape streaking by. The codes thought of everything.

Generally speaking, out-of-town duelists would take lodging the night before in *Pensionen* at the edge of forests where the duel would be held, then rise and shine at the crack of doom. In 1894, consequent of a love triangle, it was two in the campagna when a doctor from Bohemia traveled to an appointment with a veterinarian outside Berlin and cured what ailed him forever with a parting shot; that same day he was back across the border.[61] To avoid hometown suspicion and local reprisals, both duelists might make the roadtrip, as in 1899 when an officer and a civilian left Berlin with their respective entourages on a Tuesday, spent the evening in a village *Gasthaus* some miles south of the city, then sallied forth the next morning for the officer to rate a purple heart.[62] Day trips were almost the rule in Vienna. Due to the gentle character of Hungary's laws, Austrian subjects were in the habit of resolving their disputes beyond the Leitha in the Hungarian frontier town of Pressburg, just across the border from the imperial capital. Following the duel, survivors would take it on the lam back to now preferable Austrian territory.[63]

Duelists, their seconds, and a doctor—and sometimes a neutral umpire called the *"Unparteiische"*—were usually transported to the point of rendezvous in covered droshkys. Only an exagerrated self-confidence would lead a duelist to arrive on horseback and fail to commission some sort of carriage, thereby leaving no provision for the reshipment of a dreadful burden home. But it was his carcass. Punctuality was imperative. Any retinue kept waiting longer than one quarter of an hour had the right to leave and draw up a terse protocol condemning the tardiness as baneful proof of the opponent's disreputable character and unworthiness. Still, the courteous half hour was recommended.[64] But if after a half hour there was still no show, the duel was to be rescheduled only if the other party had been unavoidably detained.

Upon gaining the site, the contestants stripped off their coats and their persons were checked for watches, wallets, coins or other articles such as letters or newspapers capable of deflecting saber slashes or impeding the progress of low-velocity slugs. In 1898 in Bavaria the torso-frisk failed to reveal a key in the high pockets of a young law student. Instead of saving his life, it was driven ahead of the bullet into his abdomen, producing a wound to which he succumbed two hours later.[65] So as to avoid any possible complications arising from a bullet carrying with it pieces of cloth (often leading to infection and death from an otherwise nonlethal ball), a duelist one time bared all at the site and the duel was disgustedly scotched.[66] Barring such naked ploys, opponents would be ceremoniously led to their respective places by the seconds. It was this last moment before taking up arms, as the mood grew redolent with foreboding, that was described as the "most unpleasant and most critical" of the duel, and doctors were admonished to refrain preparing their instruments during this interval so as not to demoralize the more high-strung.[67]

The role of the doctor at duels was a delicate one. His purpose was not only to extract balls, if not too deeply embedded in tissue, and stitch up saber wounds, but he was also consulted to see if a bout should continue. If permitting it to endure too long, injuries might be incurred whose fatal complications, should the case be brought to trial, would exacerbate the criminal charge of dueling. (The death itself did not so much matter.) On the other hand, if duelists were to be sicked on one another until a serious wound was inflicted, and the doctor stopped the bout prematurely "out of misplaced sympathy," then the injured party "would be justified in demanding satisfaction from him"[68] in a way that no malpractice insurance could ever cover. But a physician was auxiliary to the duel, not its accomplice, the seventh party thrown in for good luck. Unlike seconds who were threatened with one to six months detainment by the law, doctors were granted immunity.

The leading second would make a last-ditch attempt to reconcile the opponents before joining battle. In truth, he did not usually try very hard. Apologies at the site were roundly condemned by the dueling manuals for the suspicion of cowardice they excited. The apologizer might have been playing at brinkmanship in the hope that his opponent would ultimately fold, thus gaining a cheap victory. Or he might have gotten a last-minute attack of nerves. It even caused eyebrows to elevate and tongues to wag for renowned fencers, who had often proven their mettle, to beg forgiveness at the site: the insult may have been leveled as a test to see if the adversary would have the gumption to decisively counter. And in itself the assumption that an opponent would accept an olive branch "formed a serious insult, more serious even than a physical affront, because it a priori places into doubt the courage of the offended."[69] Animosity might have dissipated, but the fear of being thought recreant never vanished. Only among old friends could supplication conscionably take place at the zero hour, and of these I have read only one example, effectuated in Berlin's Grunewald in 1896 and celebrated in the Kurfürstenpark zu Halensee afterwards.[70] Since Article 209 of the German penal code allowed seconds to evade punishment if they "had made a serious attempt to avert the duel," the peacemaking bid was more a precaution taken by these trustees to save themselves, not their charges. In actuality, an attempted reconciliation (*Versöhnungsversuch*) was a transparent formality that stood little chance against the ringing imperative of untarnished derring-do.

Reconciliation was not the object of the duel, for there were certain affronts, namely seduction, that mitigated against a restoration of amicable relations. A handshake formed an agreeable postlude to the proceedings but the critical aspect was that the duelists had been socially reinstated, not personally reconciled. There is little question that "proving oneself while in personal danger allows the issue to recede and repairs the feeling of mutual respect,"[71] but the point of the duel was not to make nice with an opponent through therapeutic mayhem. Its purpose was to scour away the black turpitude of insult, and as soon as swords or pistols were brandished cleanliness was restored. Combats were arranged only in the wake of a foundered compromise attempt,[72] and therefore a duel always expressed intransigence. But if the insult that had precipitated the challenge was based on a simple misunderstanding or stubbornness, differences could be honorably composed, and in such cases it was fitting for the healthier duelist to initiate the action by offering his hand.[73] After a rapprochement, it was acceptable to inquire after the condition of wounded opponents; however, unless the two fighting men had been old friends, it was overly familiar to pay a personal sickbed visit. If reconciliation was deemed impossible, due to the severity of the offense or the enmity which had developed between the combatants, then the duelists would leave the grounds wordlessly.

But we precede ourselves. Let us first handicap the contest. Then, like the watchful crowd at a Roman gladiatorial bout observing the manner in which men received death, we shall be better able to rate these German duelists and appraise the character their particular brand of combat invoked. Will we be one with the ancient Roman commentator who concluded, "Many spectators, few men"?

———

The motto of the German dueling codes was "Never draw your sword without good reason; never sheath it without your honor!"[74] Most German swords rusted in their scabbards. At best, one out of every four duels was carried out with this weapon, and in Germany that meant the curved saber. In 1895, the *Illustrierte Zeitung* complained that in Germany, outside of the army and the universities, and in contrast to other nations, "the noble and chivalrous art of fencing" was rarely practiced.[75] Predictably, from their modern revival in 1896, the Olympic Games foil and épée competitions were dominated by Italy and France; and Hungary, hardly a sports powerhouse in most other respects, was the clear force in saber fencing: Germany did not win a gold medal in male Olympic fencing until 1976.[76] In 1902, a Reichstag deputy confirmed that "almost all serious duels" in Germany were fought out with pistols[77]—and duels in Germany tended to be serious.

The questionable but seldom questioned syllogism for satisfaction read: The greater the danger, the greater the honor; pistols are more dangerous than sabers; therefore pistols are more honorable. Sabers were seldom rattled not only because they stipulated a verve and athleticism absent from the pedestrian pistol duel, but mainly because they were less likely to inflict mortal wounds. In a 1902 session of the Reichstag, the National Liberal Ernst von Bassermann wished aloud that German duelists would employ sabers more often to curb deaths and thereby diminish dueling's recent adverse publicity.[78] Gustav Hergsell tried to reassure an apparently skeptical readership that, as compared to pistols, sabers could test courage "in the same if not greater measure."[79] But few listened. Bravery among German prewar stock was measured not by the exhibition of physical and mental agility, flexible response and active daring, but by a bovine impassivity that could trade shots at suicidal range.

According to the codes, however, the chance and luck inherent in pistol duels was incompatible with true conceptions of courage.[80] Pistol duels—with their smoothbore barrels, arbitrary pacing requirements, and nondefensive orientation—offered too many contingent elements to merit fully the chivalrous tag. In 1896, the Justice Ministry received an anonymous yet eloquent missive condemning the duel, that excoriated pistols in particular as "a pure gamble with one's life."[81] In pistol duels it was not so much marksmanship as craftsmanship that determined the result, because the outcome of an encounter depended essentially on the quality of the weaponry.[82] The unreliability of crude smoothbores placed a very low premium on expertise.[83] The premium on bravery was equally marginal. There was fear to surmount, but duelists got over it in their own way. And terror cementing the feet, it would not have been unlikely to lock knees and convulsively twitch a trigger without coming all unhinged. Scared stiff, one could still cut a sanguine figure at fifteen or fewer paces. Such grace under pressure was not so amazing. As for dying, that was even easier. One's opponent did all the work, and "superhuman self-mastery"[84] was wasted here. In recommending sabers to the army instead of firearms for settling its disputes, Freiherr von Hodenberg told how "the coward frequently hides behind the pistol."[85]

The cult of honor was alive and well in Germany, but its supreme expression, the duel, had been dead on the vine for years. The German will to firepower was a spurious attempt to retain aristocratic values without truly embodying them. According to the old standards, the antique sword, not the pistol, denoted noble rank, and it was also symbolic of the cult of the warrior. In the British Isles, although defunct by 1850, pistol dueling had first become popular during the second half of the eighteenth century when it attracted the following of a large middle class inexpert with swords, and the nineteenth-century German bourgeoisie would appear to have done something similar as a way of asserting and achieving status in their own nation.[86] But bloodless scholars and fat businessmen waving pistols were would-be warriors, and the confrontation between frail flabby flesh and death was ludicrously inappropriate. In *Der Zauberberg*, master ironist Thomas Mann dramatizes a mock-epic pistol duel between two intellectuals wasted by tuberculosis.[87] Heroic stature has traditionally its ultimate source in powerful physical attributes and these were entirely irrelevant to a contest in which one was nothing more than a bourgeois bullseye, like a condemned man facing a firing squad. The missing props were a cigarette and a blindfold. By the late nineteenth century, disciplined cooperation had replaced heroism in the German duel. It was more proper than glorious, more dutiful than beautiful. In a historical devolution, the German duel with pistols had reemerged as its medieval antecedent, the ordeal.

While there was a much greater probability of being killed in a pistol duel, cool-hand flukes could walk away from it not only unhurt but without breaking a sweat. In lively saber matches there was at least an even chance of carrying away some nasty mementos of the occasion, because contests were continued until first blood (*auf's erste Blut*) and quite often beyond to the point that one or both of the combatants were unable to continue fighting (*Kampfunfähigkeit*). Power played a far greater role than finesse in most German saber duels and for this reason one imagines that first blood and *Kampfunfähigkeit* were often the same thing. If duelists were determined to shed blood at all costs, sabers would sometimes back up pistols. In 1892, for instance, following a political dispute, the Graf Roon fell dead to the blade of a Polish nobleman after the two had missed each other with guns.[88] Sabers were always a saving trump because they were certain to originate wounds, but, because they were not designed as thrusting instruments (the blade's curvature inhibited deep penetration), rarely killed on the spot.

The saber ordinarily used in Central European duels, a basic army-issue blade, unnotched and smooth, was a few inches short of three feet long and weighed a feathery six hundred grams. (The current fencing saber used in international competition is even lighter at five hundred grams, something more than a pound.) The center of gravity was about ten to fifteen centimeters from the guard and so not further forward than halfway up the defensive part of the blade, which made up the lower half of the whole. The notion was that "the man should wield the weapon, not the weapon the man."[89] The codes frowned upon heavy cavalry sabers, for example, because they turned combat into a "vulgar brawl," rendering the "idea of chivalrous battle worthless." Only when intelligence and judgment prevailed was courage in its "noblest form" to be found.[90] The slogging two-handed broadsword contest of medieval knights no longer set the standard by which chivalrous encounters were judged. Although the lighter, quicker swords were apt to snap on occasion, they could still inflict frightful injuries—as could attest one Hungarian officer who bid farewell to arm in an 1890 Budapest saber duel.[91]

In comparison to the swashbuckling genre of swordplay portrayed in romantic novels and Hollywood cinema, the German saber duel was ascetic in its restraint. Flynn would not have been in. There was no punching with the guard or the free hand, no kicking or pushing. It was forbidden to touch hand, knee, or any other part of the body to the ground. The duelist was not allowed to follow-up an attack which had disarmed his opponent or had caused him to stumble and fall. It was impermissible to transfer a blade from one hand to the other. Parrying of the opponent's blade with one's free hand was not allowed, something difficult in any case because this hand was usually lodged firmly in the small of one's back, in contrast to the French épée duel in which it was kept poised above one's head or splayed at a downward angle when lunging.[92] (If hopelessly reflexive, the extremity could be tied down.) There was no talking, screaming, or taunting through word or gesture. The attack was to proceed "calmly and with consideration and not bruskly,"[93] and the gaze of the opponents "should be sunk in the eyes of the other."[94] Bouts were confined to a roughly 20x6 meter area, the same length as today's competitive strips, so that a pitched running battle with duelists rushing helter-skelter about was impossible. Because advance was much more dangerous than retreat due to the chance of sudden ripostes, duelists who had been driven outside the perimeter were reprimanded and escorted back into the middle of the site. Doctors could regulate the duration of bouts for those patients with heart conditions, although two minutes was the bare minimum for any duelist. Clinches were broken up. This squeaky-clean contest was littered with rules—and they were not made to be broken.

Several precautions helped further protect participants from life-threatening injury. Swaths of silk were coiled about wrist and neck to safeguard the pulse and carotid arteries, and blades were rinsed with an antiseptic carbolic acid solution to prevent infection. After a wound was inflicted, depending on the conditions of the bout, the perpetrator would repair to a neutral corner while the doctor inspected the gash. Studded gauntlets were almost always worn by the combatants, but less as a safety precaution than as a prophylaxis against the premature ending of a "first blood" bout through a minor cut on the hand. As a rule, the larger the gauntlet, the graver the bout. Leg swipes and arm chops were discouraged because of large veins near the surface of these limbs, the prime target area being the head and the upper torso. If a duelist's saber began to sink from fatigue, if blood from a head laceration started streaming into his eyes obscuring his vision, or if any other eventuality occurred to render a combatant momentarily defenseless, the seconds would intervene.

In most saber duels thrusting was expressly proscribed, or the point might be ground down or detached to frustrate a "perfidious assassination."[95] Although some dueling codes warned that exclusion of the thrust (*ohne Stich*) was "impractical, illogical, and unjust," saber bouts employing the thrust (*mit Stich*) were always special arrangements and never appear to have caught on, perhaps for the very reason that they placed too many special demands on the dilettante.[96] The ostensible rationale, however, for the institution of *ohne Stich* dueling in Germany was to delimit the danger. As an alternative to the traditional and potentially deadlier épée duel, Chatauvillard encouraged the propagation of the saber duel *sans pointe* in his own homeland.[97] It was above all very difficult to determine the extent of a wound in duels *mit Stich* because its internal quality was apprehended only by the victim, who was often ill-suited to assess his own continued fighting capacity.[98] But though the saber duel *ohne Stich* may have been less dangerous, it deprived skilled fencers of half their technical arsenal. By altering the blade, one denatured a contest in which the defensive was normally stressed.[99] Inferior yet more powerful fighters stood a greater chance of emerging victorious by virtue of a sudden banzai charge, otherwise neutralized through a simple outstretched point that maintained a sword-length's interval between the combatants. Unlike *mit Stich*, in *ohne Stich* duels it was impossible to redirect the force generated by an inexperienced adversary so as to defeat him. Most Austrian saber duels were *ohne Stich* as well, and Schnitzler's Gustl, on the eve of his combat with a civilian doctor, reminds himself that "just these unschooled fencers are sometimes the most dangerous."[100]

Obversely, schooled fencers could be their own worst nemeses. In an 1893 Viennese saber duel, a first lieutenant of the Hussars demonstrated a superb technique but no killer instinct as he delivered blows with the flat of his blade, a habit apparently acquired from long hours in the fencing hall. His opponent, a reserve officer of the Dragoons, noted this tendency and stormed in to disable the Hussar's right arm and in the process hack off his nose, which for the balance of the combat was stuck up on the wall by an attentive second. The Hussar was compelled to continue the bout *ohne Nase*. It was stitched back on afterward.[101] Although saber duels *ohne Stich* were historically suggestive of the blunted weapons used in medieval jousting, saber duels *mit Stich* were theoretically adjured as "more chivalrous" because of the circumspect and deliberate style they fostered, giving physically disadvantaged opponents an even chance.

The implications of "chivalrous" depended, of course, on one's point of view: in saber duels *mit Stich* physically weaker duelists were compensated, while technically inferior duelists were reimbursed in matches *ohne Stich*. What was fair to the strong was annoying to the skilled—and vice-versa—therefore, neither style was as unprejudiced as pistols, in which skill and strength were negligible components and cold blood held the balance. Consequently, sabers under both species were generally disdained, and even relative experts shunned the form. Unless insulted at the critical third level, for example, fencing masters were forbidden to use the tool of their trade, and then were urged to gallantly derogate this privilege. (This was decidedly not the case in France where duelists were usually well-trained swordsmen and so fencing masters had few qualms.) Officers, often drilled in saber fencing, usually opted for pistols; in any event, they were only permitted to use sabers in the case of a first-level insult. *Mensur*-trained collegians, whose impoverished blade technique (which we will examine in chapter IV) had little to offer a more freewheeling saber match and had, moreover, greater affinity with the torpid and mechanical pistol duel, were likely as not in later life to choose firearms for serious affairs. Thinning the ranks yet further, saber challenges could be rebuffed up to a third-level insult if one suffered from a physical disability, which might mean many things to many people; and civilians had the right to reject the weapon *sans gêne* if they were unfamiliar with it, as a good many no doubt were. The field was therefore left to the blunt-tipped hackers and it is no wonder that cutlery was stigmatized as a flimsy substitute for gunpowder. Instituted about the 1880s originally as a means to reduce fatalities,[102] the *ohne Stich* duel seems in the long term to have had the reverse effect: the danger factor, as the one constant and supreme value in the German honorable equation, had been lopped-off with the saber tips, and men of honor fastened on pistols as more functional for their purposes.

THE PISTOL DUEL

German conceptions of chivalry found their natural expression in pistol dueling. Pistols were more life threatening than sabers and they were also clearly more conducive to notions of fair play. In a German pistol duel equality was the thing. Sunlight, shadow, and wind were evenly apportioned. Ideally, a clean horizon behind the duelists afforded each a sharp silhouette to aim at. Guns were to have the same form, caliber, length, weight, and bore. They were not only cleaned and oiled identically, but were also anonymously chosen to avoid unfair advantages gained through prior acquaintance with the triggering mechanism and error differential of the muzzle-loading guns.

In the late 1500s, guns with wheel-lock ignition systems were first utilized for European duels. For the next two hundred years pistol duels were carried out with these and other firearms designed for general use. By the eighteenth century the flintlock pistol had rendered the cumbersome wheel lock and matchlock designs obsolete, and in the 1770s specialty dueling pistols were first manufactured, chiefly in the British Isles. Here sword dueling had slackened and the first comprehensive code regulating pistol duels, the so-called "Irish Code," was published in 1777.[103] By the 1840s the English pistol duel was washed up, but percussion-cap dueling pistols, with their more efficient firing mechanism, were gaining popularity on the continent and remained in use until the First World War. Instead of primer exposed to a random shower of sparks, as in the flintlock variety, the percussion-cap pistol's detonating compound charged powder located in the barrel.[104]

Because a "flash in the pan"—a flintlock misfire in which only the primer ignited—was considered a shot in Imperial Germany, more dependable percussion caps significantly decreased the chance of misfire and thus increased the odds that a rencontre would end fatally.[105] (Manufacturers and merchants of these newfangled devices naturally countered that greater deadliness was rather a deterrent and diminished casualties by reducing the overall incidence of dueling[106]—unlikely.) Most misfires in the future would be the result of the percussion cap's faulty application, and Gustav Hergsell urged seconds to exercise extreme care with the operation.[107] Hergsell's admonition and the rule regarding misfires may have been attempts to avoid botches like that which occurred in 1843, during the period when percussion caps first found favor on the continent. The duel was in the Black Forest near Baden-Baden between German and Russian aristocrats at a cozy ten paces. The first exchange passed without result, but in the second round the Russian struck his opponent full in the chest. With his left hand the German pressed close the rented flesh while essaying his allotted shot, which misfired. A second percussion cap was fitted. This too failed. He was bestowed another pistol by his opponent's own seconds. Third time lucky. The Russian was mortally wounded and, buckling, gave out with the dapper exit line, "*Je suis mort!*" The German aristocrat sank quietly to the ground following his Promethean third attempt and died two days later, making the holocaust complete. As was later discovered, both German and Russian had fought the duel on another's behalf. The Russian was the last of three brothers who had likewise fallen in duels.[108]

Dueling pistols were typically equipped with octagonal barrels about twenty-five centimeters in length and a ten-millimeter bore fashioned from Damascus steel and darkened with a chemical solution to dullen glint. The pistol's metal appurtenances were usually unengraved for the same reason, and its stock and handle were of uncarved walnut. The piece was ordinarily fitted with sight and bead, but these must have been removable since most duels were prosecuted minus their aid—and for the same reason that groves of trees were avoided as dueling sites: so as not to inordinately channel one's aim. These guns of august citizens came in pairs and were stored in cases made of mahogany, oak, or walnut, lined with green or red fabric and containing special lidded compartments for accessories and fittings, as fine a receptacle as the violin case of a virtuoso's Stradivarius, only the instruments it contained were of death and one need not have been Paganini consorting with Beelzebub to make them sing.[109] Just before duels, the box would stay with seconds representing the insulted party, while their counterparts sequestered its key.

Duels with rifled barrels were explicitly denounced by the codes. But in an age that boasted semiautomatic Lugers and double-action revolvers, the single-shot dueling pistol was something of a museum piece. By the last years of the century, it was becoming increasingly difficult to procure, and one application for imperial pardon pleaded the case that, in a duel with rifled barrels, smoothbores had originally been assigned but could not be turned up.[110] The duel in *Der Zauber-*

berg is matter-of-factly fought with automatic Brownings.[111] The codes allowed for the eventuality of rifled barrels if suitable pistols or swords were unobtainable—and for ordinarily peace-loving *Bürger*, this might not have been too farfetched a circumstance.[112] The codes also extended a person offended at the third level the privilege of using his own firearm if granting a similar favor to an opponent, and this may have ushered in rifled barrels. Germany is a region of lowering skies, and frequent rainfall that wetted gunpowder or detonating compound could have given rise to the use of self-priming cartridges and their accompanying grooved bore. This might explain amphibious encounters like that in June of 1895 between the *Regierungsassessor* von Flügge and the *Kommerzienrath* Bosch. The Berlin rain poured throughout this five-pace "barrier duel," and after three exchanges with rifled barrels they were drenched but unbloodied.[113] Concern here was placed perhaps not so much on death-dealing accuracy, but on simply getting off the shots and forestalling controversies over rules of misfire. Be all that as it may, a great many German pistol duels were obviously fought with precision guns for the very reason the codes frowned upon such weapons: for possessing "a very great target fidelity and penetrative ability, so that at close range every shot is a certain hit and mostly mortal."[114]

A rifled barrel, spiral grooves cutting the surface of its bore, imparted a spin to the elongated, metal-jacketed bullet, gyroscopically stabilizing it in flight so as to ensure pinpoint accuracy. Smoothbore dueling pistols, on the other hand, had a plain inner surface that imparted no rotation to the sphere and invariably left a gap between it and the bore, called "windage." This not only greatly reduced the shot's muzzle velocity but rendered its exterior ballistics extremely fickle. Incorrect loading could throw off fire even more, powder and bullet being stuffed down the barrel of smoothbores with a plunger. Immoderate or repeated tamps could deform the malleable poured-lead balls, skewing aim. Usually the black powder charge came to about one-seventh parts per weight of the shot, but it was an imprecise science and also depended on the distance separating the combatants. When stumbling over reports of duelists zapping opponents between the eyes at a jaunty thirty-five or even sixty paces, one can be assured that these were not the result of crack William Tell shooting but rather the delicate exactitude of pure chance.[115]

The terminal ballistics of the smoothbore pistol round were influenced by two factors which distinguished it from the conventional bullet: its lack of power and spherical shape. Whereas most bullets fired from a rifled bore would have easily passed through a man's body at the close range of German pistol duels (thanks to their tapered cylindrical form and drastic force on impact), a blunt lead ball fired from a low-velocity muzzle generally lacked not only the physics but the puissance to create an exit wound, or knock a man over. There are a fair number of German dueling accounts in which an opponent was struck in a nonlethal area and remained erect to return creditable fire. In 1892 in Potsdam, an artillery officer took two slugs in the left arm and hip, and then put his tormentor, Second Lieutenant Reibnitz, out of commission.[116] An enterprising American duelist one time hoodwinked death with a long swatch of silk wrapped tightly about his torso so as to successfully deflect a ball at ten paces.[117] Devoid of such subterfuges, however, the low-impact pellets tended to lodge themselves, like modern hollow-point bullets. Consequently, lives could be cut short just as readily through infection or surgical complications as through traumatic injury. Death was seldom accomplished from the dizzying heights of the battlefield. It was very often a ghastly business in which one expired by slow half inches. Courage in the German duel came less in the event itself than afterward.

The entire body from head to toe was a fair mark. In order to decrease its surface area while firing, duelists would stand sideways with the shooting arm crooked to shield one's thumping heart from oncoming bullets. Before and after firing, they would pose with the arm compressed tightly against the pectoralis major and the slender gun barrel pointing skywards as an optimistic nosepiece for the face. It was actually a matter of debate whether the sideways posture was more prudent. By standing sideways, if not too plump, the duelist offered his opponent relatively slim pickings; but by assuming this stance he also ran the risk of having several vital organs pierced at once. In 1894 in Bromberg, for example, a man received two entrance wounds when a single shot penetrated both thighs.[118] But all things considered, the oblique attitude was probably the more advisable of the two and seems to have been the stance of choice. It was the natural one for shooting, a beefy arm could sometimes stop a ball, and with most pistols only accurate to three inches at fifteen paces,[119] the better part of wisdom decreed minimizing the overall chances of getting struck by foregoing a position that presupposed a dire result. The wounds incurred in a pistol duel were various, but because of the sidelong station assumed by most duelists, bullets would often strike home in the kidneys and the back part of the ribs. One imagines that the profile stance would have exposed the gluteal muscles as a conspicuous target, but if so, accounts are strangely quiet.

Apart from the different types of combat to be discussed shortly, there were two adjustable components of a pistol duel that could heighten its menace, thus making it worthy of German honorable conceptions: the pacing and the number of exchanges. The codified parameters for most styles of duel ranged between fifteen and thirty-five paces. The distances were normally measured at multiples of five, although in case of disagreement among seconds an arithmetic mean could be chosen. It is interesting that before the Great War, German delegations to the modern Olympic Games were completely shut out of the medals in pistol shooting, and in 1906 in Athens an event with dueling pistols was contested in which a Frenchman and a Greek won gold medals at distances of twenty and twenty-five meters, respectively.[120] Germans were accustomed to a closer range. Their duels seldom took place at a distance greater than twenty paces, and seconds habitually marked off ten or sometimes less in extreme situations, affording scarce *Lebensraum*. A not unusual case of overkill was that in 1892 of a man who had suffered a physical outrage and challenged his antagonist to a contest of rifled pistols fixed with sight and bead at a warm five paces, violating the code in every particular save the number of exchanges, three—two more than needed.[121] A pace was not a "bounding stride" ("*Sprungschritte*"), as many duels just before the First World War may have been measured in order to preserve the fiction of mortal combat while yet skirting death as dueling fell into greater disfavor among the general public.[122] Typical German duels were contrived to oust the spring from the step, a pace being figured at a scanty .75 meters; a duel at the commonplace distance of fifteen paces would place the contestants just a little over eleven meters from one another. Ten paces was a claustrophobic seven and one-half. An outstretched shooting arm narrowed the space another meter or so.[123] Even old-fashioned smoothbores were practically foolproof at so bare an interval.

Although one exchange was the standard number prescribed by the dueling codes, a great many encounters had multiple shots. A triple exchange was designated as absolute limit by the manuals, but four and five were not at all rare; and hostilities would sometimes cease only when one or another of the contestants could no longer answer the bell. In 1890, in Perleberg sixty miles northwest of Berlin, a duel between Lieutenant von Forstner and Lieutenant Frenk was conducted under such conditions, no ceiling being assigned to the number of shots. Frenk caught not one but two balls in the chest, and they dueled no more that day.[124] Things were just getting started. In 1886 in the Rhineland, a war of attrition between two officers saw twenty-seven balls pumped back and forth.[125]

All exchanges took place with a pause for reloading between. Even in revolver duels, a sole chamber was to be charged, which would then be refilled for each subsequent round;[126] this would curb any trigger-happy temptation of squeezing off stiff chasers at a fallen adversary—as once happened in Karlsruhe in 1843.[127] But dueling had become more regularized by the 1880s, and Chatauvillard's German scholiast discouraged special arrangements in which each duelist was armed with two pistols, preferring serial volleys of a single gun apiece.[128] This sort of commentary seemed to betoken more than a simple desire to preserve uniformity, prevent euthanasia, or give duelists time out to pat their backs. A duel had its drama heightened by intermissions and a division into acts, and single-shot dueling pistols were ideal showstoppers. Also, the introduction of repeaters would have robbed the duel of much of its mythic color—the formal breaking of the seal on the pistol case, the ominous loading before assembled seconds, the acrid smell and thick smoke of saltpeter and sulphur. Clapping home a cartridge would have offered a rather bleak and prosaic alternative.

To compound the danger factor yet more, the bighearted gesture of shooting over an opponent's head or firing off into the woods, as often portrayed in fantasy, was strictly forbidden by the dueling codes. Operative here was not so much the idea that it needed a stouter heart to direct a well-aimed bullet than to stand in one's path. Rather, prominent misses were perceived as a craven show of clemency in the hope that the gesture would be returned. Were the seconds to note such a conspicuous miss, it was their duty to rush between the combatants before an opponent could return fire, to reprehend the offender and begin anew, giving him a second chance to get it right—or at least near enough to look right so as not to excite suspicion of a yellow streak. Should the bad aim persist, seconds were to again foreshorten the battle and declare the transgressor *unsatisfaktionsfähig* and ineligible for further combat. So loathsome was this offense considered that if the answering shot happened to fall before the seconds could intervene, wounding or killing the Good Samaritan, a protocol would be composed blithely stating that his "shooting in the air" (*Indieluftschiessen*) had gone unremarked. This was the case of a duel at the Eberswalde in 1895 when Lieutenant of the Reserve Frueson fired glaringly over the head of his superior officer, a Captain von Stosch—who blandly dropped him dead without a twitch.[129] This unsentimental German penchant was also graphically revealed in a duel at the Hague in 1892. A tiff at lawn tennis was promoted into a match at twenty-five paces between the secretary of the German embassy Freiherr von Gärtner-Griebenow and the secretary to the Spanish legation Marquis de Vallarda. Attended by French seconds, the Marquis lobbed a shot high over von Gärtner's head, who rewarded his largesse with a sizzling ace to the hip.[130]

A duelist was disgraced by an opponent who fired visibly wide not because it cast direct aspersion on his own character but because he had exercised poor judgment by indulging an evident coward through consent to duel. Professor Medem's 1902 petition would have also augmented Article 204 of the penal code—"A challenge and the acceptance of same, as well as the *Kartellträger*, are exempt from punishment if the parties voluntarily abandon the duel before its commencement"—with the supplement, "as well as for those duelists who intentionally fire in the air."[131] The proposal was never seriously taken up, and it is highly doubtful whether this specific insert would have been at all effective in derailing deaths anyhow: it so aggravated the presuppositions upon which the entire duel was based that it would never for a moment have been considered a viable option by duelists. The embellishment might, in fact, have impelled them to take closer aim than ever so as not to appear frightened of legal recriminations. In 1893 the Belgian senate attempted to legislate this sensitive point by distinguishing between intentional and accidental homicides,[132] but such a thing was hopeless to prove one way or another and would have gotten a wintry reception from Germans whose duel was premised on shoot-to-kill. In a pistol duel that same year of 1893, two deputies in the Hungarian parliament, Julius Horvath and Moriz Mezei, stared down their barrels at one another—and they continued staring. After thirty seconds had elapsed without either one pulling a trigger, the standoff was terminated and the two men honorably reconciled.[133] Armed neutrality was not a German policy.

In contrast to sporting England of the early nineteenth century, where "it was considered extremely bad form to consciously aim the weapon,"[134] in late-nineteenth-century Germany it was advisable to draw a deadeye bead, because a miss was seldom received charitably by one's opponent, who would then proceed with equal deliberation. A favorite fighting style, in fact, bore the moniker *Zielduell*, or "aiming duel," in which the killing was done by urbane turns. In no other country was this inimitable version so often practiced and it was a delicious duel for those with sadistic tendencies. Each contestant was allotted a full minute in which to empty his pistol and so there was ample time to savor a pigeon's quiet anguish before lowering the boom.

Perhaps the most popular duel overall in Germany was the "barrier duel" (*mit Vorrücken*). In Thomas Mann's *Der Zauberberg*, the central thematic conflict of the novel finds its surreal culmination in a "barrier duel" in which one of the duelists "raised his pistol in a way that had nothing to do with dueling, and shot himself in the head."[135] Other fictionalized tableaux were slightly more empirical. Pushkin's *Eugene*

2. *Zielduell.* From Gabriel LeTainturier-Fradin, *Le Duel à travers les Ages,
Histoires et Législation, Duels Célèbres—Code du Duel* (Nice, 1890). (Bayerische Staatsbibliothek, Munich)

Onegin (1831) portrays a "barrier duel," as does Turgenev's *Fathers and
Sons* (1862), Tolstoy's *War and Peace* (1869), and Chekov's novella "The
Duel" (1891), leading one to imagine that this rendition must have also
been fairly widespread in Czarist Russia, where dueling first become
fashionable under the reign of the mystagogical Alexander I (1801–
1825).[136] When the scarce pistol duel in Austria-Hungary occurred, the
barrier style was the usual choice.[137] It was the flagship of pistol duels
in Europe during the half-century before the First World War.

  This duel took place at an official distance of thirty-five to forty
paces. Ten paces in front of each opponent lay a handkerchief or a
length of rope, or sometimes a stake was driven into the ground to
demarcate a central area of ten to fifteen paces—Germans liked reducing it to five. These two barriers marked the farthest line of advance
possible for both opponents, who faced each other across them. At the
command "Forward!" the duelists would cock their guns, the muzzles
facing upward, and advance as their pleasure dictated, but always me-
thodically, no sprinting allowed. They could fire at will, but it had to
be done while immobile. If a duelist missed his first shot, he was required to "stay standing and await the answer of the opponent in perfect stillness."[138] The opponent, for his part, had one minute to stride

3. Barrier duel. From Gustav Hergsell, *Duell-Codex*
(Vienna, Pest, Leipzig, 1891). (Bayerische Staatsbibliothek, Munich)

forward to his barrier—if he had not already done so—toe the line and
snipe away. If no longer ambulatory, he was conferred a timed two-
minute bonus to crawl there. Had both parties missed their first shots
in a planned multiple exchange, then it was a fresh deal with a clean
deck. In discussing this duel, Chatauvillard noted that "the disadvantage of firing second is compensated for by the advantage of firing at
an immobile target."[139] However, it seems that the major benefit of
firing second was the complimentary sashay to the barrier. And in my
reading of hundreds of dueling accounts, it was not necessarily desirable to get the drop on an opponent. The second shot was more than
likely to be the telling one.

There were other choices on the stylistic menu: a collateral to the
Zielduell in which opponents stood with backs turned at distance then
whirled and gave fire; an arrangement employing parallel lines in
which adversaries would be positioned diagonally across from one

4. Back-to-back. From Gustav Hergsell, *Duell-Codex*
(Vienna, Pest, Leipzig, 1891). (Bayerische Staatsbibliothek, Munich)

another at opposite ends of their respective stripes and advance and
shoot as they went; and an alternative "barrier duel" with a zigzag
approach. But the most controversial duel of all, and in stark contrast
to the *Zielduell*, was the duel "on cue" (*auf Signal*) in which the aim was
harrassed and opponents fired simultaneously at the sound of a loud,
unnerving handclap—and not a half second too soon or too late. Any
premature or tardy shootists were declared dishonorable, and if the
result of the transgression was the death or injury of an opponent, a
protocol was drawn up and the case submitted to the authorities who
would prosecute it under Article 207 of the penal code, thereby providing for its classification beneath the general headings of murder or
grievous bodily harm.

Although the *auf Signal* duel found practitioners in the *Kaiserreich*,
connoisseurs took a rather dim view of it. According to Hergsell, if
there was not a third-level insult, seconds could always reject this duel
on behalf of their client; according to the authoritative dueling code
Gebräuche, it could always be declined.[140] First of all, triggering mecha-
nisms on dueling pistols ranged anywhere from hair- to hard-triggers,

5. Duel with parallel lines. A rare duel, dangerous for
seconds who arranged these things. From Gustav
Hergsell, *Duell-Codex* (Vienna, Pest, Leipzig, 1891).
(Bayerische Staatsbibliothek, Munich)

and so there was no telling what the tension on an anonymous gun
might be. Consequently, the threadbare line between murder and
honor became even more frayed in those duels fought "on cue." Second, there was the possibility that even scattered fire might find its
mark, and a pair of corpses did no one any great good.[141] Third, the
"on cue" duel provided no real opportunity by which to demonstrate
personal courage because the simultaneous fire on command precluded what little individual judgment and initiative still pertained to
a German pistol duel, and poise was hardly a factor. Ergo, whether at
fifty or ten paces, this duel bore a tawdry aspect which was an affront
to German earnestness.[142]

The popularity of the "on cue" duel in France may have also prejudiced some. In France, this style had displaced almost every other type
of pistol combat by the 1880s when the dueling craze in that country
ran herd. Leaving nothing to chance, French seconds were not above
tampering with the weaponry to avert mortal outcomes, and firing
over an opponent's head was considered a very *beau geste*. A witticism

6. Barrier duel with a zig-zag approach. From Gustav
Hergsell, *Duell-Codex* (Vienna, Pest, Leipzig, 1891). (Bayerische Staatsbibliothek, Munich)

that made the rounds in Germany at the turn of the century was about
a famous Parisian rake, known to be a late sleeper, who wakes up
early one morning startling his wife. Solemnly he tells her, "Do not be
afraid dear child, today I have a pistol duel in the Bois de Boulogne."
"Oh," replies the wife with a sigh of relief, "you have a pistol duel!
Alright, then be careful . . . I don't want you coming down with the
sniffles."[143]

The Germans did indeed regard dueling in the Third Republic as
something of a joke because of its hilariously low fatality rate, which,
from a pool of between four and five hundred duels a year until the
first decade of the twentieth century, never exceeded twelve annual
deaths and was often as low as two per year.[144] Berlin's *Das Kleine
Journal* explained in 1901 how "the whole world knows that French
duels, be they with pistols or swords, present not the slightest danger
to their participants. In the duel protocol, one reads of at worst a prick
on the outside surface of the right index finger, or of a one-tenth of a
millimeter deep wound on the first knuckle of the thumb—the so-

7. "On cue" duel. From Gustav Hergsell, *Duell-Codex* (Vienna, Pest, Leipzig, 1891). (Bayerische Staatsbibliothek, Munich)

'wounded,' however, does not die as a result."[145] The German rate of dueling—if one excludes the promiscuous student duel, the *Mensur*—was about half that of the French, but the German combat was shockingly terminal, and this fact seems to have sired a bit of hubris in many. In discussion of the German duel in the Reichstag at the turn of the century, even abolitionists tramped the French *Scheinduell*, or "pseudo-duel," as a poor and pathetic alternative for the restitution of honor. Compared to the bitter German cup, the French combat was duel *au lait*; making the French duelist, by German standards, an automatic drip. In his 1888 *Das Buch berühmter Duelle* (*The Book of Famous Duels*), Dr. Adolph Kohut opened his chapter on the French duel by giving it both barrels: "The duel in France has deteriorated into a trivial game. Neither high-mindedness, nor noble sentiment, nor preservation of true manly honor are the mainsprings of the affairs of honor, but in most cases enormous vanity."[146] "Whoever is to any extent acquainted with Paris," scoffed another German commentator, "can point to people who have their two dozen duels behind them without ever having incurred one scratch."[147] It is curious that Frenchmen during the fin de siècle should have seen in this duel one of their "noble flowers of courage and heroism," believing that its pervasiveness would help counteract the softening effects and decadent trends they saw as having led to their country's crushing defeat in the Franco-Prussian War of 1870–71. Dueling would prepare the nation for its long-awaited *revanche*.[148] In point of fact, the French duel would indeed seem to have ultimately translated into fewer casualties among the French than among the Germans, who, if not getting pin-pricks on the pinky, were all but dying of laughter. Because of its notable lack of astringency, the French duel played into the hands of German men of honor who considered their own austere version as being somehow of a higher moral content, although whether the typical German duel, for its turn, was true proof of anything save a tremendous paucity of imagination or a manifest death wish is very open to question.

In 1896, that Boswell of the duel Albert von Boguslawski articulated the German Golden Mean in relation to the Anglo-French example: "It is as little necessary to adopt the dueling mania of the French as it is to adopt the dueling prohibition of the English."[149] Dueling in England went belly-up in 1844 through a salutary combination of public pressure and government initiative,[150] and by the time of the British Empire's proud celebration of its progress and civilization in the Crystal Palace Exhibition of 1851, England had driven the remains from its shores.[151] Writing in the 1890s, the German historian Heinrich von Treitschke had his own interpretation of the English success of the 1840s: "The old sense of honor and prejudices of the upper classes were scattering before the superior strength of money, whilst the German nobility remained poor but chivalrous. . . . [T]he duel fell into disuse and disappeared completely; the riding whip ousted sword and pistol, and this victory of brutality was celebrated as a triumph of Enlightenment."[152]

In the minds of German duelists, this so-called "victory of brutality" owed in large measure to the rise of pugilism in the British Isles at the start of the nineteenth century,[153] when aristocrats such as Lord Byron took instruction in the sport. Proper German gentlemen harbored a particular distaste for boxing and its two-fisted muscularity, considering it lower class and bestial, a one-way ticket to Palookaville. The German duel, on the other hand, was supposedly imbued with a chivalrous patina because it equalized chances between combatants and elevated them above the messy, random, and spontaneous fury of the streets by virtue of its perfumed rules, which happily also supplied it a unique legal status. But the decisive reason why duelists were so horrified by the sweet science of boxing—though they were unwilling to admit it—was that Gleason's Gym posed a greater threat to dueling's pretentious rigmarole than the most severe penal sanctions. Arrogant Germans could be humbled when leveling challenges across the Channel in Britain. "In many cases," gloated one critic, "he immediately receives for his troubles an unpleasantly hard and unpleasantly sure fist in the solar plexus."[154] But even on their own turf they were not out of harm's way. In 1883 at Göttingen, after a minor incident, three university students demanded formal satisfaction from one of England's American cousins. Much the wrong approach. All they got was a good shellacking.[155] For the German duelist, aggressive only by rote, swift and real fighting seemed a contingency beyond his spirit's reckoning. Theirs was not a can-do mentality; hidebound duelists were too preoccupied with doing nothing *wrong*. Von Boguslawski pleaded the case that the Englishman paid special attention to his muscular development, implying that Germans were not physically equipped for the rough work of light sparring.[156] The traditional affiliations signified by the synonymous equation of the word *Boxerei* with the terms *Schlägerei* and *Prügelei* (both meaning a brawl or street fight) died hard. The scrappy English way was wholeheartedly deplored by an old guard of German votaries who had long sworn their allegiance to the Comte de Chatauvillard, not the Marquis of Queensberry. "Gentleman Jim" Corbett may have been heavyweight champion of the world (1892–97), but for Germans he was certainly no gentleman. The two titles were incompatible in the minds of patrician-nosed duelists.

This is not to say that Germans were averse to getting clobbered. Just the opposite. It was better to receive than to give. One turn-of-the-century traveler remarked about student duelists that "the real victor was he who emerged from the battle with the greatest number of wounds."[157] As Freud observed, the sadist is a masochist at heart, and so duelists, instead of taking pleasure in the pain they were imparting, may have been imparting pleasure as they knew it. In Arthur Schnitzler's short story *"Der Sekundant"* (1932), a nice masochist and perennial bridesmaid, assisting at his seventh duel, entertains the thought of one day himself becoming embroiled: "I would very much have liked to have one time stood opposite a dangerous opponent, and I really cannot say what I would have preferred—to triumph or to fall."[158] There was truly something of a martyr complex obtaining to the psychology of German men of honor, in particular that of pistol duelists who were usually indifferent shots. Because of the various violations of the code in German pistol duels, the mildly surprising thing is that there were not more casualties. No coiled-spring assassins

these. Their concern was facing death, not administering it; the ex-
ecutive will was upstaged by their passionate *amor fati*. The brainy
Madame de Staël had seized upon this propensity several generations
earlier: "The spirit of chivalry still reigns amongst the Germans,—but
passively."[159] The great thing was not to surmount death or outstrip an
opponent but to scorn your trembling knees and achieve a spiritual
triumph in material disaster. Some would call this the tragic view.
Others have stated it as a general sociological principle in contending
that heroic stature is never attained through ability but through a
show of calm in the face of insuperable odds.[160] Whatever one's taste,
the German duel is a classic illustration of men who were better exis-
tentialists than fighters.

This trait is shown to best advantage in an examination of German
images of American dueling during the same time period. German
men of honor found American roughnecks who sought revenge rather
than "satisfaction" repugnant. Satisfaction for German duelists was
not achieved by seeing an enemy sprawled lifeless but through having
him personally witness one's worth while performing with aplomb
when the chips were down and one's true self was concentrated in a
single point. In America, as in England where there had supposedly
taken place "a complete transvaluation of all former conceptions of the
sense of honor," things were different:

> In North America, this archetypal land of reckless self-interest, one gains
> satisfaction for even simple putative insults at once with the revolver,
> shooting an opponent without any further ado. Through this form of
> self-help, a type of blood feud has developed in many of the United States
> similar to the Corsican vendetta. . . . [O]ne has not time there for the for-
> mal resolution of insults to honor by means of regulated self-help; if it is
> not done immediately with the revolver, then it is fought out with the
> dollar, in which one seeks to destroy his opponent through pecuniary
> means.[161]

What Germans mostly meant when they spoke of American dueling
was the high noon showdown in which both gunslingers were killed
and law-abiding townfolk were caught in the withering fusillade. This
imaginative conception, perhaps fired by the pulp Westerns of popular writer Karl May (1842–1912), was actually just a ricochet from the
truth. American dueling rested "upon a solid foundation of armed
self-reliance already developed in the American character," and it was
as pluralistic in its choice of weaponry and styles of combat as it was
democratic in its participation requirements.[162] B. Wyatt-Brown affirms that dueling in America's antebellum South "was not at all un-
democratic. It enabled lesser men to enter, however imperfectly, the

ranks of leaders, and allowed followers to manipulate leaders to their taste."[163] Social equality of the combatants in American dueling was generally an irrelevant issue—a bedevilling notion to class-conscious German duelists—and German authors recounted with fascinated horror the various ways in which "the American seeks in the duel, as in all his conduct, to appear original and monstrous so as to publicize himself."[164] Duels such as the dynamite duel, where opponents would lob sticks of TNT at one another; or the Spanish duel with dirks in a lights-out room—these and other unorthodox, yahoo forms were strictly if not expressly forbidden by the German codes.

In the 1880s a strange hybrid of duel came into vogue in certain circles in Germany. Perceived as a savage deviation from the elegant, ritualized norms of old-world Europe, it was branded searingly the "American duel." It received its appellation not through a concrete episode in American history but rather through pejorative cultural associations that led many xenophobic Germans to take its national derivation for granted. The terror of "Americanization" was very pronounced among conservative cultural critics of the era who perceived Uncle Sam as the chief patron of a diabolic modernity.[165] The "American duel" was, accordingly, viewed by one author as a "pathological phenomenon" and "the last consequence of American morals, which are evinced through the unprecedented foolhardiness and recklessness of that continent's inhabitants in their economic and other enterprises, in their peculiar intimacy with the high tide of riches as well as the abyss of impoverished misery."[166] This new form of duel became so ungovernable that by 1886 a bill was introduced into the Reichstag to outlaw it.[167] It was in essence part suicide pact and part Russian roulette, in which two men would agree to let fate harmonize their discord by drawing lots, the loser then quietly offing himself within a specified period of time.[168]

In 1883 a young university lecturer was pontificating on the "Jewish Question" in a Berlin restaurant to a group of friends when a Jewish jurist, who had been eavesdropping, arose and demanded satisfaction. Putlitz, the lecturer, freely gave the jurist choice of weaponry as the offended party. Excusing himself on anemic and myopic grounds, the jurist proposed an "American duel," which Putlitz accepted and subsequently lost. After arranging his affairs, in a remarkable display of good faith, Putlitz held to the pact and killed himself before the deadline expired, apparently none of the problematic Jewish or American elements of the affair sufficient to prod his instinct for self-preservation and countermand the death warrant.[169] In 1898 a stir was caused in Munich when the sister of the popular actress Anna Reisner, after taking up with a certain Werner Edler von Östern during *Fasching*

(Carnival), decided to follow her new flame into death when he lost an "American duel" to a student with whom she had been cohabitating. The lovers traveled together back to von Östern's native Bohemia and committed romantic suicide in his castle outside Prague.[170] Not all "American duels" ended in the rictus of death. In 1880, in a town just outside Berlin, a serious controversy erupted between members of high society, and shortly thereafter one of the two inexplicably vanished. It was discovered only later that he had been the victim of an "American duel"; but instead of blowing out his brains, his labor was to stand at an intersection of Berlin's Potsdamerstrasse day in and day out, rain or shine, for five years, a cross he had been stoically, if somewhat idiotically, bearing for the past three (at the time of the account).[171]

The dueling code *Gebräuche* was categorical in its disapprobation of the "American duel" as "standing in sharpest contradiction to those views that every officer and gentleman must have pertaining to the chivalrous execution of matters of honor."[172] This would seem an odd commentary regarding a duel that was supremely impartial, imminently lethal, allowed for such gallant behavior as that of the lecturer Putlitz, and did not entail the charge of manslaughter. Would it not be the reductio ad absurdum of the German duel, whose moral equivalent was crunching a cyanide capsule? The "American duel" was an intolerable arrangement because it had death as its *object*. Although it was Europe's most inexorable national style and could hardly be said to espouse survival, the German duel was an ostensible showcase for bravery, poise, and skill, in which the demise of one of the participants, if not unexpected, was generally basis for some consternation. The German duelist redeemed his honor by removing the blemish to it, not the source of that blemish. And the blemish was removed through an exhibition of fortitude under the stressful exigencies of an ultimate confrontation. Von Bolgar condemned the solipsistic "American duel" as having no relation to the chivalrous form simply because a duel called for seconds;[173] that is, peers to witness the proceedings— even though their commiseration actually mitigated the ordeal's pathos, for when heroically endured, suffering and death are always lonely, isolating affairs. The "American duel's" refreshing lack of hypocrisy obviously made too much good, solid American sense, for German men of honor mulishly insisted that it was a "dishonorable act of the most wretched cowardice."[174]

All three forms of "duel"—the French, British, and American—symbolized for Germans corrupt western *Zivilisation* opposing the German duel's expression of superior *Kultur*, a conceit that was actually symptomatic of what Fritz Stern has called "a partly sick society" and its resentment against "the *embourgeoisement* of life and morals . . . the culmination of the secular, moral tradition of the West."[175] B. Wyatt-Brown writes interestingly that antebellum "Southerners' touchiness over virility, stemmed from deep anxieties about how others, particularly Northerners and Englishmen, saw them."[176] Similarly, the determined snobbery of German duelists may have derived from some sneaking sense of inferiority, especially vis-à-vis the English Gentleman. But to duel in the German style was still hypothetically to define oneself culturally over and against not only a wide spectrum of social, ethnic, political, and religious groups, but whole nations as well. This general mentality emerged most catastrophically in the ideology of such radical-Right bourgeois factions as the Pan-German League (founded in 1890), which believed in war and violent conflict as a kind of "cure-all," and more specifically as a means to battle the politics of cultural encirclement allegedly being practiced by all of non-German Europe at the expense of pure—and therefore highly vulnerable to infection—*Deutschtum*.[177]

Slavs from the steppes of Russia numbered among the archenemies of German *Kultur*. However, it is a story by Alexander Pushkin (1799–1837), veteran of four duels and dying in that fourth, which depicts better than any other the psychological underpinnings of German honor. In "The Shot" (1830), the marksman Silvio becomes entangled in an affair that issues in a pistol duel at twelve paces. His opponent draws the first shot, which pierces Silvio's hat. As Silvio prepares to return fire, he sees his opponent picking cherries out of a cap and casually spitting the pits across the interval separating the two. Silvio looks for signs of fear, for the slightest hint of discomposure, but sees not a trace. "What's the use of killing him," he thinks to himself, "when he is completely indifferent to the possibility." Silvio lowers his pistol and passes his shot. Several years later he receives news of his antagonist's marriage to a beautiful woman, and so he travels to Moscow to see if life remains yet so immaterial to the cherry-eater. A second duel takes place in the cherry-eater's estate house. Even though Silvio has a right to the first shot, he waives the privilege and they draw lots for it, the lot once again falling to his enemy. But the fellow's bullet again misses, perforating a Swiss landscape portrait above Silvio's head, at which point the wife rushes in and interrupts the combat by throwing herself at Silvio's feet. His opponent demands that he at last make use of his allotted round, but Silvio replies: "I will not shoot . . . I am contented: I have seen your confusion, your fear; I have compelled you to fire upon me. That suffices. You will think of me. I leave you to your conscience." Departing, he fires casually from the doorway, replicating his opponent's shot into the hanging picture.[178]

Although the natural emotional admixtures of pique and malice were certainly present in most duels, the German combat was theoretically based not on the gratification of these splenetic drives but rather on the desire to give an enemy's imputation of cowardice the lie through a mannered show of pluck. To punish with impunity, precluding risk to one's own person—this may be the definition of revenge as elaborated in Poe's classic tale of redress *The Cask of Amontillado*. But had the duel's purpose been reprisal, or a Manichean trial to decide right or wrong, then it was a woefully inefficient device because death loomed as distinct a possibility for the "innocent" as for the "guilty."[179] Therefore, to prevent the misuse of duels as instruments of retribution and their broadening into feuds, double jeopardy was proscribed. A friend or relative who wanted to avenge at all costs the death of a comrade or loved one could conceivably incite the killer to a second duel, but such was always a third-level offense.[180] In addition, the written "protocol" of a challenger failing to receive adequate satisfaction had for him the same value as a well-fought duel. The dueling abolitionists insisted that because the duel was ill-suited as an instrument of punishment and revenge, it was devoid of validity—ethical, logical, legal, or otherwise. After all, they reasoned, the offended party might be killed and justice go unserved. But duelists did not seek justice. Theirs was an affray—if one will pardon the homely phrase—that did not determine who was right but who was left.

The German saber duel rarely made any pretense to a life-or-death struggle. The absence of a thrusting point in most duels of this type, the plethora of rules swaddling the bout, the protective silk worn around wrist and neck, the temporary stoppage of matches when one or both of the opponents was fatigued, and the optional clause in some manuals providing for cessation of the duel without benefit of bloodshed if both duelists had managed doughty showings—all testify to the fact that the duel's significance lay in its role as a proving ground of manhood and not as a gross instrument of revenge. It was usually considered bad form to leave the dueling grounds without having spilled warm blood, but unspilled sangfroid was of estimable worth.

Pistol duels were also proof against naked retribution, although at first glance this seems not to be the case, for they followed the exact opposite tendency of sabers. Tight pacing, numerous exchanges, rifled barrels, and the fact that German men of honor generally chose the more risky styles of combat and then always shot to kill, would appear to indicate a wicked taste for reprisal. But although the German duel was the deadliest in Europe, this was not the outcome of hatred for an enemy but disdain for danger. Whereas bloodshed was practically always the precondition for the completion of a saber match, volatile pistols were more than likely to miss, and so German pistol duelists nipped and tucked the rules of combat to make wounds a larger possibility. Moreover, if a gun misfired the duelist was usually denied a retake, for it was thought adequate satisfaction that an opponent have suffered the fright of a long-barreled pistol snapping in his face and expecting it to go bang. The point was not to kill him. A duelist would sooner have seen his enemy quail than merely die, as a death could complicate matters with the criminal justice system and, perhaps, his conscience. A corpse was not the goal—although it was the logical emblem of a contest emitting the death rattle of a self-conscious German masculine ideal.

The model for this masculine ideal was the German officer. Perhaps the most plausible explanation for the German duel's ballistomania is that because the officer corps habitually pressed pistols into service, firearms under virulent conditions became the natural preference for admiring German citizens, many of whom were themselves reserve officers. The use of pistols had become generalized in the Prussian officer corps from about the middle of the nineteenth century, and one author suggested that these enjoyed superior status with officers because their application helped prevent the mismatches endemic to saber dueling.[181] A 1902 student petition urging the Prussian War Ministry to promote the use of sabers in army duels perceived officers as preferring pistols because of their more lethally efficient quality in addressing weighty matters of honor.[182] In all events, it may have been felt that facing down a speeding projectile was a more honest re-creation of modern-day battle conditions than was the scenario of hand-to-hand grappling. And consonant with a career in arms, officer duels were prosecuted with unusual mortality, one military man asserting that "even the mildest form of duel between officers is more serious and rigorous than in other societal circles . . . for one must be prepared at any time to do too much rather than too little in matters of honor."[183] From a practical point of view, the duel was perhaps defensible so long as it was restricted to an officer class whose duty it was to guard personal and national honor with its lives. The code of battle owed little to moral and civil law. For precisely this reason are dicta of the warrior always miscast in society at large.

CHAPTER III

Theirs Not to Reason Why

Friend, to be struck by the public foe,
Then to strike him and lay him low,
That were a public merit, far
Whatever the Quaker holds, from sin;
But the red life spilt for a private blow—
I swear to you, lawful and lawless war
Are scarcely even akin.
—Alfred, Lord Tennyson, "Maud" (1856)

IN THE year 1890, one C. Balan predicted that, "From the moment when the conviction will have gained credence in the officer corps of the duel's immorality and expendability, the career of this practice will certainly end for the other strata within which one presently regards the duel as a necessary evil."[1] Balan's "practical solution to the dueling question" was no empty theorizing: the example of the officer in Wilhelmine society was paramount, and the fortunes of the duel waxed and waned with the course of its fate in the German officer corps. In few countries did the army exercise so unwonted a cultural influence on the bourgeois populace as it did in a Germany where "[w]ar as embodiment of the nation established identity."[2] The army war machine's prestige extended to the duel, military criteria for the execution of honorable affairs being the private citizen's touchstones. The authoritative German dueling code at the time was written by an officer for officers. Although anti-duelists often made a sound case for the necessary and inevitable abnegation of dueling in civilian circles, their arguments were predestined to failure within the army—and, by association, civil society—because the officer who defended his honor considered the duel a mere occupational hazard of his precarious profession, as the upholder and animus of values indispensable to his solemn station.

At the turn of the century, by virtue of the mammoth reserve officer corps, civilians appear to have played a more prominent role in the continued life of dueling. But the regular officer's code endured as the paragon of manly comportment and remained the private citizen's conscience in matters of honorific sensibility. For his part, the officer's tribunal of conscience was the "honor court" (not to be confused with despised public courts) an institution which had its genesis in the early part of the nineteenth century and was devised to monitor the conduct of officers and imbue them with a sense of their lofty calling. Originally designed to prevent duels through instruction of the German officer in the fundaments of dignified bearing, by the late nineteenth century the "honor court" had become more instrumental in promoting duels than in foiling them, thus keeping alive the flame at which officer's honor had warmed its hands ever since the days of the Great Elector.

THE COURTS OF HONOR: 1808–1897

After the Prussian defeat at Jena by Napoleon in 1806, the state administration was reshuffled in that idealistic eddy known as the Prussian Reform Movement. High on the movement's list of aims was to restore national confidence in the polity's armed forces by jimmying their public image. Accordingly, in 1808, Friedrich Wilhelm III (1797–1840) introduced a measure that recommended outfitting each army regiment with courts of honor composed of peers to deliberate in marginal cases of a fellow officer's proposed advancement. If found guilty of dissolute living, pettiness, or insubordination, his promotion could be denied. Although this order did not directly address dueling and honor, Friedrich Wilhelm urged his officers to "carefully watch over" one another's conduct and consider "the good reputation of the entire officer corps as the joint share of each,"[3] a clear articulation of the *Standesehre* ethos.

In the years following the Prussian victory over the French at Leipzig in 1813 and Napoleon's final defeat at Waterloo two years later, dueling surged in popularity across Europe, Germany included.[4] Documented officer duels in Prussia were occurring at about the rate of one per month,[5] and this statistic excludes plentiful run-ins between Prussian occupation forces and French patriots. Nettled Parisian fencing-masters would slip into the uniforms of French officers to incite challenges from Austrian and Prussian officers who were destined to die in battle after all, breathing their last in the Bois de Boulogne.[6] It was amid this high-flown spirit that a series of four royal proclamations were issued during the 1820s in Prussia addressing the army dueling problem. By a cabinet order of 1821, Friedrich Wilhelm formally established honor courts "which would serve the purpose of promoting morality, mediating disputes, reprimanding impropriety, and investigating blatant cases of professional misconduct."[7] Those convicted could be released from service or banished from the officer class subject to confirmation by the king, but these honorific bodies continued as optional courts of appeal.

A second declaration in 1823, on the occasion of an officer's duel with an actor, condemned dueling outright. The king prohibited his officers from seeking to maintain "caste dignity through violent response to self-incriminating insults," demanding instead that "they preserve it through decent and moral conduct and through the rejection of deeds which are reproachable from the aspect of both moral law and honor."[8] His officers turned a deaf ear but Friedrich Wilhelm did not turn a blind eye. In a third order of 1828, he noted that duels in the army had actually increased in recent years (between 1817 and 1829 there were twenty recorded officer deaths by duel[9]), and urged his officer corps to utilize the sanctioned courts of honor, even if they were still not mandatory. A fourth order of 1829 was less mealy-mouthed and promised not only to prosecute the crime of dueling but those miscreants who, through their insulting behavior, would have fomented the encounter:

> When insults take place which, according to the still prevailing opinions, injure the personal honor to such a degree that they can supposedly be cleansed only through blood, then he who is capable of so frivolously uttering such unworthy abuse shall have proven himself equally unworthy of any longer belonging to the caste for whose sacredness he lacks all sense, and his expulsion from this caste is simultaneously perfectly sufficient reparation for the unjustly offended, and so will I have it everywhere recognized.[10]

Karl Demeter views this last decree as capping the movement from an external honor of caste to an inward honor of conscience that had been evolving under the king's well-intended auspices ever since 1808. Whether or not this was the case, dueling came to be categorically censured in Friedrich Wilhelm's injunctions, and it is conceivable that his efforts may have finally gained some purchase, for in the 1830s the rate of duels among officers seems to have curtailed. Thirty-nine serious duels between officers were punished from 1817 to 1829, and twenty-nine between 1832 and 1843,[11] a period when one imagines that the courts of honor and civil courts exercised greater vigilance following the king's condemnation. Officer duels during this stretch were so rare that any such encounter was considered "a remarkable event."[12] However, those duels that were fought were carried out with a remarkable perniciousness, as in Frankfurt in 1832 when officers exchanged rounds at the homey distance of five paces[13]—nothing remarkable in the fact that a soldier died with his boots on.

In 1843, Friedrich Wilhelm's son Friedrich Wilhelm IV (1840–61) issued a fresh cabinet order which would serve as the basis of future edicts and of the honor court system in general up until the First World War. It also helped retrench the displaced caste-consciousness of the officer corps to breathe new life into the duel. The real author of this latest decree was Friedrich Wilhelm's War Minister Hermann von Boyen (1771–1848), an officer from Pomerania who was a key figure in the Prussian Reform Movement and who had fought a pistol duel in 1815 with the noted humanist educator and founder of the University of Berlin, Wilhelm von Humboldt.[14] Von Boyen, whose "entire work served the sole function of fortifying a bulwark of military-aristocratic caste consciousness,"[15] believed that "since laws were to leave every citizen the greatest possible liberty compatible with the purposes of the state, duels might be left outside the range of state interference."[16] This "military liberalism" of von Boyen's interlocked with his troglodyte monarch's own romantic-conservative tendencies, and created a fertile topsoil for the regeneration of army dueling.

The two-part cabinet order of 20 July 1843 made plain that the purpose of the refurbished courts of honor was to preserve the collective image of the officer class by discouraging disgraceful public behavior that could be witnessed by impressionable civilians.[17] All who had ever donned Prussian braid were subject to rulings of an honor court: regular as well as militia officers, pensioned officers, those discharged but retaining the right to wear their old uniform in public, and even officers of the *Gendarmerie* (I, Art. 3). Honor court verdicts ranged from acquittal or a simple warning to dishonorable discharge with loss of rank and standing (I, Art. 4). Each regiment handled its own cases (staff officers had special courts of their own), and the regimental honor court was supported in its review and investigation of cases by a three-man council of honor, or *Ehrenrat*, composed of a captain and a first and second lieutenant elected for annual terms (I, Arts. 6 and 12). The council of honor was the preliminary mediator that would recommend a formal trial for the litigants only if it was unable to reconcile the two parties or itself arrive at a decision. In keeping with the army policy of public discretion to safeguard "the dignity of the caste," the need for procedural top secrecy was stressed (I, Art. 51).

The second half of the order spoke directly to the dueling question when the king specified that "in order to prevent *as far as possible* duels among my officers, . . . the courts of honor should function as umpire in all disputes and insults among officers insofar as they are not directly connected with an act of service [my emphasis]" (II, opening paragraphs). The next thirty-seven articles described in detail the guidelines to be followed. It became a duty of the participants to promptly notify the intermediary council of honor of all snarls that might complicate (or, rather, clarify) into duels (II, Art. 2), and the inquiry of the honor council had as its chief aim pacification and reconciliation of the litigants (II, Art. 7). If the honor council deemed that there had been no intentional insult but only an unfortunate misunderstanding, for example, a first-level offense, it would suggest an apology. If this judgment was acceptable to both parties and subsequently confirmed by the commander of the regiment, the matter was settled (II, Art. 10). However, if one or both of the officers concerned declared themselves dissatisfied with the decision of the honor council, they could place the case before an honor court (II, Art. 11).

The honor court's investigation would lead to one of three verdicts: 1) that neither party's honor had been impugned, and the case would be thrown out as inappropriate object of an honor court inquiry; 2) that a reprimand be delivered to either one or both parties, with a formal apology and a handshake to follow; or 3) that someone be ejected from the officer corps (II, Art. 13). The order declared that the conflict would then find its "complete conclusion" and no further satisfaction could thereafter be legitimately claimed by either officer (II, Art. 15). However, the very next article stated that if either party remained less than pleased with the verdict "due to the peculiar relations of the officer class," the honor court proceedings would be adjourned, but not before the court had warned the co-belligerents of the legal ramifications that a duel on their part would engender (II, Art. 16).

At this juncture in the order came the clause that stood in brazen conflict with the general law and would be incorporated into future honor court edicts. Article 17 stated that should the honor council somehow learn of an impending duel, it retained the right to appear at the site of combat in order to assure a "good and proper" (*Standesgemäss*) fight. The council would, in effect, act as officious seconds, who having failed to resolve a conflict would then proceed to regulate its bloody eruption. When the smoke of battle had cleared and satisfaction was obtained, the combatants were then to be taken into custody by their accessories for breaking the law (II, Art. 19). However, a host of extenuating circumstances were eligible as at least partial excuse for the resort to violence (II, Arts. 28, 29, 30). Chief among these was the recurrent qualifier: those "peculiar relations of the officer class"—which could in certain cases be brought to bear when the duel was undertaken pro forma and did not have an "unfavorable result," or when both duelists had given impeccable account of themselves under the giddy pressure of combat. In such cases, they would escape with a brief disciplinary arrest (II, Art. 31).

The significance of the 1843 cabinet order was threefold. Ever since the abolition of the Bench of the Nobility (*Adelsbank*) from the Berlin Supreme Court (*Kammergericht*) in 1809, the aristocratic and military element, often identical, had wished to establish special courts presided over by their peers.[18] The influx of bourgeoisie into the Prussian civil service and judiciary during the course of the eighteenth and nineteenth centuries was also a cause for concern in military and other pedigreed circles.[19] By founding highly specialized courts of honor for officers of the standing army and militia, the unique and privileged legal status of the military was thus confirmed. The contrast between civilian and military penal codes was particularly crass: the civil law under the Prussian Law Code of 1794 assigned the penalty of death (Art. 671) for those duelists who had taken life themselves, whereas a minimum of one year's detention was usually deemed sufficient penance for an officer (II, Art. 22).

Second, the order made abundantly clear in its opening paragraph that the individual officer was responsible not to the evanescent "moral law" stressed in Friedrich Wilhelm III's 1823 order, but rather to the marmoreal standards of his caste. The purpose of the newly established honor courts was

> to protect . . . the collective honor of its membership, as well as the honor of the individual against those members whose conduct is inappropriate to the proper feeling of honor or relations of the officer class, and, where necessary, to request the removal of the unworthy member from the corporation so that the honor of the Prussian officer caste can be maintained in its purity and the good reputation of each member as well as the whole remain unblemished [I, Art. 1].

The definition of honor elaborated in the 1843 order had more affinity with notions of social prestige than the demands of individual ethics.[20] Consequently, Friedrich Wilhelm III's plea of 1828 to reject the "decadent prejudice" of the duel found little resonance in the 1843 decree. To assert that in 1843 the officer duel was "more or less" legalized[21] is scarcely an exaggeration, for there is no question that tacit approval for the duel could be found in the order by those officers determined to avenge with a vengeance their personal honor—though always in the name of their grand corporate body.

This was the third effect of the order. The new king never stated unconditionally to cut out the fighting, and the mere presence of the honor council on the field of honor to ensure smooth execution was the duel's first-class ticket to respect and legitimacy. By going so far as to supervise the combat, the honor council acknowledged its own sterility and gave undeviating recognition to the duel's superior competence in the restitution of tainted honor. Moreover, cool posturing during the duel and strict observance of its prescribed rules could lead to a lightening or even complete erasure of possible sentences.

It soon developed that the honor council was not beloved by Prussian officers. Appeal to its wisdom was regarded as a pusillanimous evasion of the more time-honored method of settling scores.[22] Even if a fractious pair temporarily placed themselves at the disposal of the council or court, they would in most cases reject the ruling and duel anyway—their option—and solicitation of these bodies quickly assumed the dimensions of a pathetic transparency.[23] To avoid demotion from the ranks, all an officer need do was calmly wait until the paperwork had cleared and a cameo verdict was rendered. He could then openly attend to the duel devoid of qualms about dismissal and with the added attraction of an official referee in attendance—the honor council. In the thirteen-year period after 1843 the number of duels reported in the army rose at least 25 percent over those documented in the decade previous to Fredrich Wilhelm IV's toothless measure.[24] Generals were not subject to the courts of honor, but this did not exempt them from the implications of an insult or the consequences of a challenge, and by 1861 chiefs of the Prussian Military Cabinet were dueling.[25] Just twenty years earlier had one English maven observed that "duels are rare among German officers."[26] Something had happened in the past two decades, and that something was Friedrich Wilhelm IV's obiter dictum, which would prove to be the thin edge of the wedge.

On 2 May 1874, Kaiser Wilhelm I reiterated the honor court principle in yet another decree. By this order, and in tacit recognition of the de facto situation, honor court procedural guidelines became so attenuated as to reduce consultations to the sheerest formality. Reports were to be made "no later" than the official delivery or reception of a challenge, at which point the honor council was to make "an attempt" at reconciliation before completion of the duel "if possible," and only "where caste mores allow."[27] Mores not allowing, the honor council would then superintend the combat to insure a proper gravity, as called for in the 1843 ordinance. Councils and courts of honor in the 1874 order, however, were no longer regarded as dueling surrogates but as alternative advisory organs. Whereas the 1843 council/court always arrived at a peaceful settlement of the conflict, the 1874 bodies decided whether a peaceful resolution of disputes between officers was an actual possibility in accord with the "interests" of the officer class. Hence, the situation could and often did arise whereby an officer was forced to duel against his wishes through an oblique suggestion of the honor court. Dueling in the 1843 order was nominally discouraged, but in 1874 it was only denounced "when one or the other of the participants, in the origins of the dispute or in its settlement [meaning a duel], has been found wanting in his obligations toward caste-honor."[28] This was a conveniently fluid criterion, appropriately expressed in Wilhelm's viscous statement that, "I will just as little tolerate an officer in my army who is capable of wantonly injuring the honor of a comrade as I will an officer who does not know how to defend his honor."[29]

Because of the enigmatic wording, the 1874 decree was open to varying interpretations and these later excited a great deal of polemical exfoliation in the Reichstag. There is, however, little doubt that the 1874 order was a basic recognition of the duel's legitimacy. Since 1843, three decades of sorry experience may have convinced the army that very proud officers would duel heedless of the repercussions, and Wilhelm's untidy phrasing can be interpreted as a concession to these. But the 1874 order also offered little in the way of support for those officers who held anti-dueling convictions, because one could now be dismissed from service for refusing to scrimmage. Even less pacifistic officers would find themselves in trying situations whereby their honor demanded an expiatory duel ultimately in conflict with the law. It had, in effect, become a formal part of the officer's job description to *schlagen*, one of his professional hazards, clearly sanctioned by the fact that duels ordered by the honor courts took place in army barracks so as to avoid meddling police,[30] and officers maimed in duels were granted leave and pensions.[31] Although as of the previous year, 1873, officers had been made technically subject to the general dueling clauses in the *Reichsstrafgesetzbuch*—effacing their singular legal status of 1843—the cleft originated in 1843 between the law of the land and the dictates of the officer class had by 1874 evolved into unbridgeable and frank opposition. (Two decades later, these dueling imperatives were clearly ascendant, a fact recognized by the legal state in 1893. Insulted by his employer the Graf Reden, the *Forstminister* Berthold issued a challenge. Reden fired him for the challenge; then he accepted it and a bloodless duel took place. Alive but jobless, Berthold sued his former employer for damages, basing his suit on the circumstance that as a reserve officer he had been compelled to challenge by his local honor council. Berthold further argued that Reden, being a reservist himself, should have foreseen this dueling eventuality and therefore refrained from canning a comrade. The case was kicked up to the Berlin Supreme Court, which decided that Berthold was right.[32])

Wilhelm's essential motives for revising his brother's 1843 order are impenetrable, but the result of his action was to demarcate the privileged corps even more unmistakeably from the rest of society by installing the duel as an indispensable component of the officer's code. The officer class had always pitched its political base camp just out of parliamentary striking distance, but now it emerged more than ever as an institution unto itself, pledging allegiance not to the *Rechtsstaat* but solely to its hereditary sovereign. Also, by bolstering the duel's standing within the ranks of the army, which had garnered prodigious status through the wars of unification from 1864 to 1871, the 1874 order lent the practice social distinction through the vaunted military affiliation. A general disrespect for the law was thereby fostered among the German middle and upper classes, loyal followers of army fashion. It may therefore be regarded as the official watershed for the cascade of duels in the next two decades.

The 1874 order was incorporated into the military constitutions of the three other German states possessing administrative rights over their own territorial armies: Saxony, Württemberg, and Bavaria. The Bavarian example helps shed light on certain peculiar aspects of the 1874 order which contributed to the duel's proliferation in the Prussian officer corps up until the turn of the century. Distinct from the in camera sessions of the Prussian Army courts, beginning in 1870 the proceedings of the Bavarian Army courts were made public. Bavarian honor courts had been first established in the 1820s, and before 1870 there was proportionately more dueling among the officers of the Bavarian Army than among those of the Prussian. After 1870, however, when the minutes of the honor courts became public domain, the number of duels sank, plaintiffs apparently finding sufficient satisfaction in a public humiliation of their antagonist. The Bavarian Army adopted the 1874 order on this open secret basis; but only after it had rejected the provision that the accused should be allowed solely a written defense, and also the provision which recognized the court's verdict as legal and binding without referral to constitutional law. Berlin ratified the Bavarian reservations, and this last one could well have made courts chary of proferring implicit recommendations to duel in their published verdicts. Also of note is the fact that Wilhelm's introductory remarks were replaced by those of Ludwig II (1864–86), and these did not contain a similar veiled sanction of dueling.[33] This courtly ritual was apparently too grim a reality for even the perfervid imagination of the "mad" king.

It is difficult to say how much overall dueling rates among German officers rose after Wilhelm's decree. Some statistics are available: from 1862 to 1886, 360 officers were punished for dueling; between 1890 and 1894 there were 68 duels from an active officer corps of thirty thousand members; and from 1874 to 1897, a period that may be regarded as the high red tide of German officer duels, around 250 active officers were punished for the activity.[34] None of these numbers are definitive. The last one, for example, excludes reserve officers, those not punished, those not prosecuted, and those duels that escaped detection or were conveniently ignored by the authorities. The two prior figures are equally cryptic.

An order promulgated by Wilhelm I's grandson Wilhelm II does, however, serve to illuminate these numbers. On 1 January 1897, after a turbulent year of sensational duels, noisy Reichstag debates, and thorough reappraisal of the government's official position toward the duel in the Ministry of Justice, Kaiser Wilhelm II authorized a nine-point supplement (*Ergänzung*) to the 1874 order. As to be expected from the word "supplement," it modified the old decree hardly at all, but the new document did express Wilhelm's qualified displeasure with the quantity of duels among his officers:

> The officer must recognize as an injustice the infringement of another's honor. If he has erred on the side of haste or excitement, he behaves chivalrously not by holding fast to his mistake but by offering his hand in apology. No less must he who has suffered an insult accept the proferred hand, *insofar as caste honor and good morals allow*. [my emphasis][35]

The most expedient courts for thwarting duels were those that never licensed dueling as an ultimate possibility, as under Friedrich Wilhelm III; those whose consultation was mandatory, as under Friedrich Wilhelm IV; and those whose decisions were binding, as under Wilhelm I. Wilhelm II's order confirmed none of these things. He emphasized that "henceforth the honor council should play a fundamental role in the settlement of affairs of honor," but this statement was also abridged by the old 1874 proviso: "caste morals permitting" (Art. 2). If officers were bent on dueling, his only request was that they kindly notify him of their intent (Art. 7). In other words, there were still exceptional cases of a less tractable nature that could only be settled on the field of honor. Jealous of his command and disciplinary prerogatives, the emperor was still reluctant to deny his cherished officer corps—"the heart and soul of the army"[36]—the anointed means by which it defended its bright honor.

Surprisingly, the number of officer duels after 1897 appears to have declined—as they appear to have multiplied after 1874. Wilhelm II's essential objection to the practice and increased efforts on behalf of the councils of honor to hammer out compromises may very well have contributed to the decline in the rate of officer duels. Although the statistics are skewed, ministerial quotations in the Reichstag indicate few duels between active officers occuring after 1897: 1898—three; 1899—eight; 1900—four; 1901—five; 1902—zero.[37] Once again, these numbers fail to include those many duels between active officers and civilians, reserve officer duels (considerably higher than the regular officer rates after 1897), and those that went unnoticed or were purposely overlooked. But in relation to the available pre-1897 numbers, which indicate that officer duels averaged between ten and fourteen annually,[38] a dip seems to have occurred. In 1901, Minister of War Heinrich von Gossler adduced the 1897 order as the effective reason that officer duels had "so substantially dwindled."[39] Whether this apparent trend can be attributed exclusively to Wilhelm's regulation is doubtful, but his measure was the most unswerving condemnation of the duel since the series of orders promulgated by his great-grandfather Friedrich Wilhelm III during the 1820s, immediately following which officer duels also tapered. Combined with the recent public ferment over the issue, one may conclude that Wilhelm's 1897 decree was a decisive catalyst hastening the duel's abstemious usage among active German officers.

It might have gone further. Dueling, as widespread in England in the early nineteenth century as it was in Germany later on, vanished from the British Isles in 1844 as the result of a trenchant measure that successfully nullified the duel in a manner "C. Balan" (quoted at the head of the chapter) would certainly have applauded. According to Antony Simpson, the measure made dueling unacceptable by lending it "the color of a practice whose tyranny could extend to the families of its practitioners."[40] Swept along by a wave of anti-dueling sentiment similar to that which moved Wilhelm II to action in 1897, Prime Minister Robert Peel in 1844 instituted the unprecedented policy of denying an army pension to the widow of an officer killed in a duel the year before. Queen Victoria gave it her blessing. The genius of the intervention was that an "institution predicated on the affirmation of courage and the demonstration of manliness could . . . be subverted if it brought destitution to the dependent and the weak." As this notion was now "publicly and safely expressed" in Peel's enactment, the practice of dueling "could be rejected by individuals without the worry of taint attaching to their reputations."[41] Dueling came to an end permanently. Although honorable alternatives to dueling did exist in the German officer's courts of honor, these very bodies could still try an officer for "conduct unbecoming" when failing to come out and fight like a man, as will be shortly seen. This certain clause had been carefully excised from the English Articles of War simultaneous with publication of Peel's revised pension plan. And a challenge in Germany still could not always be spurned in graceful fashion because German officers were not given to understand, as English ones were a half century earlier, that the consequences of their valiant spasm could

8. "Consolation." "We can give you the comforting as-
surance that your son behaved quite well when he took
the fatal ball." By W. Schulz, in *Der Student: Kulturbilder
aus dem Simplicissimus* (Albert Langen Verlag, 1905).
(Staatliche Museen zu Berlin, Kunstbibliothek)

be to make victims of the blameless. On the contrary, no matter whose
heart a duel might break, ridicule and contempt were the invariable
consequences of a challenge scorned in the Fatherland. Certainly German officers in 1897 were not so politically prepared to abandon the
duel as were their British counterparts in 1844, and the jackboot-lick-
ing German bourgeoisie was more committed to dueling than had
ever been the English middle class.[42] But the underlying reason why
the duel in Germany did not suddenly expire in the late 1890s—the
main reason why German officers were not inoculated against challenges—is that the perception never gained general currency that dueling was a selfish and not a selfless act.

The response to Wilhelm's order was split in the Reichstag's anti-
dueling faction. Apart from their basic political antagonisms, the divergent perspectives of the SPD and the Catholic Center Party on this
particular question undermined a coordinated attack on the duel
from its two leading opponents, the nation's two mass parties. Except
for the Right—which felt that harsher slander and libel laws were
greater dueling deterrents than the threat of prison—the balance of the
Reichstag generally clustered about the two polar views represented
by these parties. The Catholic Center, from whose membership were

drawn many adherents of the Anti-Dueling League,[43] declared itself satisfied not only with the wording of Wilhelm II's palliative but also with that of his grandfather's 1874 decree. As far as the Center Party was concerned, both ordinances categorically condemned the duel and imposed no illegal obligations on the officer. Their only grievance was that enforcement of these measures, as with the general dueling law, was unusually lax and they urged rigid application.[44] The Social Democrats took a more jaundiced view, considering the edict defective from Wilhelm II's opening sentence, "I desire that duels among my officers should be *more than ever avoided* [my emphasis]." To the socialists, this phrase smacked of a dilletantism and equivocation that gagged the document throughout. In their opinion, the 1897 decree failed to address decisively the 1874 order's glaring deficiency which gave dueling a de facto blank check, and Articles 2 and 7 were perceived as outright compulsions to duel. August Bebel declaimed against the 1874 measure as standing "in contradiction to all law, above the law," and he pronounced it "unworthy of a civilized state."[45]

As already noted, objections of the SPD were of a less ingenuous character than those of the Center Party. All the quibbling from the socialist contingent was less a direct preoccupation with solving the dueling question than it was a difference of opinion about the preferred legal and constitutional status of the army and its officer corps. The SPD realized that the duel was the mere chancrous nub of an elitist code and autocratic system it had sworn to upset. As a member of the German Conservatives accurately described it, the entire left side of the chamber wished to "destroy the prevalent spirit of the German officer corps, we wish to maintain it; that is the dramatic difference that separates us from you [the Left] in this question."[46] Accordingly, the socialists often sniped at the peripheral flanks of the dueling issue, seeking a pretext by which to throw the state's entire authoritarian superstructure into disequilibrium, as in the sinuous argument that neither the 1874 nor 1897 order had been countersigned by the Minister of War, thus making them both unconstitutional. But in his capacity as commander-in-chief, the Kaiser was under no constraint whatsoever to acquire such approval. The SPD's motive was clearly a sidelong assault on the government's obstinance to real ministerial responsibility.

The cheap shots of the SPD, then, were tenuous and misleading. Because neither the 1874 nor the 1897 decree entailed explicit coercion to duel, the debate perforce devolved—as the Center Party unflaggingly and rightly pointed out—on the issue of enforcement. The edicts were not unconstitutional because, although failing to damn the duel, they in no way gave positive guarantees to duelists. True, the 1897 order was aimed not at the duel's total eradication but rather at ablating its frivolous, careless usage. But although the two edicts were not in seamless harmony with the law, the more salubrious effects of Wilhelm II's declaration helped ultimately to enforce it. In optimistic statements a year before the 1897 decree, Chancellor von Hohenlohe and the Prussian Minister of Justice Schönstedt assured their skeptical parliamentary auditors that the forthcoming imperial pronouncement would affect the dueling question not only in the army but in society as a whole.[47] Their confidence was not misplaced. Civilian and officer dueling rates receded in unison. Almost every contemporary impression—of politicians, generals, government ministers, journalists—concurred in the judgment that annual dueling rates had suffered a perceptible, if hardly precipitous, drop since the turn of the century, and they would invariably point to the order of 1897 as the manifest reason for it.[48]

Karl Demeter suggests that after 1897, unconditional obedience became conflated with the *point d'honneur*, thus paving the way for the notorious *Kadavergehorsamkeit* ("cadaver-like obedience") of the German officer corps under Adolf Hitler.[49] There is little doubt that by the turn of the century the courts of honor had become authoritarian agents for the inculcation of that "lacky morality"[50] so much a trademark of Hitler's generals, products of this prewar generational cohort. But by tracing, as well as can be done, the ebb and flow of officer dueling rates in conjunction with royal and imperial decrees throughout the nineteenth century, it appears that the sovereign's pleasure was in each instance generally heeded. The German officer had *always* been beholden to more than just a code of honor; as a soldier he owed first allegiance to his *Oberbefehlshaber*. During the Franco-Prussian War and the First World War the German supreme command decreed a moratorium on dueling so as not to detract from the national effort, and officers docilely complied.[51] Likewise, the order of 1897, despite its equivocation, was a clear statement of preference by the Kaiser for temperance in matters that might precipitate a duel, and, generally speaking, the officer corps tried to follow Wilhelm's lead. Demeter notwithstanding, it was really business as usual: duty before honor. And in the short run, it mattered little how many duels were fought by officers after 1897. Such plenteous combats that did yet occur were informed by the same indomitable sense of honor prior to 1897, and were often fostered by those very honor courts that had originally been designed to forestall resort to arms. An officer's imperative of unconditional obedience can prove itself a Janus-faced virtue, depending on who is ordering what.

TRIAL AND ERROR

The Prussian court of honor records have gone missing since the Second World War. An analysis of those extant in Bavaria, Baden, and Württemberg, however, is revealing in several ways that surely parallel similar aspects in the irretrievable Prussian files. In this respect, Baden's records are of primary importance because the Fourteenth Army Corps received orders directly from Berlin, while Bavaria's and Württemberg's forces had their own ministries of war. Likewise, Karlsruhe's honor court verdicts were dispatched to Berlin for confirmation from the Kaiser, whereas Munich and Stuttgart disciplined their own malefactors. But all three records lend themselves to certain generalizations about the function of the German officer's courts of honor.[52]

The first statistic of note is the volume of honor court trials preceding and subsequent to 1897. There were more or less—Bavaria more, Württemberg less—dramatic increases in the number of cases brought to trial after 1897 in all three armies, certainly contributing to the sag in duels which occurred. Honor courts resolved controversies on an unprecedented scale through the imputation of dishonorable conduct to one or the other parties to the dispute, making a duel untenable by revoking half its honorable complement. If a man had no honor, he had none to defend. After 1897, therefore, potential army duels were not strictly forbidden but hamstrung, for behavior tolerated in former years that would have instigated a duel became grounds for dismissal.

One should not, however, allow German War Ministry statistics to pass unquestioned. While more and more cases were being submitted to the honor courts, these boards were not always instrumental in sabotaging duels between belligerent officers. The cardinal rule, again, was that those determined to duel would duel, and apparently always in the lull between honor council and honor court procedures, which could sometimes be delayed for weeks or months at a time.[53] As the rehabilitation of an officer's honor brooked no more than a forty-eight-hour deferment, this was asking for trouble. In 1914, a commissioner from the Prussian War Ministry conceded in a Reichstag caucus that he recalled no instance whereby an officer had patiently awaited an honor court verdict after the honor council had disqualified itself from the case. Moreover, after referring cases to an honor court, honor councils never expressly prohibited duels between litigants in the interim.[54]

A typical example of these bureaucratic foibles occurred during *Fasching* of 1914 in the garrison town of Metz. When the Second Lieutenant Haage discovered the infidelity of his wife with a Second Lieutenant La Valette Saint George, he called upon the gentleman caller with riding crop and pistol. La Valette reported the incident to his commanding officer. In the meantime, Haage had issued his challenge: five exchanges at fifteen paces with rifled pistols and sights. That same day the honor council met for several hours to arbitrate the case, finally concluding that it was incompetent to resolve it and that an honor court ruling was in order. Apprised of Haage's challenge and the impending duel, one of the honor council's representatives supervised the combat in which Haage crumpled at the second exchange.[55]

The order of 1897 fostered a welter of confusion in the officer corps over what constituted dishonorable behavior. If the document did not exactly founder and reel with ambiguity—the glib socialist depiction—it was simply not lucid on this point. The confluence in Wilhelm's order of older, less compromising conceptions of honor with more contemporary and liberal views turned regulation of officer's conduct into a haphazard business, and made the honor court verdicts farragos of contradiction. In a drunken stupor at a Metz celebration in 1901, a young second lieutenant manhandled a First Lieutenant Hoffmann. It was impossible to be insulted by a drunkard—the code said so—and Hoffmann ignored the provocation. The next day he communicated to the second lieutenant how he had already apprised his regiment's honor council of the case. The second lieutenant begged pardon, and the honor council, after issuing him a warning, pronounced the affair settled. However, the Metz regimental commander was unmollified and submitted the case to the district commander, who obtained a veto of the original honor council decision through an appeal to His Majesty, the King of Saxony. The case was retackled by the court of a Leipzig regiment, and Hoffmann was busted down to private citizen: as the "insulted" party, he had betrayed indelicate eagerness by initiating the reconciliation. Upon hearing the verdict, the Metz regimental commander reportedly warned his officers, "Gentlemen, all I can say is: In all cases, challenge at least to sabers!"[56]

Sometimes the procedural snafus engendered by the 1897 order could result in grotesquely tragic incidents that left not only chaos but decimation in their wake. In July of 1898 in Munich, a Major Ludwig Seitz exploited the absence of the First Lieutenant Eugen Pfeiffer to broach intimate relations with his wife. Returning home, Pfeiffer soon learned of the infidelity and the matter was referred to his regimental commander, Colonel Killinger. Alluding to the Kaiser's 1897 order, Killinger dissuaded Pfeiffer from sending a challenge, and then introduced an honor court proceeding against Seitz. Before the trial could begin, however, in August while on maneuvers the two antagonists had high words when Pfeiffer called Seitz a "scoundrel" and a "coward." Seitz now judged himself the offended party and would have bruskly issued a challenge had not Colonel Killinger again intervened, this time on the grounds that Pfeiffer had momentarily taken leave of his senses. In September the honor court process against Seitz began. Although he was advanced a "warning" for his adultery, he was found innocent of any dereliction of duty for not forwarding a challenge in the name-calling episode.

Now comes the kicker: In December the case was exhumed by the Bavarian War Ministry, which decided to honorably discharge Seitz and to now try not only Pfeiffer but Killinger as well. They were both rebuked for laborious adherence to the 1897 order: "There are certain instances in which a duel is unavoidable, and when this is the case it is better that it take place sooner rather than later. If First Lieutenant Pfeiffer had seriously wanted a duel, which, in his situation and from the standpoint of the officer, would have only been natural, it would have no doubt taken place despite [the order of 1897]." Pfeiffer's challenge was anticipated by Seitz and a duel took place a week before Christmas at fifteen paces with three exchanges. Seitz was killed. The next day a fresh court of honor trial was opened against Pfeiffer. The verdict was dishonorable discharge because of Pfeiffer's cursing of Seitz on maneuvers the previous summer. In February, Pfeiffer was tried for his December duel by a military court but was acquitted. In the same month, Killinger was given a warning by an honor court for having misled Pfeiffer, and later that summer he resigned his commission, certainly gnashing his teeth over the madness in his army's methods.[57]

The honor courts were as influential in stimulating as in squashing many duels. In 1899, a Captain Hönig published a scholarly work analyzing Vionville and Mars le Tour, battles of the Franco-Prussian War. His portraits of the deceased father of Colonel von Schwartzkoppen and that of General von Bernhardi were unflattering. Both scions took umbrage and challenged the partially sighted historian to duels, which he was forced to reject out of hand. The honor court proceeding that followed found Hönig truant in this blind refusal, and he was stripped of his uniform.[58] Not only did honor courts soft-pedal the 1897 decree and order up duels, they snazzed-up their conditions. In one swell editing job of 1901, the Lieutenant Döring and a student Klövekorn were ready for reconciliation after three exchanges, but the committee in attendance bade that further shooting be done, and at the fifth salvo the student was dashed to the ground.[59] As late as 1914 it was still incumbent upon Wilhelm II to remind his honor courts not to convict an officer for refusing to issue a challenge.[60] But the Kaiser himself did not always set the most sapient example. In 1907, following the discharge of an officer, His Imperial Majesty overturned the particular honor court verdict and fatuously pardoned the offender. Having been rehabilitated and recommissioned, the officer's *Satisfaktionsfähigkeit* was no longer suspect and the object of his insult was now compelled to send a challenge, which ended in fatal gunplay.[61]

Violations of the officer's code of ethics were protean, for general guidelines were rather obscure: his behavior was to proceed from "the code word: chivalry," and remain free of "all that dirties and stinks."[62] With indeterminate pointers such as these, there were few things not subject to the scrutiny of an honor court because the criminality of particular acts was predicated on little else besides the extent of their public exposure, their degree of flagrancy. Chivalry and smelling good aside, the officer's watchword was discretion.[63] Yet the honor court's eye was kept perpetually to the keyhole as well. Homosexuality, illicit relations with the wife of a comrade, intercourse with liminal social elements and women of dubious reputation, sexual trafficking with a subordinate—these were among the more frequently litigated cases. Carnality in general was foul play for single officers who were officially expected to remain celibate until—in this exceptional context it seems to bear saying—they wed, and nuptials were strongly discouraged before their thirties.[64] Needless to say, such a state of affairs fostered more hypocrisy than purity. But amorous license was certainly not the only area of grave concern. As mentioned, almost anything could be construed as inflammatory behavior. Sometimes complaints would be filed by private citizens, as in two instances where the unsubstantiated "charges" were screaming and a reneged promise of marriage.[65] According to Rumschöttel, duels in the Bavarian Army increased in the 1880s largely due to the proliferation of trivial taboos such as these.[66]

Although the chief hallmark of honor court decisions after 1897 was their inconsistency, they pretended to perform the pedagogical duty of educating junior officers to a uniform standard of comportment befitting their rank. Wilhelm I's order of 1874 urged older officers "to oversee and to educate their younger comrades," and this paternal responsibility fell institutionally to the honor courts,[67] which had very long arms and prosecuted wayward sons in such far-flung locales as Romania, Buenos Aires, and Samoa.[68] In 83 percent of all cases from 1888 to 1914 that went before Bavarian honor courts, lieutenants were the defendants; and in roughly two-thirds of all cases, junior-grade lieutenants were involved.[69] In Badenese honor court proceedings from 1879 to 1918, lieutenants stood in the dock approximately 70 percent and junior-grade lieutenants 55 percent of the time. In Württemberg honor courts from 1871 to 1918, lieutenants were accused in 77 percent and junior-grade lieutenants in 66 percent of all cases. A yet more revealing statistic is that in Bavaria 53 percent of all cases were prosecuted against reservists. Almost 70 percent of all honor court cases in Baden concerned officers of the reserve or militia, and 42 percent of honor court trials had junior-grade lieutenants of the militia or reserve standing trial. In Württemberg, the numbers were less striking but still noteworthy at 44 and 33 percent, respectively.[70] The prime target of honor court trials, therefore, was the obstreperous reservist or militiaman with a second lieutenant's commission. It is no accident that these officers bore the brunt of the anti-dueling invective in the Reichstag. The Austrians had their own problems with these enfants terribles, and in a Reichsrat debate over the duel in 1884 the Minister of War affirmed that Habsburg officers were never enjoined to "turn the other cheek." Whereupon his interrogator sneered: "So Christ would not have become a second lieutenant?"[71]

With the Army Reform of the early 1860s, Prussia established her reserve officer corps to supplement and partly replace the outmoded Landwehr militia units. The traditionally aristocratic army was thus laid open to a greater bourgeois influx, this apparent capitulation allowing a militaristic bridgehead into civilian society.[72] By 1914 the proportion of reserve to active officers was three to one.[73] In view of this ratio, it comes as little wonder that by the 1890s, and particularly after 1897, the reserve or militia officer hoisted the army's dueling standard. There was almost universal consensus on this particular among both pro- and anti-dueling groups. In an 1896 debate, it was basically the sole point of agreement between Conservatives and Social Democrats.[74] In a concurrent issue of the respected publication the *Preussische Jahrbücher*, historian Hans Delbrück affirmed that it was not the frontline officer but his reservist auxiliary who was the greatest source of mischief.[75] By 1902 the reserve officer's reputation had so far preceded him that one Reichstag deputy was hesitant in approving a proposal to eject dueling officers from the army because he feared that reservist malcontents might seize upon this new regulation as a form of highly honorable discharge.[76] On the eve of the war, the reserve officer was still the principal troublemaker, and von Krafft's primer for young officers warned lifers to beware the part-time soldier and grant him a wide berth.[77]

The likely reason for this circumstance was the greater discipline of the regular officer and the limitation of his daily routine to a circle of fellow officers who possessed a single standard of conduct. The reserve officer, on the other hand, was likely to have irregular dealings with an eccentric range of personalities whose deportment just might be based on criteria other than an imperial commission. "They are continuously sitting on the powder keg," summed up one contemporary.[78] The reserve officer may also have experienced periodic bouts of social insecurity that left him more susceptible to veiled digs and otherwise good-natured japery than his careerist associate. A component of officer's honor was the ability to defend it against attacks, a fact that may have unconsciously induced the aspiring reservist to confirm his stripes through gasconading hijinks that would provoke a challenge. Additionally, and unlike the case of active officers, conflicts with civilians were not under the jurisdiction of the courts of honor. In lieu of a martial court umpire, therefore, reserve officers were expected to take independent action either through a civil process or by settling, as it were, out of court.[79]

These were words to live by for the reserve officer because honor court procedures could be Kafkaesque in their lunacy. In Dresden during the early 1890s, a district judge who was also a captain in the Landwehr received a pistol challenge from a legal clerk after he had scolded the clerk for snotty remarks in court. But the judge declined the duel based on the fact that his comments were uttered in the line of duty, and he was supported in this position by his superiors. The irascible clerk then penned several letters to the judge's district Landwehr commander, heaping abuse upon the junior officer. The commander showed the letters to his captain and ordered him to duel. But he once again rejected the idea, correctly perceiving this most recent affront as an extension of the first affair. The judge was then brought before an honor council. It ordered him to finally put an end to it all and duel. He dueled. Because the clerk had been sentenced to prison for his challenge, special dispensation from the Saxon Minister of Justice gave him a day of vacation to carry out the combat. The judge was later chewed out before several official bodies and finally reprimanded for his initial hesitation to take up the gauntlet.[80] You either took it up or you ran it.

The bungling arbitrariness of honor court decisions was only compounded in the case of reservists who lived in two worlds. In 1905 an officer of the reserve named Feldhaus received an epistolary insult from a Dr. Alfred Göpel. After gaining a promise from Göpel to submit to the verdict of his local honor council, Feldhaus presented it with the incriminating evidence. But at the last second Göpel backed out. Feldhaus then correctly undertook to press private charges and eventually received the highest compensation of six hundred Marks in damages after Göpel admitted that, keenly aware of Feldhaus's pacifistic nature, he had written the offensive letter simply to jeopardize his Landwehr officer status. Meanwhile, Göpel in revenge had in-

formed Feldhaus's district commander of the private charges his officer was bringing, and the commander then notified the concerned
honor council, submitting a plea on Feldhaus's behalf. Feldhaus was
nonetheless reprehended for not extracting "satisfaction befitting
one's rank" (*standesgemässe Genugtuung*) and was handed a dishonorable discharge. In the Reichstag interpellation of the Ministry of War
concerning the incident, its representative declared that Feldhaus,
aware of the consequences of not dueling, should have been exceedingly careful in his dealings.[81] This, again, in 1905—eight years after
Wilhelm II's pronunciamento.

The miasma of caprice surrounding honor court decisions did nothing to instill reserve in reservists, who inured themselves to the idea of
dueling at the slightest pretext so as to avoid possible condemnation.
While unwonted tolerance might well lead to a dishonorable discharge, reserve officers were rarely cashiered for combativeness, and
theirs was fabled. At the society club "Börsengarten" in Königsberg
during the summer of 1895, a reservist's behavior prompted a board
member to politely but firmly request he leave the premises. An exchange of words ensued and the testy officer challenged his interlocu-
tor to a seven-pace barrier duel. The member indignantly rejected the
challenge on the basis that he himself was the insulted party and was
only performing his job. The reservist raised a stink, and the result was
a full-scale army boycott of the society, in which even the chairman of
the regional council and the *Oberpräsident* unilaterally revoked their
memberships.[82] In another incident, a lawyer and a judge had an antic
squabble over the proper color of the former's tie. In the course of the
argument the attorney reminded his antagonist to exercise caution, for
he was a reserve officer.[83]

Gentle reminders were not inadvisable, for unlike the regular officer, reservists were not compelled to wear their livery off-duty.
Tongues may have had a tendency to loosen when not confronted
with insignia. But uniform or no, reservists adored displaying their
credentials for all mankind to admire. They were fond of inscribing
visiting cards with their rank, and even Protestant vicars who were
reserve officers gave unseemly precedence to their army title.[84] The
engagement announcement of a certain reserve lieutenant left one recipient to wonder how the reservist would support his bride, since
only this status was mentioned on the announcement and reserve officers drew neither sinecure nor pension.[85] In an 1893 court proceeding,
a well-to-do factory owner defended the veracity of his testimony and
that of his wife by invoking his commission: "I am a reserve officer,
my wife is the spouse of an officer, and so you must believe us." Had
not the star witness been a sergeant in the reserve, the court may likely

have believed them.[86] Exasperated by such unmitigated foolishness, once in the midst of a dueling debate August Bebel sighed, "We really live these days in the Reserve Lieutenant Era."[87]

After Wilhelm's order of 1897 the incidence of dueling in regular army circles declined. Although the continued proliferation of duels among reserve officers blurs distinctions, by 1900 civilian dueling rates were apparently surpassing those of the army. In 1901, Graf Bernstorff of the conservative *Reichspartei* voiced his opinion that most duels were occurring outside the army. In that same session a member of the Liberal Union went so far as to declare that the duel was more widespread in civil life than ever before.[88] Although this was an exaggeration because civilian rates had tailed-off some with those of officers, by 1906 the emboldened War Ministry had the temerity to suggest that the army could not afford to alter its dueling policy so long as society at large clung to the practice, thus placing the onus of responsibility on the common *Bürger*, an inversion of the patent causal relationship scarcely ten years before![89]

The German situation was paradoxical. Whereas in such places as France and Hungary the duel was plainly a civil phenomenon, in Germany, even though it was largely the civilian populace that lent dueling the vivacity it enjoyed in the immediate prewar years, the regular officer and his uncompromising code remained its inspiration, the mighty imperial reserve officer corps serving as vector for the exuberation of such tenets to the upper flights of society. The officer was still the glittering paragon and his punctilious habits the pervasive standard before which the German man of honor unabashedly kowtowed. "All those must be regarded as *satisfaktionsfähig* who come from the best circles of society," testified one expert shortly before the war, adding, "and who . . . share the same conception of honor as the officer."[90] Speaking of the turn of the century, Isabel Hull has observed that "the more the nobility and its most purified sector, the officer corps, raised its standards, the harder the bourgeoisie tried to live up to them, particularly in the form of the reserve officer."[91] But as compared to their role models, reservists tended to chase the phantom glory and never mind their p's and q's. Henry Pachter has summed up the motivation behind a German middle class who "imagined that by donning a reserve lieutenant's uniform they were the barbarians whose dawn Nietzsche had predicted."[92] Blond beastliness did not necessarily lead to the propagation of glassy-eyed killers, but it hardly made for dispositions as sweet as mountain lilac. The Sunday duelist, the weekend warrior, was now the pacesetter.

All this makes some sense if one grants the duel's fairly obvious relationship to bellicose tendencies. There is an analogue to officer/

reservist dueling in what Stig Förster has called the phenomenon of "double militarism" in Wilhelmine Germany. Especially after 1905, those who were most vocal in support of a preventive war or even a war for its own sake, hailed from the bourgeois radical Right, whereas the aristocratic general staff tended to hold itself aloof from such reckless thinking. The hawkishness of representative figures like Heinrich Class, leader of the Pan-German League, was motivated by the aspiration for a type of reform in the *Kaiserreich* that would mainly profit the bourgeoisie. Of this bourgeois-reformist *Primat der Innenpolitik*, Förster writes:

> [A]n aggressive imperialistic foreign policy, inclusive of the risk of war was a decisive vehicle in the enactment and legitimation of those changes. War, and even world war, seemed to the *Rechtsradikalen* in this respect not only an unavoidable, necessary evil, but as a desirable means to groom the German people to accept the domestic political objectives of the Pan-Germans and their allies.

These allies included the party par excellence of the educated and wealthy middle class, the National Liberals. Naturally, the nation's nonradicalized conservative sector, including the regular officer corps, was not only wary of this amateur war ideology, but was equally mistrustful of any so-called "domestic political objectives."[93] The point is this: Maybe the disproportionate rates of dueling between reserve and regular officers in Germany after 1900 can be partly explained from the condition of "double militarism," the bourgeoisie perceiving in dueling, as they perceived in war, a means of social advancement, therefore using it not as a last line of honorable defense, but as an extension of politics by other means.

THE MILITARY ETHOS

"War is nothing," professed the military theorist Carl von Clausewitz (1780–1831), "but a duel on an extensive scale."[94] The duel was war in microcosm, a kriegspiel ideally suited to an officer class trained in the art of mortal engagement. It was celebrated as the actuating spirit of martial virtues that achieved their highest expression in battle, in dangerous self-exposure, in destruction of the enemy. The logic of the war-duel symbiosis was conspicuous to observers at the time:

> If one therefore speaks of war, one may not speak of justice. War is the right of the stronger, whether he is justified or not—it is the "ultima ratio" in the resolution of opposing interests. The duel, resting on the

same natural law, is the "ultima ratio" in the resolution of quarrels and affairs of honor. . . . Battle gave birth to the chivalrous ethic. . . . The officer class's ideal attitude toward life, based on true chivalry and high-mindedness, this most noble achievement of genuine manliness, comes from the principle of struggle. The duel is a call to battle.[95]

As armed defender of his country's sovereign integrity, the officer found it natural to repulse in a similar manner attacks upon his own prickly honor, "or rather, the armed honor [*Waffenehre*] of the state."[96] Von Boguslawski stated the issue most plainly when he observed how it was eminently understandable for "the man who has made the career of arms his life's occupation [to] make resort to weaponry more often than others."[97] Naturally, this situation could arouse a certain "pathological proclivity" to conceive a grave affront in affairs of a petty and ticky-tack character.[98] But because honor was considered "the foundation of the healthy spirit in the army,"[99] it was essential that it be well guarded, and with a warlike pugnacity. The army had a hard time disabusing itself of the opinion that cooly standing fire in a pistol duel or cooling someone with your blade in a saber contest was not in some way an uplifting experience for a man whose life gained in meaning directly inverse to his power to deride it. Immolation in a duel was a shortcut to Valhalla, and not just a nameless death in battle either.

The question is, therefore, how much did the officer's honor really owe to the duel? Would his honor, and his fighting capacity, have been diminished had the duel not been present to fund it with the absolute integrity that came from risking one's life? Was the duel a vainglorious appendage or an indispensable prerequisite of honor? To answer, in an army which regarded "the soiled glove as a harbinger of the failed campaign,"[100] the duel was seen as a consummate tool for the maintenance of combat readiness (*Kriegsfertigkeit*), to kill or be killed at a moment's notice. If a man was able to gaze dispassionately into the artless eyes of a fellow officer—or simply a fellow German—and, while placing his own breast at the disposal of his opponent's bullet, perfunctorily commit a form of fratricide, he probably would have little compunction in leading a charge of cavalry or fixed bayonets into the serried ranks of a faceless foe. As an articulation of the officer's vocation to risk all for the sake of an abstract idea or an emotional symbol, the duel exemplified what the nationalist historian Heinrich von Treitschke described as "the majesty of war," in which a man "must murder an opponent whom he highly respects and toward whom he feels no real hatred; this type of struggle entails a greater moral effort than those of the barbarian."[101] In a certain way, the dueling principle was a conventional takeoff on the venerable Prussian doctrine that a soldier be trained to dread his own officers more than the enemy; in this case, that an officer should be more terrified of flinching at a challenge to duel than any challenge the field of massed battle might present him. V. G. Kiernan speculates that the duel may have

> helped to keep the German army keyed up for action, in the years be-
> tween 1871 and 1914 when German officers saw scarcely any active ser-
> vice, and had to fall back on other ways of manifesting courage. A soldier
> who never fights comes to border on the ridiculous, or must feel that he
> does. Meanwhile French, Russian, and above all British officers had con-
> tinual opportunities to distinguish themselves in colonial wars, and pile
> up ribbons.[102]

Germany had not given its officers a good "show" since Bismarck's wars of unification, and their warring instinct was not likely quelled by attitudes flowing from High Command. Though not in the same jingoistic league with Heinrich Class, Marshal Helmuth von Moltke, the elder (1800–1891), held the conviction that, "The perpetual peace is a dream and not even a beautiful dream, and war is an element of the order of the world established by God. In war the noblest virtues of men unfold, courage and renunciation, duty and self-abnegation with the sacrifice of one's life: Without war the world would sink into mate-rialism."[103] By 1898, idealistic German officers were so spoiling for a fight that when the United States declared hostilities against Spain, scores of them stampeded the U.S. embassy in Berlin to offer their services in Cuba.[104] War was hell, but peace was overrated. Soldiers languishing in some desultory post on the Russian frontier could have dueled to purge the *taedium vitae* of the barracks, choosing the pros-pect of rigor mortis over the deathly certainty of remaining bored stiff. Plentiful enough were the officer skirmishes reported from East Prus-sia, Posen, and Silesia.

International rivalries managed to rationalize the army duel among sympathizers. During a Reichstag debate, in a patriotic show of hands by the Right, Ernst Bassermann of the National Liberals cheered the "sense of honor of our officer corps, which has made our German offi-cer corps the first in the world." A Conservative deputy arose to cite officer duels as the acme of those attitudes which were mainstays of national greatness, "for these views have helped us to win our bat-tles. . . . [O]ur officer corps unconditionally demands from each of its members that he stake his honor with his life." A representative of the Prussian Minister of War, shutting hard his eyes to moxie British in-fantry squares, mentioned dueling in the French and Austrian officer

corps as reason enough for its preservation in the German army.[105]
Again, such advocacy had its source in the apprehension that were the
German officer to scuttle his sacerdotal rite, he would lose his combat
edge. In time of peace the war gods must still be oblated. However, the
important distinction was that in the French and Austrian armies dueling was officially restricted to the épée and the saber, respectively, in
order to avert death. German officers, therefore, if not sacrificing their
combat edge, were the only ones routinely forfeiting their lives—and
to friendly fire.

Attempts to abolish the duel were perceived by the military leadership as extravagant ex parte plots to subvert traditional values. To
some extent, they were. In the spring of 1914, during one last prewar
push by the Reichstag to pass effective anti-dueling legislation, the
sagacious Minister of War Erich von Falkenhayn (1861–1922), responding to an in-house governmental survey undertaken by Chancellor von Bethmann-Hollweg, acknowledged the need for tougher
dueling laws. But he rejected the particular parliamentary proposal at
issue on the basis that "the roots of the duel grow in the soil of the
notion of honor. This notion is a valuable one, and for the officer an
irreplaceable good. To destroy or at least transform this notion is the
goal of the Reichstag." He concluded: "I am unable to grant the legitimacy of this enterprise."[106] Scarcely feigning the fiction of ministerial
responsibility, von Falkenhayn was adamantly opposed to any suggestions emanating from the Reichstag concerning the topic:

> One is probably not wrong in assuming that the Reichstag, at least in its
> democratic sectors, is less concerned with combatting the duel than in
> battling the caste views of the officer corps. . . . I consider it . . . my duty
> to counter all direct or indirect parliamentary attempts to exert a pressure
> on the views and spirit of the officer corps. I especially believe that all
> legislative bills touching upon the officer corps and so warmly supported
> by the *Demokratie* must always be met with powerful distrust.[107]

Von Falkenhayn apprehended what was at stake in the dueling
question. The left-wing parties, particularly the Social Democrats,
who labeled dueling the wicked outgrowth of a militarism closely en-
twined with the ethos of *Standesehre*, were fond of drawing attention
to the fact that the concept of *Satisfaktionsfähigkeit* rested not on an
inward feeling of personal worth but on a highly cultivated sensibility
of caste. In 1902 one SPD deputy could contain himself no longer and
cried, "If you want to eliminate the duel, then depose the Junker!"[108]
The unofficial dueling code of the officer corps, *Die conventionellen
Gebräuche beim Zweikampf*, gave propitious occasion for such blasts,
stating in its foreword: "The unusually high and respected position

that the officer occupies in our Fatherland demands that, next to his competence and devotion to duty, his most solemn obligation be the 'painstaking preservation of his caste-honor.'"[109] In 1914, in the wake of the Zabern Affair, another socialist deputy chided the bourgeois parties for prostrating themselves before militarism. He maintained that in order to enforce the existing dueling laws it was first necessary to throttle the military oligarchy holding the German nation in thrall. With respect to the most recent dueling bill under discussion by the Reichstag, "revision of the penal code must likewise remain unsuccessful . . . so long as the power stronger than the legal paragraphs remains unbroken; namely, the absolute will of the military establishment."[110]

But the eventual rejection by the government of this new dueling bill of 1914, which among other things would have automatically cashiered all officers for dueling, was bound up not only with the concept of *Standesehre*. It was intimately conjoined to principles of monarchy. The French philosophe Montesquieu elaborated this link in his 1748 *L'Esprit de Lois*: "Honor is the motivating force behind monarchy. . . . The bases of the monarchy presuppose hierarchy, outward honors, and even a hereditary aristocracy. All these things spur ambition, and if ambition brings about corruption in a republic, it obtains to good effect in the monarchy."[111] The paradoxical flip side of duelists' insurgence against the constituted state was their pledge of allegiance—through their honor-based sacrificial rite—to its designated monarch, who was inclined to show his appreciation with pardons.[112] Von Falkenhayn feared that incorporation of the new law into the penal code would lead the beneficent Kaiser to exercise his right of reprieve for convicted duelists even more so than in the past, therefore offering the opposition parties, whose persistent chatter he hoped to muffle, an "always welcome occasion for the contestation of monarchical ideas."[113] After ascending to the throne in 1888, in one of his more coherent outbursts, Wilhelm elatedly declared: "We belong together, I and the army."[114] The army was indeed a sort of imperial escort. A commissioned soldier in this Praetorian Guard was entrusted with his "King's jacket," and any unexpiated insult left the garment soiled, the sovereign importuned, and the officer with the stigma of turncoat. King and country were thereby implicated in every honorable affair involving an officer. In this sense, dueling for the Wilhelmine officer was a statement of principle and "a confession of faith."[115] It is important to recognize that the army duel was never a test of backbone as in student and civilian rencontres, because the fortitude of the Prussian officer was held a deathless verity transcending validation.[116]

He was denizen of a higher realm—but not a higher income bracket. The Frankfurt philosopher Arthur Schopenhauer (1788–1860) speculated that had the German state been less parsimonious, honor and its accessory duel would certainly have been more easily expendable: "Yes, if officers were better paid, if they received the wages they deserve in return for the sacrifices of health and life to their country, then one would not need to salary them with special honor for which they can pay so dear a price."[117] It is true that German officers were miserably compensated for their pains, though not because their service was considered valueless, but invaluable. This custom's origin may have been in the old Prussian tradition of plying the wealthy aristocracy with commissions, the position of officer bringing its own psychic rewards and thus obviating the necessity for generous remuneration. By the Second Empire, however, these skimpy emoluments were unable to vie with the earning power of other professions, and the gradual increase in civilian living standards before the First World War must have rendered the opulent category of officer's honor an even more distinct imperative. Unless they were tendered the special honorable status affiliated with epaulettes and brass, many potential officers would surely have thought twice before choosing an army career.[118] In lieu of money, the officer class derived its prestige through a moral superiority naturally accruing to grandees whose principles were backed unconditionally by the purity and super-logic of force.

This might serve as a partial explanation for the increased tenacity with which the officer corps clung to the idea of dueling until the very last days of peace, for with the exception of the cavalry, bourgeois arrivistes composed the majority of German officers. As the Prussian Reformer Scharnhorst termed it, that "aristocratic something" attendant to the officer's code[119] must have been a highly coveted perquisite for the roturier hot to embroider his escutcheon. Even chastisement was heartening. A member of the German Liberal People's Party dubbed dueling the "noble crime," and protested that incarceration was a point of pride for many, equal to a semi-patent of nobility.[120] It was described how—aside from the Club-Med Getaway aspects—"a couple weeks of honorable detention sometimes constitute the most pleasant memory in the life of a reserve officer."[121] An officer's duel-based honor distinguished him from the venal civilian rabble, and this fact was emphasized in army circles as an antidote to abolitionist agitation. In his order of 1874, Wilhelm I implored officers to steer clear of get-rich-quick schemes and questionable business ventures, and he prohibited any and all indulgence in luxury. The danger was "a complete disruption of the ground and foundation upon which the officer caste stands, in consequence of the striving after profit and sumptuous living."[122] In 1914, a missive from the Bavarian War Ministry condemning the publication of marriage offers was prompted by the advertisement of a "pretty, young Bavarian officer" seeking any woman of means worth at least one hundred thousand Marks.[123] Honor, not love or money, was the proper nexus among men. Officers were taught to "despise the materialistic,"[124] and this was precisely the ontological endowment upon which the dueling ideology rested. Happiness was not a suitable preoccupation for a man, and so officers closed their Byron and took pleasure in renunciation. This attitude sunders them more sharply from our consumer age than does the enormous fact that they dueled.

In 1889 the moral philosopher Friedrich Paulsen admitted that the army duel was an abused privilege but steadfastly refused to throw out the honor baby with the dueling bath. "An evil that prevents a greater evil," he proclaimed, "is a good."[125] And by estimations of the military, where casualties were a quotidian fact of life, the lesser evil was a rather miniscule one at that. By the turn of the century, when both the army and its duel had become objects of public scrutiny and disputation, the documented rate of officer duels was almost negligible. If lives had been lost on a daily or even weekly basis, a firm and vigorous crackdown by the Kaiser would surely have followed. But this was not, and never had been the case. From the army's point of view, the officer duel never became such an irksome problem that it warranted uprooting those martial values and ethical absolutes that nourished the custom. Dueling was perceived as an indispensable correlate of honor, and the rapport between the two may have helped lend the German officer corps at this time a sort of epic grandeur that more than compensated for the relatively scant fatalities. What was good for officers, however, was not necessarily suitable for the lay public, where casualties were higher and the duel's rationale simultaneously less justified. Civilians derived a role that for them had little pragmatic subtext. These imposters transcribed literally a stern code that even for the military profession was the exaggeration of a possibility. The appropriation of the officer's code of honor by the German civilian elite was as ill-advised and risible as would be the scenario of Spanish bullfight aficionados adopting the preening bravura and reckless *pundonor* of their matador idols, whose defiant poses are efficacious within the confines of the bullring but of dubious utility and worth beyond its portals.

Up until the First World War, the duel was retained in the officer corps and was represented to civilian society on the strength of the well-known formula: Love me, love my dog. And by 1897, the old

adage about new tricks notwithstanding, the cur had been to obedience school and was more or less housebroken. Allowing for low estimates, out of a pool of seventy-five-thousand officers both active and
reserve in 1913, only sixteen duels were recorded.[126] Yet for those
thousands of others whose code of honor was likewise guaranteed,
dueling remained a sincere possibility—if it worked out that way. On
the eve of the First World War, von Falkenhayn stressed in a speech to
the Reichstag that physical courage was still "the prerequisite of the
soldier's raison d'être . . . upon which he has accustomed himself to
place the supreme value," and he spoke for the officer corps and perforce much of bourgeois society when he concluded, "I personally
would regard an extirpation of the conception of honor, which now
and then unhappily leads to a duel, as a misfortune."[127]

***

For those who thought the officer's code of honor was a quaint and
ultimately harmless pretense so long as its dueling ramifications were
limited to a top-lofty stratum, there was yet one aspect that made it the
business of the mangiest guttersnipe—especially the mangiest guttersnipe. A rather bizarre facet of officer's honor was the practice of
Ehrennotwehr, or, defense of one's honor in extreme emergency
through unusual measures. *Ehrennotwehr* was a device technically reserved for those occasions when the physical integrity of the officer
had been violated by a member of the unwashed horde who could not
render formal satisfaction, but liberal interpretations led to its indis-
criminate use as an effectual method for teaching any upstart his place.
Although it was theoretically impossible for an officer to be given affront by an inferior, he was still granted special immunity to punish all
manner of insolence. The exercise of *Ehrennotwehr* in suitable circumstances was not a mere right but an "obligation" of the officer, integral
to the special distinction conferred upon him by the wearing of His
Majesty's swagger coat.[128]

When social pipsqueaks got a shade too bossy, an officer was to
unsheath Excalibur and correct the nuisance as someone might swat
a pesky fly. No swallowing hard and counting to ten—it was an
emotional reflex. In contrast to dueling where feelings were checked,
frigid restraint was inappropriate for saucy lesser mortals—although,
being an unconsidered action free of rational forethought, *Ehrennotwehr* in one way epitomized the duel's military-aristocratic ethos of
heedless and prodigal disbursement opposing a bourgeois pack-rat
ethic of calculated accumulation.[129] Apropos, there were two conditions to keep in mind: 1) because any hesitation constituted a premedi-

tated assault, the officer must react at once; and 2) he must not merely wave his sword about threateningly or spank his victim with the flat of its blade, but act with paralyzing resolve—proceeding "with his entire energy and with the highest degree of brutality of which he is capable."[130] It was especially important to combust spontaneously when civilian witnesses were around to impress upon the public that "such gross injury to caste honor does not for one minute remain unexpiated."[131]

Unlike his Austrian counterpart, whose military penal code made express provision for the possibility of *Ehrennotwehr* and its legal exercise, the German officer was not exempt from prosecution. He was to bear his vocational burden and "calmly accept his punishment,"[132] for "there are cases in which little remains to an officer outside of instantaneous infliction of corporal punishment upon his opponent with the use of his sword."[133] Denuded of uniform, however, officers would have looked silly lugging a sword, and this is one of the reasons why they were enjoined to always style full regalia, especially when appearing in society. Buckling a sword was a privilege restricted to the officer class, harking back to the Middle Ages when only knights were afforded a similar distinction, but on a practical level, *Ehrennotwehr* was only effective when one had a sharp-edged sidearm at hand. "In mufti . . . the officer is always at a disadvantage. It can come to genuine brawls, and in such a case the officer's future is, as a rule, finished."[134] To help enable his officers' prospects, an 1880 cabinet order of Kaiser Wilhelm I restricted Prussian policemen from interfering in cases of *Ehrennotwehr*; only after someone had been polished off were they permitted to restore order—as if at that point it needed restoring. Officers were moreover given the right to turn their blades on overzealous policemen who refused to sit by and watch military personnel slash defenseless civilians.[135]

Half-measures were inconsonant with the officer's strict conformity to an intemperate code, and sometimes the bloodletting could originate through the most trifling of episodes. In one instance in 1892, a first lieutenant strolled down Berlin's fashionable Potsdamerstrasse, his unleashed dog at his side. Along the way, they encountered a large Leonburger fastened to the wrist of a man who, while attempting to pull his dog away from the other animal's snapping jaws, inquired if the lieutenant would not restrain his pet. No sooner had he uttered these words, then the lieutenant, who had stood placidly by, drew his saber and commenced to rain down blows upon the man, who fought back desperately with his umbrella. He suffered several gruesome cuts before a gendarme sauntered by to intervene. The incident would have in all likelihood been forgotten except that the first lieutenant's dog had been barking up the wrong pedestrian. The unfortunate civilian emerged as an inactive major. The matter, therefore, became province of an honor council inquiry that did not augur well for the junior officer.[136] *Ehrennotwehr* required an officer to make impromptu judgments as to the *Satisfaktionsfähigkeit* of his antagonist, and to err in one direction or another could prove ruinous to his career.

Two cases in the year 1895 were equally flagrant. In Hamburg an officer demanded apology of a man who had jostled him while exiting from a streetcar. Apologies were not immediately forthcoming, so the officer buried the edge of his persuader in the man's scalp. He elicited the desired response. The same officer then kindly assured that his victim received proper medical attention. People have moods.[137] In Königsberg later that year, an inebriated Second Lieutenant Burmeister of the Sixth East Prussian Infantry insulted a crowd of people returning through the city gates at the end of a Sunday in the country. His comments were chiefly aimed at the women in attendance. Their escorts called him to account. Burmeister drew his sword and stumbled after them braying, "You damned dogs, I'll make mincemeat of you," prompting the company to laughter as they scurried before him. While Burmeister thrashed wildly about, he had the bad luck of reconnoitering with a couple of proletarian toughs, one of whom captured his sword and snapped it like a breadstick. Although the ensuing honor court trial naturally took place behind closed doors, subsequent rumors in Königsberg were that Burmeister was later discharged from the army not for his embarrassing behavior but because his sword had been wrested from him and cropped.[138]

The Berlin, Hamburg, and Königsberg vignettes were not untypical of episodes that occurred with regularity across Germany during this period, and in October 1896, the year of the first great dueling debates in the Reichstag, a case detonated that propelled the officer's code into the national limelight. It took place in Karlsruhe, the provincial capital of Baden: While prowling the streets late one October evening, a Lieutenant von Brüsewitz encountered a worker named Siepmann who brushed by using an epithet; or perhaps just brushed by. Accounts varied. Siepmann continued along his way. Having failed to react instantly to whatever offense von Brüsewitz imagined Siepmann had committed, the confused officer brooded: "I am now a lost man, my career is finished." Finally bracing himself to action, von Brüsewitz raced after his provocateur. Picking up two other junior officers along the way, he finally cornered Siepmann in a courtyard. At sword point, he forced the worker to stammer apologies.

Satisfaction?

Hardly.

Von Brüsewitz had his job, his reputation, his communal esteem to consider. He considered them, and then made a surprising decision. He did not slash Siepmann to ribbons: He dealt him the blow of the matador. Wiping his sword, he was said to have muttered: "I've redeemed it."[139]

The *Fall Brüsewitz* became a *cause célèbre* in the press, and was appropriated commercially when "Brüsewitz plates" and "Brüsewitz bowls" were hawked to capitalize on the public interest. In addition, a scandal ensued when the Berlin police, supposedly acting on orders from a very high source, illegally confiscated an issue of the newspaper *Der Reporter*, which had printed a lurid illustration of the incident. Agitation in the Reichstag for greater delimitation of the officer's violent prerogatives—dueling and *Ehrennotwehr*—found its focus in the *Fall Brüsewitz*, and the resultant ruckus kicked up by the left side of the chamber in November of 1896 undoubtedly played a role in the timing of Wilhelm II's honor court promulgation several weeks later on New Year's Day 1897.

Why, one may well ask, should von Brüsewitz have taken so personally an alleged insult to which there were no witnesses? Arthur Schnitzler's "*Leutnant Gustl*" (1900) is the story of an Austrian officer whose *Ehrennotwehr* riposte is stymied when its intended victim, a powerfully built baker, prevents the officer from drawing his saber by laying his heavy paw on the hilt. While people in the concert hall's cloak room mill about, the baker says in low tones: "I don't want to ruin your career . . . so, behave yourself! . . . Don't worry, no one's heard a thing." And soon thereafter he releases his viselike grip and disappears into the crowd, leaving Gustl in a state of shock. Gustl spends the evening replaying the nightmarish incident in his head, considering the alternatives. He cannot, of course, challenge the lowly baker to a duel, and therefore conventional means of satisfaction are ruled out. The critical aspect of the episode for Gustl is not the fact that he has suffered a personal humiliation of the first order (or, third level) but rather the possibility that bystanders may have witnessed the disgrace. "I must at least be glad," he says to himself, "that he didn't speak loudly! If someone had overheard us, I'd be forced to shoot myself without further ado." Gustl, however, is not reassured: "But what guarantees that he won't tell anyone, today or tomorrow, his wife, his daughter, his acquaintances in the café." Most disconcerting about his knowledge of the affair is not the fact that he will be saddled with a nagging conscience the rest of his life, but that he will long be plagued with anxiety of disclosure. "I'd never have another moment of peace in my life . . . I'd always have the fear that someone else would learn of it, one way or another." After spending the entire evening on a park bench in the Prater, early the next morning he enters a café with the firm intention to do his duty and take his own life as soon as he indulges in one last meal. In the café he learns that through some miracle the baker—whose rolls he is munching—has suffered a heart attack and died after the concert. Gustl is transformed. Dead men tell no tales and his secret is safe in the grave. In matters of honor the world was not big enough for two: "The main thing is that he's dead, and I may live, and everything belongs to me again!" As the story ends Gustl is in a splendid mood and begins to savor the thought of his dueling date with a doctor later that afternoon.[140]

Ehrennotwehr and dueling were twin facets of the officer's quest for purification through spoliation. As armed custodians of a German Empire—and before that, a Prussian State—which owed its existence to military force, a certain logic inhered to these apparently ruthless conceptions. And the civilian leadership of this German Empire was drawn largely from the universities, whose student fraternities likewise fostered notions of moral cleansing through physical demolition. Their expression of this idea, however, was slightly different from that of the officer corps. It was neither dueling nor *Ehrennotwehr*, but rather a hybrid of the two: an *Ehrennotwehr* encounter in which both parties were armed. If this seems like a funny arrangement, it was.

CHAPTER IV.

Graduation with Honor

Shot? so quick, so clean an ending?
Oh that was right, lad, that was brave:
Yours was not an ill for mending,
'Twas best to take it to the grave.
—A. E. Houseman, *A Shropshire Lad*, XLIII (1896)

MARK TWAIN, in *A Tramp Abroad* through Heidelberg, found the action "wonderfully stirring."[1] In 1897 the visiting Japanese politician To-mofusa Sasa wrote home from Germany, "My poor pen is incapable of describing how impressed I was with this brave spectacle."[2] A skeptical French journalist in 1893 found the drama to be "not without a certain magnificence,"[3] and in 1900, even the sardonic Englishman Jerome K. Jerome conceded that if on first viewing he felt "a mingling of disgust and pity," as the evening wore on, "I wanted more."[4]

The object of these international hurrahs was the German student duel, which was at its height a century ago in the Second Empire of Kaiser Wilhelm II. Of the Wilhelmine dueling culture's myriad facets, this one stands out as the most uniquely German. Beyond German borders the student duel, or *Mensur*, was to be found at the universities in the Austrian half of the Dual Monarchy and in select regions of Switzerland and Poland. But nowhere did the *Mensur* flourish as it did in its homeland. As a surrogate duel without the accompanying mortality, the *Mensur* served as an academic proving ground for future duelists, imbuing them with caste consciousness and acculturating them to the social punctilio of honor. Every year at graduation, these well-trained bravos were dispersed into German society's upper echelons, where they assumed positions of power and authority. As a result, state offices were staffed with civil servants who not only candidly endorsed the practice of dueling but were just an insult away from turning common felons themselves. This situation had no parallel in any other European country. Nowhere was the duel so well established in the state apparatus as in Germany; consequently, nowhere did the duel receive greater philosophical justification from neo-Hegelian pundits. And, because the *Mensur* functioned as an affi-

9. "The *Corps* man." Illustration by C. W. Allers, 1901,
in Allers, *Das Deutsche Corpsleben* (Stuttgart, Berlin,
Leipzig, ca. 1902). (Staatliche Museen zu Berlin,
Kunstbibliothek)

davit of manhood, it is little conceivable that anywhere else were
career, position, and status so intrinsically related to one's virility
quotient.

THE *MENSUR*

The *Mensur* (from the Latin word *mensura*, to measure) was and remains to this day a phenomenon specific to Central Europe. Its roots,
however, can be traced to French and Italian universities of the late
Middle Ages, which offered fencing as a part of their curriculum and

whose classes were patronized by large numbers of enthusiastic German scholars who transmitted what they learned to their native land. By the late 1500s every German university boasted a fencing master, and by the middle of the eighteenth century, under the leadership of the Kreussler family in Jena, German fencing had progressed so far that its technique, an aggressive and elemental attack shunning the lace and ruffles of the French school, was regarded as the finest in Europe. The skills of the student fencers, who trundled their rapiers to class, would usually come into play as the result of spontaneous challenges issued in the marketplace or other public venues, whereupon the good citizens (and constables) of the town would form a circle around the combatants in order to better view the action and spur on their favorite.[5]

Following the Seven Years' War (1756–63) Friedrich the Great of Prussia prohibited the carrying of weapons by the student body of his universities, and street fighting (*Strassenrencontre*) soon became a thing of the past. Although duels in the late eighteenth century continued to be fought in much the same way as before, they would ordinarily take place the next day and proceed in a more orderly fashion, with seconds in attendance and certain rules observed, such as the number of rounds to be fought, the regulation of the distance between opponents, and the delimitation of lateral and backward movement through a small circle drawn around the combatants, outside of whose boundaries they could not step without incurring shame. The protection worn was minimal, consisting of a sort of codpiece-cummerbund that safeguarded the lower abdomen, a gauntlet, swaths of silk around the throat, and a wire-formed cap or top hat to protect the eyes.

The weapon of choice among most student dueling fraternities continued to be the rapier (*Stossdegen*), whose proud virtue lay in its ability to inflict the notorious "punctured lung" (*Lungenfuchser*), an internal wound that tended to show itself only belatedly through gory froth at the lips. Due to the high incidence of fatalities from this style of dueling, Breslau banned it in 1819, and gradually other German universities followed suit. Venerable Jena was the final holdout, but in 1840, in the wake of eight *Lungenfuchser* and two deaths within the space of three months, it declared that henceforth all rapier duels would be reported posthaste to the authorities. The last student death by rapier was in Munich in 1847. By the second half of the century the rapier had been completely displaced by the *Schläger*, a straight-edged cutting weapon bereft of a point. Also, the *Schläger*'s next of kin, the curved saber, supplanted the rapier for serious duels among students in which no protective padding of any sort was worn.

Coincident to these developments, pistols began to enjoy mounting

10. An early *Schläger* match at Göttingen in 1847. Lithograph, 1847. (Bildarchiv Preussischer Kulturbesitz, Berlin)

popularity with officers and grown-up men of honor, and so the fine art of parry and thrust declined on both the collegiate and general dueling fronts. The volume of student bouts rose rapidly through the 1850s and 1860s because the cruder movements of a *Schläger* combat were more easily assimilated by novices than the dexterous and subtle rapier technique. Little prowess was now required. Virtuosity plummeted as contestants were swathed from neck to thigh in wadded silk and rolls of bandages and padded leather. The only target remaining on these knights in nerf armor was the bare head, thus eliminating the threat to other body parts and considerably vitiating the repertoire of assault and parry. In fact, parrying was now rendered moot by dint of the heavy upholstery swaddling the arm and the bell- or basket-shaped coquille cradling the hilt and covering the hand—arm and hilt being now used to absorb blows previously thwarted by a blade. Since the entire head could now be protected by simply arching the arm over it with the blade of the *Schläger* angling downwards (*verhängte Auslagung*), the need for advance and retreat was nullified. Footwork became obsolete, and immobility usurped movement. Even fidgeting was taboo: one stood transfixed to the floor like a stone pillar, the sole body part activated being the arm, which was pivoted into striking position by a lateral snapping movement of the elbow across the face and then a downward flip of the wrist to deliver the blow—then back

11. A *Mensur* at the fin de siècle. "The Mensur," from a painting by
M. Kupfer, ca. 1900. (Bildarchiv Preussischer Kulturbesitz, Berlin)

again to fend off the opponent's counterstrokes and as wind-up for
another smack. Because of the immunity afforded by the *verhängte
Auslagung*, it was incumbent upon each combatant to repay every
blow forthwith or else rate the collective scorn of comrade and foe.
Hence, in order to assert their fortitude beyond any shadow of a
doubt, it became the habit of both fencers to simultaneously mount a
headlong attack as soon as the signal to begin was given, thus exposing their faces to the jagged lacerations on which every student duelist
plumed himself.

Collateral to the phenomenology of the emerging pistol duel, the
best defense in the student *Mensur* became a good offense; although,
paradoxically (and like the pistol duel) the emphasis was on sustain-
ing, not delivering hits. An opponent's blade was now literally parried
with the face. So as to protect the eyes, in 1857 a Heidelberg doctor
named Immisch developed a pair of makeshift iron goggles held in
place by means of a leather thong which also helped safeguard the
ears by pinning them to the sides of the head. Although noses could
still be sliced away and mouths transformed into gaping maws, the
fear of blindness was alleviated. Fencers thus felt all the more obliged
to engage in an increasingly aggressive, reckless, and—as a consequence—lackluster style of swordplay that, like pistol duels, tested

12. A student challenge. Illustration by C. W. Allers, 1901, in Allers, *Das Deutsche Corpsleben* (Stuttgart, Berlin, Leipzig, ca. 1902). (Staatliche Museen zu Berlin, Kunst-bibliothek)

high on careless disregard for self and on the art of unflinchingly taking it. Also, most bouts were no longer primarily based on real or imagined slights but were arranged, either through the artificial insults issuing from the special pub evenings (*Kontrahierkneipen*) in which rival clubs would meet to pick up opponents, or through formal challenges tendered by leaving one's calling card at a corporation's dwellings. The *Mensur* now became *Bestimmungsmensur*, or *Mensur* by agreement.[6] The result of all these changes in the middle years of the century was to create a contest as sanguinary and brutal as it was dispassionate and robotic.

At this time there were three main dueling associations a student could join: the *Landsmannschaften*, the oldest; the *Burschenschaften*, the least conservative; and the *Corpsstudenten*, the most elite. Each organization had subdivisions called corporations, and a given university might sponsor any number of these. Other groups permitting extracurricular dueling existed, such as the *Turnerschaft* (Gymnastics Union) and the *Sängerschaft* (Choral Union); however, the aforementioned trio constituted the Holy Trinity of *Mensur*, and of these the *Corps* was godhead. With the infusion of this "club" aspect, at the founding of the German Empire in 1871, the student duel had assumed the dimensions of a sport, regulated by the *Comment* (literally, "know-how"), the incorporated student's junior code of honor. Occasional serious affairs were played out with curved sabers and no upholstery, and sometimes with standardized dueling pistols (*Paukpistolen*), but the vast percentage of so-called *Ehrenhändel* among German students after 1871 was confined to the formal *Mensur*.

For most of the nineteenth century the *Mensur* was usually ignored by the authorities, but government control made itself felt during the *Gründerzeit* as the activity earned an increased following among a generation of students whose appetite for blood and iron had apparently been whetted by the wars of German unification. It was in 1876 that the state intervened forcefully for the first time, after a Göttingen student's skull was cleaved by a stalwart *Schläger* blow. Later, the wound was aggravated through the victim's continued immoderate beer intake: meningitis set in and shortly killed him. Because the duel had taken place minus the protective caps that would have prevented the encounter from being classified as a duel under Articles 201 and 205 of the imperial penal code, a Göttingen tribunal and its court of appeals found the survivor, Carl Wiechmann, guilty of dueling with a "deadly weapon" and he was awarded the minimal sentence of three months. The student *Schläger* automatically became a mortal implement when utilized without benefit of the conventional enwrapments and prescribed head-covering; as the headdress had been long ago abandoned in order to ensure wounds, the absence of "protective precautions that rule out any danger" now classified the *Mensur* as "a punishable duel." In arriving at this decision, the Göttingen court also asserted the supremacy of the state penal code over local university by-laws, and in June of 1877 this verdict was confirmed. Henceforth students would be subject to the civil courts in all but purely academic matters.[7]

Incorporated students, however, paid little heed and continued to duel unremittingly. It was during this period that expensive and frequent roadtrips were undertaken to other university towns to spar with rival corporations.[8] The activity was more popular than ever, as was dueling in general, and soon the *Mensur* would share its parent institution's fugitive status. On 6 March 1883, in a decision of the German Supreme Court (*Reichsgericht*), it was concluded that in order to expedite prosecution of more conventional duels, it was necessary that a "duel" be defined as a rendezvous with implements designed for the specific purpose of inflicting grievous bodily injury. It was then stated that, abstractly considered, and regardless of the quilted cushioning donned by students, the *Schläger* was indeed a deadly weapon, therefore subsuming the *Mensur* under the criminal dueling rubric.[9] The 1877 verdict, which allowed the *Mensur* with requisite padding, was thus overturned and the student duel was outlawed.

Although still unauthorized, *Mensur* participation continued unabated after the First World War in Weimar Germany. Only weeks after Hitler's appointment as Chancellor, on 6 April 1933 the student duel was legally incepted when the Prussian Minister of Justice notified his district attorneys that henceforth, in the public interest, the *Mensur* was to be officially celebrated. "The joy of the *Mensur*," announced the order, "springs from the fighting spirit, which should be strengthened, not inhibited, in the academic youth. *Mensuren* steel personal courage, demand self-mastery, and fortify strength of will."[10] Glossing the fact that the activity had been originally banned under Wilhelm I, the National Socialist mouthpiece, the *Völkischer Beobachter*, invoked the imperial dueling heritage as historical clearance for resuscitation of the free and open exchange of facial cuts:

> Above all, the road is once again paved for the healthy idea of standing up against a personal offender with weapon in fist instead of with the paragraphs of the justice of the peace. Only an insult washed away with blood counted as expiated in the code of honor of the old Germany, and this idea must be granted full recognition for it also promotes the ability and preparedness of young Germans to defend themselves.[11]

In 1935, Article 210 of the penal code forbidding the duel was supplemented with sub-article "a," which qualified the *Mensur* as an exception. But National Socialism was as confounded by the institution as had been previous regimes, and in 1937 the *Reichsstudentenführer* re-outlawed it.

In 1945 the Allied occupation forces reintroduced punishment for the *Mensur*, and in 1953, following another controversial Göttingen incident—the so-called "*Göttinger Mensurprozess*"—the dueling albatross was lifted once and for all from the *Mensur*'s neck and the pastime designated as *Sportmensur*,[12] under which title it is still practiced today. In the former German Democratic Republic, the *Mensur* was banned, no doubt because of its feudal-fascist-capitalistic onus. From unregulated scrap to illegal *Zweikampf* to sporting event, the student *Mensur* had assumed various forms. But where did it actually stand in relation to the duel?

SCHOLARS, OFFICERS, AND OTHER GENTLEMEN

By prosecuting the *Mensur*, the imperial authorities were likely working at cross-purposes to their alleged object of stamping out the duel, for by affiliating the two they made bedfellows of kissing cousins. On the one hand, the *Mensur* was encouraged because it was married to the debonair duel, and on the other, the duel gained credence as a logically coherent extension of the *Waffenspiel* engaged in by the students with so much naive zest. This reciprocity may have exacerbated the dueling problem that emerged in the 1880s and 1890s. It certainly does not appear to have curbed it, and after 1883 undergraduates and mature men of honor were at the very least united in their disdain for the law evinced every time they drew swords or wielded pistols.

Although periodic efforts were made after the Supreme Court ruling of 1883 by both university officials and police to tourniquet the bloodshed, their surveillance was always rather lukewarm, in particular because the Supreme Court decision was almost unanimously repudiated by criminologists and subsequent jurisprudence.[13] The police would intentionally avoid places such as inns and wood clearings where *Mensur* bouts were reputed to take place. The new regulations were only arbitrarily enforced and kid glove treatment was standard. Even if a student was unlucky enough to be snared in one of the sporadic and short-lived police dragnets, and even were he to be prosecuted and convicted against the better judgment of sympathetic public prosecutors and judges, he was invariably dealt the minimal sentence of three months' internment which, barring any extenuating circumstances, was practically guaranteed a magnanimous parole upon appeal to imperial clemency.[14] One half of all pardons dispensed by the Kaiser in, for example, the year 1898, were for the student *Mensur*, this rarely prosecuted crime.[15] In one case, the sentence of four months was not commuted but the convicted party was given the option of imprisonment between semesters[16]—thus, along with his studies, the weekly *Mensur* regimen would not be interrupted either.[17]

That civilian dueling rates seem to have outdistanced those of active officers after Wilhelm II's cabinet order of 1897 is partly explicable from the fact that the monarchical principle in Germany was alive and well and that both officers and civilians took their Kaiser at his word: Wilhelm, who as a student-prince learned to be a regular guy with the crack Corps Borussia in Bonn the year of the landmark Wiechmann decision in 1877, was an outspoken booster of dueling fraternities. In a pep talk before assembled *Corpsstudenten* at his alma mater in 1891, the Kaiser conveyed his wish that "as long as there are German *Corpsstudenten* the spirit which is fostered in the *Corps*, and which is steeled by strength and courage, will be preserved, and that you will always take delight in handling the *Schläger*."[18] Riding the crest of such imperial encomiums, students and former students unhesitatingly invoked Wilhelm's name in support of their unlawful practice. In 1896 at the Berlin Technical University, where an assembly of undergraduates had gathered to vote on an anti-dueling petition, one of the speakers pitched the ignoratio elenchi argument that because His Imperial Majesty was a friend of dueling and the Kaiser's word was blameless, it was traitorous for his subjects to denounce the institution. The students denounced the initiative.[19] Similar to the case of officer dueling, the divine right principle was effectively employed as a defensive buffer by proponents of the student duel. Just five years after Wilhelm's honor court order of 1897, in a panegyric before one thousand *Burschenschaften*, an attorney from the public prosecutor's office lauded the *Mensur*'s many and varied charms and championed dueling in general. He then punctuated his address with a toast to the Kaiser.[20] The Wilhelmine judiciary was replete with former Mensurians whose fondest youthful memories, like those of their emperor, were mingled with a supposedly criminal act they were hearkened to condemn. Most desisted from defiling those memories and the sentiments they represented, which were, if little else, *kaisertreu*.

The Kaiser may have been a pal to dueling but—and contrary to government legal findings—the *Schläger* could hardly be considered an ally of the Grim Reaper. The *Mensur* was not a duel with "deadly weapons."[21] Periodic deaths might intervene as the result of freakish accidents, yet almost never did one perish at the battle venue itself.[22] As in pistol duels, death would often befall the casualty days or weeks afterwards due to lack of appropriate medical care. Blood poisoning was commonly responsible. One day in 1882 in Jena, following a series of blood feasts in which the chopsticks had not been properly sanitized, about forty students were shipped to the infirmary and several of these to the funeral home.[23] Rare, however, was the young Siegfried who was powerful enough to penetrate his opponent's cerebral cortex and cut him down in the May of life—although it could be done.[24] The argument that "the danger for the spectator of a *Bestimmungsmensur* is greater than that for the so-called duelist because of the blades that tend to fly off," was, in fact, dragooned as an ironic defense of the practice in the Reichstag in 1886.[25] (If I might bring my own deposition to bear, at a *Mensur* viewed in West Berlin over a century later in 1988, about a third of the way through the last bout of the evening the flurries became so spirited that a blade did indeed snap and a splinter from it shaved my temple, the larger fragment fortunately staying out of the throng of spectators; a fresh blade was fitted, the fraternal pummeling recommenced, and I, who had been standing very close to the action, chose the better part of valor by fading discreetly into the crowd.) In a petition submitted by students of the Technical University at Aachen to the Prussian Minister of Justice in 1912 to make the *Mensur* legal, it was claimed that of the ten thousand or so student duels annually, not a single death had occurred in the last decade. It also cited statistics from 1908 of 19 deaths and 150 severe injuries contracted in the American collegiate pastime of football.[26] In figures published in 1930, the *Mensur* ranked penultimate on a list that had track and field and bicycling as more profligate killers.[27] In that same year the German Society of Surgeons, whose membership undoubtedly knew whereof it spoke by virtue of their status as former students rather than practicing physicians, rejected the legal ban on the *Mensur* stating that the causes of death were almost always indirect, mostly the outcome of blood poisoning or secondary hemorrhaging, and that by comparison the fatal effects of boxing were always the immediate result of fractured skulls or shock. If the *Mensur* were banned, warned the surgeons, consistency demanded a similar censure of boxing, which was just as much a duel with a lethal weapon—the bluff human fist—as was the student-gentleman's swordplay.[28]

Whatever the effect of the 1883 decision on the correlation of duel to *Mensur*, fraternities requiring the ordeal of their membership were perfect academies for aspiring duelists. It was a running debate in the Reichstag as to who contributed the most to dueling's popularity— officers or students—but the two main abolitionist parties, the Catholic Center and the Social Democrats, were in the habit of pinpointing the duel's seed in the university dueling clubs. In 1894 in the Bavarian Chamber of Deputies, Georg von Vollmar of the Social Democrats easily judged that, by comparison to the German officer corps, "the dueling trouble predominates to a much greater degree at the universities."[29] Even though Bavarian officer dueling rates were substantially lower than Prussian ones, in 1896 in the Reichstag a Catholic Center deputy also castigated the *Mensur* as "a preparation for the duel."[30] Though probably impelled by a desire to siphon-off criticism of the army, more conservative circles also targeted students. The university professor and National Liberal editor of the *Preussische*

13. "Academic bloodbath." "On both sides, no noble
parts injured!" By Bruno Paul, in *Der Student: Kulturbilder
aus dem Simplicissimus* (Albert Langen Verlag, 1905).
(Staatliche Museen zu Berlin, Kunstbibliothek)

Jahrbücher, Hans Delbrück, found that, as in the officer corps, the dueling organizations fostered the notion of honor and the duel as complementary concepts, and he concluded that "the entire institution of
these corporations rises and falls with the duel."[31] After the First
World War, the duel shriveled up and blew away while the *Mensur*
grew fat, but there were so many former Mensurians who as medical
doctors and jurists ignored their Hippocratic and legal oaths by dueling that it would be preposterous to assert no causal nexus linking
the two. Students and former students together seem to have constituted not only the vanguard but moreover the body of the empire's
dueling elite.[32]

If the students supplied the duel's phalanx of manpower, the German army and its officer corps carried, as ever, the gleaming standard. The student was much like the reservist in this respect: emulating the officer's code in every detail save that of restraint. Never a shrinking violet, the student would place himself at a stranger's disposal as systematically as a streetwalker. In 1896, eighteen saber challenges were issued one day in Berlin consequent of student elections.[33] In 1898, in another spectacular incident out of *schlagfertig* Berlin, a disgruntled law student challenged his examiner to pistols after failing his boards.[34] In Bavaria a *Corpsstudent* once goaded a family man to a saber duel, wounded him, and then browbeat him into another challenge. The second duel was hardly over when the *Corpsstudent* commenced hounding him yet again.[35] As a collegian, the historian Friedrich Meinecke once exchanged calling cards in the street with an incorporated student after having accidentally brushed his sleeve in passing.[36] Schnitzler's physician in *"Traumnovelle"* ("A Dream Tale," 1925) experiences these kind of bullyboy tactics when he

> crossed the Rathausplatz, which shone dully like a brownish pond, and turned homeward in the direction of the Josefstadt and saw, still some distance off, just then rounding a corner, a small gang of incorporated students coming toward him, about six or eight of them. As the youngsters fell under the light of a street lamp, he thought to discern the Blue Alemannen. He himself had never belonged to a dueling society, but he had fought a couple saber *Mensuren* in his day. . . . The students were very near, they spoke loudly and laughed. . . . He had to squeeze close to the building so as not to bump into the last one, a lanky type in an open greatcoat, a bandage over the left eye, who seemed to intentionally fall back a ways, and who then, with an outstretched elbow, jostled him. It could be no accident. "What is the fellow trying to prove?" Fridolin thought, inadvertently stopping in his tracks; after a couple steps, the other did the same, and so for a moment they stood staring at each other across a small interval. Suddenly, however, Fridolin turned and continued on his way. Behind him came a short laugh—he was about to turn around again to confront the scamp, but there was this strange beating of his heart—exactly like twelve or fourteen years ago when had come a violent knocking at the door with the lovely young thing by his side who always loved talking some drivel about a vague, probably nonexistent fiancé; actually the menacing knock had only been the postman.—But just like then, he now felt the pounding of his heart. "What is that?" he asked himself annoyedly, noticing now that his knees trembled a little.[37]

But, to return: *Satisfaktionsfähigkeit* was an ideal cookiecut by students from the officer corps. Because many reserve officers were concurrently incorporated students, academic circles felt the under-

14. "In any event."
" 'Sir, you were staring at me.'
'I hardly think so.'
'So, you're calling me a liar—I request your card.' "
By Bruno Paul, in *Der Student: Kulturbilder aus dem
Simplicissimus* (Albert Langen Verlag, 1905). (Staat-
liche Museen zu Berlin, Kunstbibliothek)

standable need to bring student regulations into sync with those of
the officer class.[38] The reverse was naturally inconceivable and conflicting codes were a proven nuisance. Consequently, Wilhelm I's
honor court decree of 1874 was adopted as a guideline in 1889 for the
student's own councils of honor by the central committee of Germany's student dueling organizations, the *Kösener Convent*.[39] For centuries, students had been struggling to put the university on the same
footing with both the nobility and the officer class,[40] and because of

the student inclination to sedulously ape army mores, it was generally believed that as soon as the army cashiered the duel it would at once "forfeit its nimbus" in the scholastic milieu.[41] Prima facie, this seemed not to be the case, for, after Wilhelm's decree of 1897 when officer duels sank, there was no discernible diminution in the rate of student *Mensuren*. But so long as the prospect of a duel still underscored the incorruptibility of an officer's honor, still technically endorsed it, the student did indeed look to this alter ego for his cues.

Consanguinity between student corps and officer corps did not, however, imply intimacy; as is rather so often the case, it begat friction. In the Bavarian Chamber of Deputies in 1894, it was noted how most duels involving an active German officer were with either a student or a former student.[42] Since most all officer duels used pistols, it would make apparent sense that students should eventually have also adopted these implements so as to preserve that longed-for equal status with their role models. This, however, seems not to have been the case—college life could be rather idyllic, and pistols were notorious killjoys. But for whatever reason, pistol duels among students did flare briefly around the turn of the century—with officers as frequent opponents;[43] and, it appears, students as not infrequent fatalities.[44] Dismayed by this trend, in November of 1902 2,318 incorporated and nonaffiliated students from Berlin filed a grouch with the Prussian Ministry of War. They exhorted the army to make the saber the priority weapon in such affairs as those in which students had played recent sad roles. The petition invoked the saber's "chivalrous" quality (the ubiquitous legitimator) and urged that "the similar views of officers and satisfaction-giving students" not reach an impasse on the issue of sidearms. It granted the necessity of pistol duels, but only in cases of shameless insult to one's family; in cases of physical inability to handle the demands of saber fencing; or, as plasma tended to spray quite freely at these functions, if one of the combatants was afflicted with a "contagious disease communicable through the blood."[45] After 1902 the pistol challenge was held to be adverse to the student code (*uncommentmässig*) and unworthy of members of a student fraternity.[46] (Illustrative of the type of situation pistol-dueling German officers wished to avoid, in Austria-Hungary in 1897, as a consequence of that year's controversial Badeni language ordinances, there were frequent hostile encounters between German-nationalist students and Habsburg officers leading to sword duels in which the officers fared poorly. Officer casualties were so great that provisional fencing schools were established by the army in such hot spots as Graz and Vienna. This ameliorative did not help much. Even though pistol duels were ex-

15. "A judgment of God." "Student and officer dispute which weapon is most suitable for the carrying-out of affairs of honor. Since they cannot agree, they decide to ask Holy God for His opinion. And so they pose the question: 'Saber or pistol?' Comes the reply, 'Malacca cane!'" By Th. Th. Heine, in *Der Student: Kulturbilder aus dem Simplicissimus* (Albert Langen Verlag, 1905). (Staatliche Museen zu Berlin, Kunstbibliothek)

pressly forbidden in the Austro-Hungarian army, its leadership was eventually forced to decree that in future duels with students officers should forsake cold steel for shooting irons.)[47]

Although German officers and students shared the same code of honor, their weapon of preference was curiously at odds, for ostensibly gun-shy scholars were the ones most likely to proffer a challenge to pistols later on in life. They did not stay true to their duel. One explanation for this drift may have been their unstated recognition of the *Mensur*'s puerile quality and an attempt to demarcate with more implacable and scientific weapons their solemn affairs of honor from earlier cutting capers. Additionally, sedentary *Schläger* fencing, despite the aforementioned Austrian example, would seem to have been an ill discipline to train one for the saber dance. Pistols, on the other hand (which enjoyed an increasing vogue around mid-century simultaneous with the institution of *Schläger* fencing), were as easy to master for critical affairs of honor as the *Schläger* was for trifling ones. Hence, the *Mensur* was *not* a prophylactic against weightier duels with deadlier hardware, as frequently maintained by defenders of the student practice. Had the student been unable to resort to his beloved *Schläger*, the art of real saber fencing, without padding, would no doubt have been more assiduously cultivated, and fewer post-graduate affairs would have escalated into shooting wars. Seen from this perspective, the *Mensur* was an incipient pistol duel.

If the *Mensur* seasoned students for actual life or death encounters, there remained a substantial difference between the two phenomena that resists the most dogged lumping. Whereas the duel issued from insults and incidents of a delicate personal nature and was generally regarded by both parties as an inconvenience, the *Mensur* was a communal celebration of a shared experience. In the *Mensur* the duel's means and ends were reversed. The duel's design was to terminate a dispute; in student circles, disputes were devised to foster phony duels. Adversaries were on confidential terms. Although there were elements of the duel's *Standesehre* ethos that paralleled the elaborate associational act of the students, in the *Mensur* there existed a literal esprit de corps between the mutual assailants that tempered the devastation taking place. Even though such attitudes might be carried over to some extent in a student's later shootouts with the label of class solidarity, this clubby fraternal element was decidedly lacking in pistols at chilly break of day.

Students and former students alike shared a deep affection for their ritual, and Friedrich Meinecke dreamily recalled youthful days at the *Mensur* site "on the Venusberg, where the sun shone through the green branches upon the place of battle and where black-white-red fought a chivalrous, today I would say historically symbolic battle against the black-red-gold of the Bonner Alemannen."[48] The German's vaunted singular relationship to Nature blossomed "in the splendid green of the forest, where you showed that you had not only learned the art of fencing but also the art of self-mastery, to employ your entire strength of will and to keep your head perfectly still when the sharp blade of your opponent flashed above it. How wonderfully beautiful is such a *Mensur* outing in the forest."[49] In Wilhelm Raabe's (1831–1910) short story "Die alte Universität" (1862), the return of an elderly former student to the town where his old college once stood is a triumphant rebirth and a journey back to a better time, even if mingled with rueful memories of his brother's death in a sword duel with a close friend:

> The old times had returned—grey-headed gentlemen threw kisses up to the windows just like twenty or thirty years ago; cloudy eyes became clear and bright, the feet won new strength and sturdiness upon the familiar cobblestones—every heart thumped and beat livelier within the breast. . . . O happy time! Time when every nerve, every muscle obeyed the spirit, and the spirit seldom demanded what did not tauten every nerve, every muscle.[50]

One student duelist declared that "with heart and soul I have been a *Corpsstudent*," but then conceded that "there are yet other goods in the world before which the *Corps* must modestly bow"—namely, family and country.[51]

Each participant in the *Mensur* was sentinel not only of his own honor but that of his comrades.[52] This mutual vigilance was also a hallmark of the German officer corps, which in honor court decisions continually stressed caste honor as opposed to a more private, self-reliant variety. "Collectivism" and "the subordination of the individual to the whole" were leading motifs of both the officer class and student life.[53] In Heinrich Mann's actually understated caricature *Der Untertan* (*The Straw Man*, 1914)—provisionally subtitled a "History of the public soul under Wilhelm II,"[54]—his protagonist Diederich Hessling experiences an infinite moment upon realization that he is at last a member of the Neuteutonia, a dueling corps: "He was submerged in the corporation, which thought and willed for him. And he was a man, with deep respect for himself and he had his honor, because he belonged!" In a similar outpouring upon commencement of his stint as a one-year volunteer (*Einjährig Freiwilliger*) in the army, Hessling exults: "Principles and ideals were clearly the same as those of the Neuteutonians. . . .'The absorption in the great whole.'"[55]

Enthusiasm such as Hessling's was also funded by a beer-drinking rite that would have sent Carrie Nation on a spree. Rabelaisian quantities were consumed in single sittings on command and in unison with the group, improvised vomatoriums and pissoirs at close ready, while rollicking challenges to "beer-duels" flew about the table. One contemporary owning that "the German student will never be a teetotaler,"[56] was like hazarding that Falstaff would never be a Tibetan monk. But oiled to the gills, Hessling undergoes his own kind of spiritual growth:

The beer! . . . You swallowed: and then you'd gotten somewhere, you felt transported to life's summit and were a free man; inwardly free. The tavern might have been surrounded by police; the beer that one gulped transformed itself in inner freedom. . . . You stretched yourself from the beer table out over the world, had presentiments of great correlations, were one with the world-spirit. Indeed, the beer elevated one so far above oneself, that you even found God![57]

The alcoholic debauch was only the more dubious half of the corps' prescription for personal enrichment and noble cast of mind. The *Mensur* composed the other half, the sobering half. Hessling is reminded by his recruiters that head-splitting hangovers would not be all he would suffer, that incapacitation would assume other forms: "the purpose of the student amalgamation, namely, the education to manliness and idealism, through the tavern alone—as much as it contributed— was not fully complete. Diederich trembled; he knew only too well what this meant. He would fence!"[58]

STUDENT HONOR: MASCULINITY AS SOCIAL STATUS

Every aspect of the student's life was organized around and subordinated to his fencing fetish because "the single thing in a student corporation that is given attention and respect is honor."[59] The typical day of a mildly committed *Corpsstudent* went something as follows: Mornings he would arise together with his fifteen- or twenty-soul contingent of "actives" (there were usually twice as many inactive members) and then breakfast in a common mess. The next couple hours would be devoted to fencing practice, which I myself had occasion to take in 1988 and mastered in all of ten minutes. Afternoons he would reassemble with his comrades for a walk, in his tiny visored cap and tricolored ribbon slung like the title of a beauty pageant queen, maybe chaperoned by a gigantic canine mascot. The students would stick to themselves, carefully disregarding the nonincorporated and those members of rival clubs also displaying their colors, which left a few pretty girls to look at. The evening festivities would vary from night to night between suds and singing in the *Kommers* or hops and chops in the bi-weekly *Mensur* matches. Any spare time was dedicated to the preparation of fêtes, banquets, balls, parades, or receptions for parents, friends, and authorities.[60]

What about coursework? Amidst this feverish onslaught of social obligation it was frankly admitted by most student duelists that the books were sacrificed. Something had to give. Bismarck, a regular

16. "New Year's eve pub." "Not a trace of that cor-
rosive carping spirit in us; through us still wafts the
fresh pure breath of idealism. We are always ready
to prove that there are still people who excite for
the beautiful and the noble, that there are still men
who are forever ready to stand up, through word
or deed, for the nation's most sacred goods—that's
why we drink so much beer." By Bruno Paul, in *Der
Student: Kulturbilder aus dem Simplicissimus* (Albert
Langen Verlag, 1905). (Staatliche Museen zu Berlin, Kunstbibliothek)

demon at the *Mensur*, whose considerable skill was acknowledged by
experts and who throughout his life bore only a single tiny scar on his
cheek as testimony, wistfully recollected his stint at Göttingen with
the *Landsmannschaft* Hanoveria. Yet he regretted that he had studied
too little and piled up too many debts.[61] Little had changed since Bismarck's time. The acclaimed freedom of learning (*Lernfreiheit*) of the
German university (where lecture attendance was optional and the

17. "The kingdom of beer." "Are we not born to
greatness?" By Bruno Paul, in *Der Student: Kulturbilder aus dem Simplicissimus* (Albert Langen
Verlag, 1905). (Staatliche Museen zu Berlin,
Kunstbibliothek)

only examinations administered were at the end of the three-year college term) was improved upon by the incorporated student to signify
freedom *from* learning.[62] The only time when studies could realistically
be squeezed into the hectic schedule was during semester breaks, or
after three or four semesters when one declared his status as honorary,
thus relieving himself of the heavy drinking and fighting demands
placed on actives so that he could bone-up for his university leaving-
exams.

But even if students were consumed by their dipso-duelingmania to
the exclusion of studies, the fact is that at the *Gymnasium*, the German
preparatory school, the student had toiled so diligently and been so
fortified with learning that he could afford to loaf and probably considered it his well-earned right to do so. The student duelist, in any
event, was less concerned with conventional knowledge and erudition

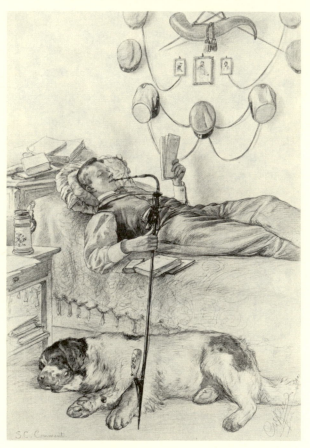

18. Studying the *Comment*. Illustration by C. W. Allers, 1901, in Allers, *Das Deutsche Corpsleben* (Stuttgart,
Berlin, Leipzig, ca. 1902). (Staatliche Museen zu Berlin, Kunstbibliothek)

than he was with molding a certain attitude toward life. In a Junker
adaptation of John Henry Newman's *The Idea of a University*, Bismarck
believed that the college student should "not only be educated in his
special field but should simultaneously receive the foundation for his
whole future destiny." For this the *Mensur* was vital.[63] In his Bonn
peroration, Wilhelm II accorded that the dueling clubs were "the best
education which a young man can get for his future life."[64] Practitioners saw it as fulfilling an auxiliary pedagogical function: as an "educational device for manly courage."[65] It was a martial compensation
for the softening effects of book-study, of the merely intellectual life,

and just as it toughened the body, it also steeled the will and showed the world that even callow scholars could be obdurate in the face of something more daunting than Greek and Latin grammar. As an antidote to the pedantry of soulless erudition, the *Mensur* was "a moral examination."[66] Clash was in session.

Unlike other one-on-one sporting contests, the *Mensur* was a discipline in which there was neither winner nor loser. Bouts might be stopped on the basis of blood loss, and there were head-cut tallies, but everybody emerged victorious for having gamely stood the test. The mutual drubbing was not to teach your opponent a lesson but to learn one together. In the Aachen Petition of 1912 it was asserted:

> There is not a single student corporation which would enjoin its members to step onto the *Mensur* site in order to inflict as much damage upon the opponent as possible. Certainly every combatant may rejoice in victory. But this aspect never stands in the foreground in assessing a *Mensur*. It is only required that each combatant 'stood up well,' that he betrayed no fear of the blows, of the wounds, that pain elicited no cry.[67]

In a Reichstag discussion of the duel in 1886, the former Mensurite Freiherr Langwerth von Simmern dilated in a similar fashion on the school of hard knocks:

> It exercises manliness, it steels the character, it breeds able men, it is a schooling that I prefer personally to that of the military: for the very reason that it is a schooling that rests upon old German tradition, because it is a natural schooling . . . . it is a school of strength, of manliness and of German fidelity, and if we banish it, then we will make our lives yet more toneless, yet more arid, yet more dreary.[68]

The affiliation with *Deutschtum* and old German customs was an endless refrain, betraying the student corporations' nationalistic bias. The *Mensur* supposedly instilled a particularly German brand of valor, and one hard-headed "pragmatist" lightly dismissed the notion that "our student *Mensur* is of French origin and one is unable to note the resonance of German medieval chivalrous tradition in it."[69] The *Mensur* did indeed enjoy certain correlations with the German Middle Ages and celebrated a sort of Gothic identity alien to the duel. It retained, for example, the merely symbolic retribution of medieval chivalry, and the scholar-knight's *Schläger* technique was a latter-day rendition of the broadsword scrimmaging of his mounted forebear,[70] swapping blows with loutish unconcern for the art of defensive parry. Furthermore, the custom allowing an unpracticed opponent six weeks in which to brace himself for the appointed match was a tradition from the days of the feudal judicial duel when noblemen were given three

19. "The essential." "You can believe me, dear Madame, the *Corps* is the best school for life. Ability matters very little later on, as it's always one's cast of mind that counts." By E. Thöny, in *Der Student: Kulturbilder aus dem Simplicissimus* (Albert Langen Verlag, 1905). (Staatliche Museen zu Berlin, Kunstbibliothek)

fortnights to report for combat.[71] Students would venture forth early mornings into the enchanted German forest, or hold bouts in the vicinity of castle ruins to give them that Caspar David Friedrich feel. Jakob Grimm (he of the fairy tales) was an advocate of the duel's preservation for romantic reasons,[72] and the student love for his own ritual was motivated by similar longings for a mythical precapitalist past when the world was young and knights would brandish their swords just by way of saying hello.

Shrouded in the autumnal mist of a pristine German yore, the student duel was invariably compared to other modern, allegedly degenerate national styles. The gaudy Franco-Italian épée duel, to the German student mind, lacked the hazy, dulcet quality of a pure and noble struggle. It was lousy with ruse and deception. But the *Mensur* was a contest wherein courage and resolve were the only prerequisites, and just as Waterloo was won on the playing fields of Eton, Sedan had been warranteed *auf der Mensur*. The students' Grand Guignol ritual was not terrifically suave but it displayed "steadfastness" (*Standhaftigkeit*),[73] the lodestar of their reverie and the crown of German manhood. Like the code of honor it served to enunciate, the *Mensur* was anchored firmly in the so-called "male" virtues—construed as eminently "German" ones—of directness, resiliency, and determined self-control. It was most important that one learn to tame one's fearful instincts, and the path to this fixed purpose was laid with iron rails that made no allowance for cutesy feints and dodges. A fictional student duelist in Herbert Hoerner's *Die letzte Kugel* (1939) sums up the corps philosophy when he explains: "Nature is for humans that which must be overcome. Each must overcome the Nature in himself. . . . Self-possession—self-possession in life is the main thing."[74]

At my 1988 Berlin *Mensur*, I was furnished an opportunity to lay eyes on the Buddha-like composure of these *Wunderkinder*. The evening's main event was a grudge match in which a *Landsmannschaft* member was pitted against the affiliate of a *Sängerschaft*, or choral union, one of the smaller dueling societies. The choirboy himself was rather diminutive, but he rose to the occasion by standing on a wooden platform about eight inches high which brought his eyes level with those of his overgrown Aryan opponent. The *Landsmannschaft* student was clearly the more powerful of the two, and in the demoniac blur of blades he managed to deliver a couple of stinging telegrams to the left side of Herr Glee Club's noggin, who got about as flustered as a side of beef. It was all *Wurst* to him. It was a minute or so after the gash was suffered before you finally realized he had been crocked, since it took that long for the blood to course through the thick dark hair and paint with vermilion strands the pale skin of his face. Otherwise there was no outward clue given as to the carnage being inflicted. Toward the end of the match our hero's face was a bloody sponge, its fluid spilling over from the wad of padding around his neck and onto the floor in heavy drops that between rounds made rhythmic splashing sounds in time with what one imagined was the controlled steady cadence of his pulse.

Frightful? By comparison with other accounts that one peruses from the turn of the century, what I beheld was kid's stuff. Today's *Mensur*, if nasty and brutish, is mercifully short. Bouts in Imperial Germany were gruelingly long, engendering some hellish mutilations as contestants wearied. Whereas today the normative match lasts thirty rounds (*Gänge*) of five strokes apiece for each opponent (with a short pause at the halfway mark), the duration of Wilhelmine contests was usually between sixty and eighty rounds. This means that the number of whacks per contestant today comprise a mere half of the bare minimum in Imperial Germany: 150 compared to 300. Occasionally matches back then would be lengthened to 120 or even 160 rounds, which, in the case of the latter number, translated into 800 whacks apiece in the space of little more than half an hour.[75] For others, a timed twenty-five minutes (pauses not included) was the only parameter.[76]

To have forcefully delivered eight hundred blows and to have received same must have been no facile undertaking, and added to the moral-educational benefits were the rewards of fitness, not to be minimized in Wilhelmine Germany where physical culture was already making substantial inroads.[77] One huckster fancied the muscular advantages of the *Mensur* to the gymnastics of the traditional German *Turnbewegung*:

> First of all, and similar to dancing yet more energized, fencing strengthens the collective musculature of the body: the leg, neck, and back muscles are tightly tensed for long periods of time through a steady, forward-bent stance. The body is thereby kept erect, the chest freely exposed and the right or left arm brought into muscular-building action. The gaze is open and calm; passionate action is mastered through precise fencing training. Moreover, the bodily exercise at the fencing site is preferable to that in the *Turnhalle* for purely practical reasons, since it accustoms us to the handling of a defensive weapon which can frequently protect us against open hostility, and in addition enables us to call an offender to account in a class-approved manner.[78]

Gliding over the law as was his custom, Otto von Bismarck in 1896 averred that, "No other bodily exercise, be it ever so useful for its own sake, such as riding, rowing, or the like, benefits to so favorable a degree . . . as the exercise with the sword." He also advanced the same practicable application: "It can come into play in [the young student's] later debut as a man . . . by not returning an insult but in seeking satisfaction for it."[79]

The equation of the *Mensur* with such sports as gymnastics and rowing was willful claptrap. It was about as useful to all-around physical development as arm wrestling, and, I might add,—and despite Twain and company's gushings and my own overwrought description— about as visually stimulating for the spectator. To compare the physique of the beer-swilling student with that of a well-conditioned oarsman or even a fledgling gymnast was hysterical posturing. But sporting criteria in Wilhelmine Germany were of an idiosyncratic nature. The standard of physical excellence was not the rippling mesomorph, not the Greek Adonis. It was the combat-ready soldier, able to stand at ramrod-straight attention for extended periods, prepared to endure the hardship and privation of long campaigning, and equipped to absorb punishment and wounds incurred in battle—making the *Mensur* the ultimate Teutonic tonic. The yardstick was cannon fodder. Attributes of the trooper were admirably cultivated in the *Mensur*, where "one is systematically accustomed to face-off just as cold-bloodedly with an inferior as with a superior adversary," and in which it was all-important "even in the midst of the most furious combat [*Draufschlagen*] to respond at once to the commands of the referee and the seconds, to bear pain—even the greatest—without the twitch of a muscle, without the slightest outer demonstration."[80]

The militarization of Wilhelmine society was so far-reaching that even the abolitionist Heinrich Graf Coudenhove was fain to cite the "many moral advantages" entailed in the *Mensur*'s facility for accustoming young men to "the wielding of weaponry . . . to bear pain manfully, to see flow his blood and that of the other, to administer first aid to wounds."[81] In *Der deutsche Student* (1902), Professor Theobald Ziegler maintained that the student duelist "is a soldier, who wants to be an officer; therefore he prepares himself for this through fencing practice."[82] A Professor Moldenhauen also saw the *Mensur* as teaching students "to learn command through obedience."[83] Despite their more athletically taxing exertion, even the *Turnerschaft* (German Gymnastics Union, which allowed its members to fence) persisted in disparaging sports such as soccer, tennis, competitive swimming, and boxing as "un-German, materialistic, meritorious, and lacking in any higher ideals such as service to the *Vaterland*."[84] In his *Deutsche Geschichte im Neunzehnten Jahrhundert* (*History of Germany in the Nineteenth Century*), Professor Heinrich von Treitschke compared mid-century English youth who "pursued their sport as a business and competed for valuable prizes," with their opposite numbers in Germany, who "shred their faces for the sake of real or putative honor."[85] The *Mensur* was self-consciously German, and celebrated as such.

Alluded to by Treitschke, most German of all were the livid scars students received in the *Mensur*, which, due to medical advances that could safely heal the most dire wounds,[86] became more hideous and copious as the century progressed. By the early 1900s, representations depict otherwise handsome young men with visages so outlandishly abused—mostly the left sides of their faces, where blows would fall from right-handed duelists—that they appear to have been the victims of some appalling industrial mishap. But the students liked it that way. They preferred a mean, well-blighted face. The *Mensur* was not only a test of courage, not only an end in itself; it was also the way to acquiring a "badge" of courage. The dueling scar (*Schmiss*, often called *Renommierschmiss* or "bragging scar"—and it was not misnamed) was of inestimable value because it was the upscale tatoo, borne by a generation of doctors and jurists and professors and officials, certifying the proprietor's claim to both manly stature and cultivated rank. This is a great part of the reason why these boys, who were "better looking than the average run of German students,"[87] did not avail themselves of alternate and more gracile methods of distinguishing their manhood that would have proven gentler on their complexions.

20. Cosmetic surgery, Wilhelmine style. Illustration by C. W. Allers, 1902, in Allers, *Das Deutsche Corpsleben* (Stuttgart, Berlin, Leipzig, ca. 1902). (Staatliche Museen zu Berlin, Kunstbibliothek)

The tantalizing combination of virility and breeding that the *Schmiss* delineated was catnip for young ladies of the era who by all reports would go limp with desire upon sighting one. The *Schmiss* was loaded with connotations for women and signified, among other things, potency, good connections, and status: the bearer had the potential to be a good provider. One dollface, a veteran of some eighty Heidelberg *Mensuren*, could rely on an uncritical swarm of girls every afternoon stroll.[88] But even nineteenth-century German women were not total

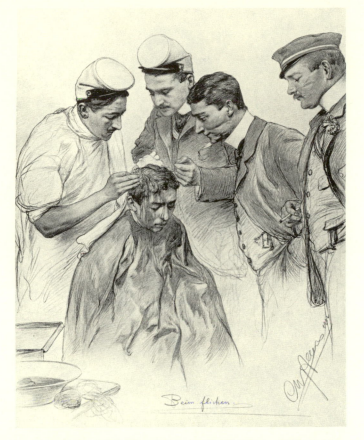

21. "Patch-up job." Illustration by C. W. Allers, 1902, in *Das Deutsche Corpsleben* (Stuttgart, Berlin, Leipzig, ca. 1902). (Staatliche Museen zu Berlin, Kunstbibliothek)

pushovers when it came to noseless or lipless physiognomies or heads without ears, which were considered deplorably passé by the turn of the century.[89] On the other hand, German females were apparently so enamored of the standard zipper-look that there was one reported case in 1894 of a student approaching a doctor to acquire what the *Schläger* had failed to dispense; and another in 1902 in which the three-inch deed (usually scars of this length the result of a *Durchzieher* or drawing-stroke across the face) was self-inflicted by a teenager with a straight-edged razor.[90] Those who received their engravatures in a less artful fashion would often pull the wound apart over long periods of time or pour wine or some other toxic irritant into it to make it suppu-

22. "You get a straw!" Illustration by C. W. Al-
lers, 1902, in *Das Deutsche Corpsleben* (Stuttgart,
Berlin, Leipzig, ca. 1902). (Staatliche Museen zu
Berlin, Kunstbibliothek)

rate and induce yucky healing. All this trouble could be avoided, however, had one the simple foresight to instruct the attending physician,
whose fingers might be grimy with pipe tobacco and who made a
point of being as rough and clumsy as possible (the *Mensur* was a
twofold ordeal, with both participants, following the bout, being automatically constrained to have their heads examined), to sew a thick
horse's hair into the gash. This dainty expedient guaranteed students
an active and effortless love life for the rest of their days. They had
some bona fide etchings to show.

Rather than tokens of self-effacement, *Schmisse* were products of
male vanity, were "regarded as jewelry" and considered "fashionable."[91] Furrowed cheeks (not to be confused with brows) were particularly swank in the three decades of Wilhelm II's reign.[92] In 1900,

Jerome K. Jerome estimated that one-third of all German gentlemen he observed in the street paraded at least one of these glamorous gee-gaws about with them.[93] In Austria, the *Schmiss* was equally coveted: Arthur Schnitzler reminisced that in his first year as a medical student, a well-meaning colleague in the dissecting room tried to enlist him for a dueling fraternity with the adroit reasoning that "he thought a du-elling scar would look well on me!"[94] German students enjoyed strut-ting the effects of their mettle and newly bandaged warriors were a common spectacle in the public gardens, cafés, theaters, and concert halls of German university towns.[95] Heads were utterly mummified in dressing, which would be drawn lockjaw tight above and below the mouth to prevent the ripping open of cuts through an inadvertent yawn; sufficient latitude remained to wedge a straw and inhale the favored restorative. They never broke training.

In a 1912 session of the Reichstag, one deputy contended that hardly anyone achieved high state office who had not undergone the requi-site facial, and that "the precondition for a better career in the high state offices is membership in a dueling organization."[96] Affiliation with a dueling corps was a major boost for any young man intent on a successful professional or business career. In this sense, because the cornerstone of their clubs was the *Mensur*'s manly art, surcharged masculinity was the passkey of character that enabled ambitious ca-reer goals in Wilhelmine Germany. Brethren from the dueling organi-zations, and particularly the B.M.O.C. *Corpsstudent*, were pantingly snapped up by the judiciary, bureaucracy, and government. In Prussia in 1903, twenty-one of thirty-five chairmen of regional governing councils, and between 31 and 64 percent of the other chief administra-tive vizierships were in the trust of *Corpsstudent* alumni.[97] The *Corps-student*'s apolitical yet patriotic tendencies made him not only the per-fect civil servant but the "ideal specimen of the Wilhelmine era."[98] The *Corpsstudent* enjoyed a regal status in later life, and *Corps* membership was greatly overrepresented in the upper echelons of industry, ad-ministration, and diplomacy.[99] Organizations such as the *Verband Alter Corpsstudenten*, an alumni club for ex-*Corpstudenten* inaugurated in 1888 to care for its own post-graduate, helped smooth the way to these pampered posts,[100] and the lists of former *Corpsstudenten* read like a "Who's Who" of German high society.[101] *Corpsstudenten* were usually to be found in the distinguished fields of medicine and law, and it is no happenstance that doctors and jurists composed the main occupa-tional cohort of civilian duelists.[102] Medicine and law were also cus-tomary courses of study for most *Burschenschaft* members. From this standpoint, and similar to American fraternities,[103] the dueling clubs were "not a haven from the demands of society but a vehicle in order

23. "Among children." " 'Oh, I should think it heavenly to be a *Corpsstudent*!' 'Flattering, very flattering! It's always agreeable when young people show an understanding for higher things.' " By E. Thöny, in *Der Student: Kulturbilder aus dem Simplicissimus* (Albert Langen Verlag, 1905). (Staatliche Museen zu Berlin, Kunstbibliothek)

to facilitate a relatively effortless transition into the professional world."[104] In *Der Zauberberg*, Thomas Mann compares the dueling clubs to those Masonic Lodges rumored to exercise undue influence on the course of world events at the time through their conspiratorial penetration into the highest echelons of power. Members "stuck together throughout life and knew how to take care of their people, so that only with difficulty was it possible to bring someone to something good in the hierarchy of officialdom, who had not been a *'Corpsbruder.'* "[105]

Although the number of university students in Germany doubled in the thirty years between 1884 and 1914, the number of active *Corpsstudenten* remained stable, constituting about two thousand members from a student body of some sixty thousand, and this derived from a total population of well over sixty million on the eve of the First World War.[106] It was a choice group. *Corpsstudenten* generally hailed from the moneyed, property-owning bourgeoisie, or *Besitzbürgertum*. Their stature was yet further enhanced by the fact that at the turn of the century around 8 percent of all *Corpsstudenten* were drawn from the nobility.[107] Some *Corps*, such as those of the so-called "White Circle" consisting of Borussia Bonn, Saxo-Borussia Heidelberg, and Saxonia Göttingen, carried overwhelmingly aristocratic memberships, even though by 1914 only 2 percent of the student population was of a sufficiently noble stamp to furnish the necessary raw recruiting material.[108]

In actuality, however, there was very little recruitment necessary in the years prior to the Great War when unqualified reverence for the *Corpsstudent* peaked. During these years, the organizations had the luxury of drafting their squads along strict lines of ancestral lineage and financial clout.[109] The *Burschenschaften* and *Landsmannschaften* were possibly not as finicky about whom they accepted into their stables, but from a demographic point of view they were equally exclusive as the *Corps*, carrying in 1913 memberships of 3,300 and 2,000, respectively. *Burschenschaften* recruits were enrolled from the more cultured circles of society, from the educated middle class, the *Bildungsbürgertum*, and they do appear to have been more diligent in their studying habits than the other two aggregates. The *Landsmannschaften*, for their part, had roots predominantly in the commercial and industrial sectors.[110] Although the *Burschenschaften* and *Landsmannschaften* reaped deference and social kudos like the *Corpsstudenten*, they were generally regarded as second-class *Corps*,[111] probably owing to the dearth of blue blood circulating through their ranks. All three of these organizations were, after all, primarily concerned with cultivating, through the *Mensur* discipline, an aloof aristocratic air among their membership, and a club such as the *Corps* possessing a large number of personnel to the manor born, had in large part already justified its existence.

Not surprisingly, most incorporated alumni in the Reichstag belonged to the conservative or the non-Catholic middle parties, where dueling was anywhere from staunchly defended to remitted as a necessary evil. In 1896, a Reichstag dueling debate intensified to the point that the Graf Mirbach, member of the German Conservative Party and an unreconstructed *Corpsstudent*, grandstanded by challenging a deputy on the moderate left—who laughed in his face, calling his behavior

24. "Drinking ceremony of old and young *Corpsstudenten* in Berlin." Wood engraving from an illustration by H. Lüders, 1875. (Bildarchiv Preussischer Kulturbesitz, Berlin)

"ungentlemanlike."[112] Five years later in 1901, the Social Democratic leader August Bebel questioned the legality of "Old Gentlemen" (*Alte Herren*) such as Mirbach who served in an official state capacity. He accused these permanent juveniles of being in technical violation of the law through continued allegiance to their fraternal colors and the statutes of the student dueling associations as set forth in articles of the *Kösener Convent*, whose *Comment* required the *Mensur* of all its members and which prescribed adjudication of intransigent disputes by means of formal duels as ordered by student courts of honor. Fidelity to the *Comment* thereby placed even former students on an illegal footing with respect to Article 129 of the penal code forbidding "the participation in a fraternity to whose purposes or occupation belong the obstruction or weakening of government rules or execution of laws through unlawful means."[113] As of 1883 and the Supreme Court decision, one could indicate a ship of state piloted by a piratical crew of cutlass-swinging hearties.

Even though approximately one-third of all Germans were Catholic, the great majority of confessing students involved in dueling fraternities were Protestant. In 1869, Pope Pius IX had reaffirmed Church con-

25. "Catholic corps." "At today's rosary Windhor-
stia once again emerged with a dazzling victory. In
its honor, a hearty *Salamander! Ad exercitium sala-
mandris eins-zwei-drei—eins!—Gsuffa!—Amen!*" By
Bruno Paul, in *Der Student: Kulturbilder aus dem
Simplicissimus* (Albert Langen Verlag, 1905). (Staatliche Museen zu Berlin, Kunstbibliothek)

demnation of the duel and threatened with excommunication all those
in breach of the sixth commandment;[114] he also threatened excommunication for accessories failing to frustrate a duel.[115] Banishing any lingering confusion on the subject of student duels, in an 1891 encyclical
to the German bishops, Pope Leo XIII expressly interdicted the *Mensur*.[116] Already in 1855, however, the student fraternity "Unitas" had
been formed for nondueling Catholics.[117] Formations such as these
were loathsome to most of the university's dueling faithful.[118] In 1901
in Cologne, three reserve officer candidates and members of Catholic
university organizations were improperly grilled by examining officers for their attitudes toward the duel and whether they would in

26. "A changing wind." "Yes, old *Leibfuchs*, what dashing *Corps* men we once were! And now our sons are involved in that Catholic club pretentiousness! And they think to forge careers." By R. Wilke, in *Der Student: Kulturbilder aus dem Simplicissimus* (Albert Langen Verlag, 1905). (Staatliche Museen zu Berlin, Kunstbibliothek)

principle accept a challenge. Their reply was that they stood upon the principles of their fraternities. When they later came up for selection they were denied commissions.[119] *Das Kleine Journal* sarcastically observed in 1893 that the "Jesuits will gain entrance into Germany before a pious Catholic who rejects the duel gains entrance into the ranks of the Prussian Army."[120] A favorite *Corpsstudent* prank in Austria was to challenge Roman Catholic reservists, thus jeopardizing either their standing as *satisfaktionsfähig* officers or their immortal souls.[121]

At the 1877 Kösener Congress a resolution to blackball Jews from the *Corps* was rejected with an appeal to the stated principles of equality (*Gleichheitsprinzip*) in the corporation statutes.[122] But Jews, like Catholics, were still generally barred from the delirious pleasures of the *Mensur* inner sanctum. Although there was no formal boycott of Jewish students by the collective German dueling organizations—as was partially the case in Austria—starting from the 1880s and the immigration of *Ostjuden* into the *Reich*, Jews were systematically discouraged from membership and statutes required that Gentile affiliates renounce amatory traffic with Jewesses.[123] By the 1890s, the *Burschenschaften* and *Landsmannschaften* had established the practice of listing religions next to names in the club roster.[124] But even though banished from the major dueling societies, Jews formed their own fraternities, and on the eve of the First World War, in an undoubted attempt to obliterate the "coffee house Jew" stereotype, they had carved out a ferocious reputation as duelists.[125] To fortify his son for any future dueling eventualities, Schnitzler's father assured that young Arthur was well trained in the art of fencing, and the young medical student in the 1880s regarded the duel as an integral part of his Jewishness.[126] The Zionist visionary Theodor Herzl also entertained the possibility of dueling about this time, believing that "a half dozen duels would very much raise the social position of the Jews."[127] Unlike in Austria and in France where there occurred quite a few "anti-Semitic" duels,[128] German Jews who had little access to the chief dueling socializers—the army and the university clubs—were not therefore among that country's chosen people. Whether "anti-Semitic" or not, a duel with a Jew was at least a recognition of his honorable status, of his claim to a certain esteem. This kind of nonprejudicial esteem appears to have also been present in Hungary and Italy.[129]

The Protestant Church, for its part, had divided loyalties. As a backer of the prevailing order—of which the duel itself was an adventitious strut—German Evangelicalism was riven between allegiance to divine law and devotion to its earthly incarnation, the Prussian State. A typical example of the Protestant knack for modus vivendi with respect to the duel occurred at the University of Jena shortly following the institution of *Schläger* fencing: because those with *Schmisse* were debarred from the ministry, the rectors for a time authorized theological students to run each other through the body.[130] The Lutheran "Wingolf" society, founded in 1841 as an anti-dueling organization, in 1895 spared its members the conflict of conscience Catholic officers often suffered in that most delicate of dilemmas—honor versus catechism—by allowing its adherents to engage in the *Mensur* and thereby assure their futures as imperial reservists.[131] Protestant clergymen, who enjoyed the status of quasi-state officials,[132] gave the duel qualified support in the Reichstag, and books with titles such as *Der Student der Theologie und die studentische Satisfaktion* wrestled with the issue.[133] "The pastors condemn the duel in principle," accused one critic, "but they do not have the courage then to take the appropriate steps, as is the case in the Catholic Church."[134] It was rumored that devout Protestants would receive communion on the eve of a baptism by fire,[135] and pastors stood ready to sanctify Christian burial for co-religionist victims of duels.[136] As a result of this *Kulturreligion*'s secular expediency, very few Protestant duelists (most duelists) had the repentant streak of the narrator of Tennyson's "Maud," who, after killing in a duel, retreats to a faraway land bemoaning "the Christless code/That must have life for a blow."[137] Although Protestant clerics cannot exactly be depicted as defenders of the practice, they did tend to grant duelists special dispensation. Consequently, Jews who as a rule were circumscribed from the *Mensur* and the Prussian army and its duel, and professing Catholics who eschewed both species, by default gave Protestantism a confessional monopoly on studliness, licensing it as the spiritual prefect of essential masculinity in Germany.

Manliness meant wielding "an intrusive weapon,"[138] something women were not physiologically equipped to do. There were more than just social and denominational strictures in the dueling associations. In sort of a Philistine version of the George *Kreis*, gender was delimited. The orgiastic activities of the students may have been the *soif du néant* of a displaced or sublimated sexuality that had its root in an inability to cope with women. This is neither a shameful nor unusual ailment in post-adolescent males, but when it does occur, according to psychologists, "collectively and individually, men submerge their fears into an overestimation of male sexuality. . . . Out of this emerges the individual and collective male pride in some version of 'machismo' sexuality, no doubt reinforced by male gender socialization or 'male bonding.'"[139] There was a kind of affection between these gay blades in their *Mensur* trysts, and plunging a sword up and down and in and out of an opponent's face might be classed as one of the more striking symptoms of male co-eroticism. A canticle warbled by the *Burschenschaften* was "The Sword Song" (*Schwertlied*), in which the soon to be bloodied implement is likened to a woman on her wedding day: "The bridal night's red morning/Breaks to the trumpet's warning;/When cannon peals begin/Fetch I the loved one in." The intended replies: "O sweet embrace! untiring,/I tarry still desiring;/Then bridegroom fetch thou me,/My garland waits for thee."[140]

It was often necessary for the priapic preppies to get very drunk, very fast. It was wine (*sic*) and song, but as for the women . . . "The German student does not dissipate his virility in the *Quartier Latin* like the French," a *Simplicissimus* caricature of the time has a sodden son of Bacchus gurgle: "As unweakened guardians of pure ideals, we go forth to face life. Hic!"[141] The student tavern was the traditional refuge

27. "Educational deficiency."
"'I believe you are quite terribly bored?' 'Not at all, my dear, but what do you discuss with such young ladies? They don't even know the first thing about fencing!'" By E. Thöny, in *Der Student: Kulturbilder aus dem Simplicissimus* (Albert Langen Verlag, 1905). (Staatliche Museen zu Berlin, Kunstbibliothek)

of these self-styled Platonists, misunderstood by a materialistic world and its maddeningly sensual ladies. Fleeing from his sexual *Weltschmerz*, Mann's Diederich Hessling finds ambrosial sanctuary in "[t]he alcohol! One sat there and you could always have more of it. Beer was not like coquettish women, but true and comforting. With beer you had no need to cope, nothing to desire, nothing to attain, like with women. Everything came of itself."[142]

Few student duels appear to have been on account of women. In Berlin in 1898, one angry young man even threatened the weaker vessel with a challenge.[143] But these ungallant swain would grow up to concern themselves an enormous deal with the opposite sex: in the relative majority of real duels in Wilhelmine Germany, women were the origin of the dispute. The redoubtable Viennese intellectual Rosa Mayreder perceived in the student duelists and their code duello "the most perverted and ludicrous caricature of the primitive masculine instincts."[144] And it were these very boys in later life, still armed with their college code, who would assume that "frivolous and hypocritical attitude [which] bestows upon woman the mere semblance of pre-eminence in order to really push her back and into that place among children and minors which masculine lordship is determined she should occupy."[145]

CHAPTER V

Les Belles Dames Sans Merci

O what can ail thee, Knight at arms,
Alone and palely loitering?
The sedge has withered from the Lake
And no birds sing!
—John Keats, "La Belle Dame Sans Merci" (original version,
28 April 1819)[1]

IT IS DIFFICULT to say whether female provocation was as seminal in other national duels as in Germany, but nowhere was it so conspicuous. In three countries, Hungary, France, and Italy, the journalistic and political duels were more prominent, whereas there is no question that in Germany women were central and the dubious beneficiaries of this self-consciously "chivalrous" institution. The German duel was Europe's most virulent because its practitioners were perhaps informed to a superior degree by a chivalrous ethos upon which was placed a most stringent he-man emphasis.

The German duel had its basis in gender relations that were reminiscent of a feudal bond and its asymmetrical tie of personal dependence—men being the protectors and women the protected. Violation of a woman's physical or moral integrity was conceived as the vilest of crimes, demanding a most extreme form of redress on the part of her titular guardian. A recognition of chivalry's essential contribution is indispensable to an accurate picture of the dueling phenomenon and the way that German men of honor understood themselves, especially in amorous and confrontational relations where the duel catered to their romantic notions of gallantry in love and war. Certain bourgeois moral-educational precepts might have brought one to theoretically accept the idea of dueling as the ultimate assertion of a free personality; but arousal to dangerous action, squaring off at ten paces with rifled barrels—this required a headier stimulus that had direct affiliations with masculine courage and fighting and dying for the sake of female goodness.

The technical term for induction of a young man into the knighthood in medieval Germany, *"zu man werden"* (to become a man) was a synonym for *"swert leisten"* (carry a sword) and *"ritter werden"* (become a knight), and the two concepts of chivalry and masculinity became inextricably linked if not interchangeable over time.[2] The degree to which a similar binary idea predominated in Wilhelmine Germany is striking. Not only in dueling manuals but in the general literature and journalism of the period, abundant discussion of what constituted "chivalrous" and "unchivalrous," "honorable" and "dishonorable" behavior was informed by an obsession with manliness. Experts were accustomed to remark that in particular bravery "surrounds the duel with the aura of chivalry and so makes it attractive for just those strong, open, and noble personalities."[3] As discussed in chapter II, the supreme shame for the German man of honor was engendered not through imputations of moral depravity but through the ascription of physical cowardice, and in a very real sense the latter implied the former. Particularly in gender relations based on power and intimidation, to be *sans peur* was infinitely more desirable than to be *sans reproche*.

In duels over women, this imperative attained a white-hot intensity that fired traditional sexual stereotypes: Distressed damsels needed intrepid knights to protect them—a wife's weakness and helplessness, in fact, was proof of her spouse's masculine stature.[4] *Ehrenmänner* had their female complement in *Ehrendamen*, ladies-in-waiting, an apposite description of the general role that most bourgeois women occupied in relation to their spouses. This marked sexual polarization was the result of a chivalrous code that albeit idealized women and required consorts to occasionally risk their lives for the sake of their chimera; but in so doing, it simultaneously placed an emphasis on hard masculine values, invariably attended by a concomitant denigration and subjugation of the female. Dueling was an exalted hoax that ostensibly vindicated the moral and physical integrity of women against male encroachment, while in fact reinforcing the thankless patriarchy of German society. Contempt for women went hand in gauntlet with their elevation because German men of honor possessed what John Keats termed "negative capability," the talent for holding two contradictory ideas in the mind at the same moment, and to credit each of them equally. For German men of honor, a woman was an object of worship *and* an object of scorn. And for this reason she was the exquisite object of a duel, which pretended to save her honor but really pronounced her shame and fastened her yoke. Judging from their deadly duels on account of women, this mental schizophrenia among German men of honor was very acute indeed, and helps to flittingly elucidate contradictory statements by bourgeois duelists concerning a woman's sacrosanct purity on the one hand and her genetic inferiority on the other.

THAT CERTAIN TYPE OF INSULT

"First of all," wrote one authority in 1889, "the fact must be emphasized that in the majority of serious duels the fairer sex serves as the
immediate cause of the conflict. In most cases, without their knowledge and without direct responsibility."[5] Twenty-three years later, the
leader of the German Anti-Dueling League Karl Fürst zu Löwenstein
was able to confirm this judgment, finding that "the reasons for the
duel are primarily insults, adultery, and other violations of marital
fidelity."[6] The next year in the Reichstag, the Prussian Minister of War
cited "illicit traffic with women" as the motive in over a quarter of all
officer duels in the few years previous,[7] and the actual figures were
certainly higher. Sexual jealousy was at least as likely to incite someone to a verbal or physical assault (constituting the other two categories of insult on the War Minister's list) as any other possible sentiment, and a man whose "tenderest and holiest feelings" had been
savaged still retained the status of the "offended" in duels where, in
the incident prior, he had inadvertently cursed or struck the spoiler of
his "domestic bliss" (häusliche Glück).[8] Therefore, duels that were the
product of simple insults were undoubtedly less than official estimates and those whose real cause was women were certainly more
than formally credited. In the German military courts of honor, for
example, "seduction" was not a prosecutable crime (if the girl was
over eighteen): only the insults or cursing consequent of the sexual
encounter could initiate proceedings.[9] Hermann Rumschöttel does
cite adultery and verbal injury as the two leading causes of duels
among Bavarian officers in the 1880s.[10] Because of their illegality,
duels in general were kept as secret as possible and this was even more
true of duels over a women, whose reputation could be smeared by
knowledge of the affair. Even if the duel did wind up in court, other
reasons could be invented by discreet men of honor to obscure the
dispute's provenance. Armed confrontations only took place after a
peacemaking effort had collapsed, and so by definition a duel meant
irreconcilable differences. Without question, the most irremediable
rifts were caused by broken hearts. Cherchez la femme had its German
equivalent in the maxim, "Es steckt ein Frauenzimmer dahinter."[11]

The court system and its refined slow penalties were abjured as inappropriate and insufficient recompense for the man whose wife or
lover had been insulted or seduced. There were few dissenters to this
point of view in bourgeois German society. Legal experts judged that
stronger fines for insult might hinder other types of duel, but never
those showdowns born of seduction.[12] In 1896, Graf Mirbach of the

Conservative Party conceded that verbal injuries should not invariably issue in challenges but cautioned that "there are then still other cases which reach into the family, into the marriage, where in my opinion it is impossible to follow the commandments of religion."[13] The *Vossische Zeitung*, a solidly liberal periodical, declared in one of its editions that, "There is one circumstance, but only one, in which, although not approving of it, we are able to understand the duel in human terms: when the family honor of a concerned party is thrown into question, when it has to do with his wife, his sweetheart, his daughter, his mother, his sister. . . ."[14] And at a congress of the German Anti-Dueling League shortly after the turn of the century, a petition that would have forbidden any member from engaging in a duel was indignantly rejected by a majority of the confirmed abolitionists. Instead, the resolution was voted to condemn dueling in principle and to fight the practice with all possible means, but to still allow for the existence of certain cases in which duels might be judged unavoidable—the stock euphemism for cases of seduction.[15]

In the dueling codes of the time, "seduction" (*Verführung*) was rated an odious third-level insult, placing it on a par with theft and cheating, both synonymous with the outrage of female allurement in Wilhelmine Germany. The third-level insult also encompassed a slap or blow, and thus the theft of one's wife or daughter through cheating behavior constituted a literal slap in the face "endangering the entire moral existence of the insulted."[16] In his 1888 edition, the German annotator of Chatauvillard's 1836 *Essai sur le duel* glossed this Frenchman's discussion of grades of insult with the anxious proviso that the third-level offense should include not only blows but also the "seduction of one's wife or daughter."[17] One codifier stepped completely outside the debate and went so far as to invent a sui generis fourth category of insult: for those cases in which "the family honor is injured."[18] In these circumstances, a contrite apology was never adequate balm for the injured party, whose opponent could only make amends "through force of weapons."[19]

The third-level insult was an important classification since it gave the woman's titular representative a choice of weaponry and style of combat, but there was scarce doubt about the reaction a man of honor should register to the seduction of his daughter or the extra-marital fling of his wife: settle accounts "with pistol in hand."[20] In duels where women upped the ante, pistols were standard equipment, and not only was the male defender conferred the first shot in alternate exchanges, he was granted the additional privilege of determining the number of paces separating the rivals. Needless to say, these close encounters of the third kind were frequent effusions of blood. "Those who tread upon the sanctity of the family," explained one dueling code, "can never claim any rights when he is disciplined by the legal guardian of the family."[21] As in material ways, the middle-class patriarch was completely accountable for the moral welfare of his female brood, thus eliminating any possibility of autonomous action for the woman, who was drained not only of direct responsibility but—having been "seduced"—of personal volition for her transgression. Had she been considered a significant actor in the affair, the husband might have made short work of her instead of her partner—as is still today the more efficient custom in the Islamic world.[22] Terminating the woman finished the matter, whereas the serial killing of lovers might go on indefinitely.

Vulgar murder, whether of the wife or her lover, was never condoned. Even a member of the Reichstag who was leading an anti-dueling interpellation in 1902, praised the character of a man who had learned of his wife's seduction and then exercised his *droit du seigneur* by challenging the culprit instead of going berserk and outright killing him.[23] In 1895, the thirty-five-year-old attorney Ernst Zenker showed typically admirable restraint when he found his wife disporting with a crewmember of the Kaiser's royal yacht, all hands this day far from being on deck. Employing the strong-silent mode, he calmly showed the sailor the door and then instructed his spouse, "Get dressed, we have a visit to make." He escorted her before her parents and then departed with the *auto-da-fé*: "There. I bring you your daughter; she'll explain the rest herself." After separation from his wife, Zenker was killed by the naval officer in a no-fault fight at twelve paces in the Potsdamer Forest, his doctor-brother in attendance to confirm the cause of death—a bullet through the heart at the third exchange. The Kaiser, concerned for his able-bodied seaman, was kept abreast of the affair throughout its development.[24]

Unvarnished murder was perceived as an illogical step for sore husbands, not because of its basic reprehensibility and the accompanying legal risks, but because that "certain type of insult" demanded restitution having little in common with wholesale revenge.[25] Recriminations were of little avail. For one, the guilty party was by no means preordained; the husband may have alienated his wife's affections through neglect or mental cruelty. But most important, a woman's guardian allegedly entered the fray "solely with the intention and thought to offer up his breast and to place his life behind his honor."[26] Unwillingness to do so was testimony to the sexual interloper's latent assertion that one was powerless to defend against such treachery. The intimation of a "sexual insult" was that its male object once-removed was incapable of redress and by equation a moral eunuch. The shameful thing was not that one was a cuckold; what excited jeering was *admission* of the fact through craven inaction. One authority observed that "there was a time when the honor of the man remained intact so long as he proved himself courageous. And it is this logic that still underlies the duel today."[27] Consequently, "the greatest insult that one can receive is the reproach of cowardice,"[28] and this reproof bulked very large in cases where female affections hung in the balance. In 1914, General Erich von Falkenhayn, author of Verdun two years later, patiently described to the Reichstag how the duel

> is a wholly inappropriate means to punish the guilty party, and just as inappropriate in exacting revenge. Such thoughts play only, if at all, a peripheral role. It is an entirely other feeling that animates and forces the insulted to set himself above law and order. It is the feeling that the insult is a double disgrace, because it is simultaneously a questioning of the masculinity of the insulted.[29]

Not surprisingly, masculinity could never be questioned—the "reproach of cowardice" could never be leveled—by women who purportedly had little understanding of such matters and who were, in any event, regarded morally and intellectually as infants. As sexual objects subordinated to masterful masculine tutelage, women acted as efficient conduits of insults between men, and chance remarks in their presence could bring bosom friends to blows and a duel.[30] But as independent free personalities they were incapable of doing an *Ehrenmann*'s pride any unmediated hurt. The lofty citadel of his male integrity proved invulnerable to the petty salvos of a niggling woman, and he was therefore allowed to regard with supreme indulgence any little outburst. "Insults from a lady, no matter how deserved," counseled one dueling code, "cannot be taken seriously and therefore do not concern the gentleman."[31]

This "categorical imperative in our hearts"[32] to call marital poachers to task through challenges was further reinforced by the convoluted laws regarding prosecution of adultery (*Ehebruch*) as an insult (*Beleidigung*), the latter a misdemeanor in Wilhelmine Germany. If a husband wished to file for divorce but it was demonstrated that the wife had been a willing partner in the adulterous liaison, it was impossible for him to sustain *Beleidigung* charges against her Lothario because the affair had been one of mutual consent. This fact was perhaps an even greater insult to the cuckold, but there was no legal "satisfaction" to be obtained against the homewrecker. If it was somehow ascertained by the husband that his wife had been the initially unwilling or at least passive party to the episode, it might be in his interest to exercise forgiveness and save the marriage, especially if there were children to consider. However, legal recourse against her paramour was once again denied the husband, because by remaining married he obviated the charge of *Ehebruch*, literally meaning the breaking up of someone's marriage. The only occasion whereby a husband could attain the requisite legal "satisfaction" against an interloper was by divorcing an "innocent," that is, a woman who was established to have been the victim of an unethical seduction. Such a proven infamy, however, ipso facto required that the man of honor challenge the villain. There are instances of such duels taking place only after the critical revelation had come to light in a public trial of divorce.[33] If the husband was then slain in the duel, it necessitated the immediate withdrawal of *Ehebruch* charges, because by destroying the husband of his mistress, the so-called seducer tidily freed himself from charges of destroying a marriage: no husband, no marriage.[34]

The extraordinary measure of a challenge was perceived as an entirely justifiable course of action in expunging a shame the courts were powerless to touch, and therefore Germans were apt to take solace in a duel to heal a wounded heart. The same civil law and judicial system that treated the duel with relative forbearance characteristically imposed rigorous penalties for adulterous women and marginal ones for their knights errant. In 1848, Friedrich Carl von Savigny (1779–1861), the most influential German jurist of the nineteenth century, enumerated three reasons for harsher penalties for women found in breach of the marriage contract: 1) the woman sank lower than the man when she committed such an act, because her career was chiefly encompassed by duties to her family, "while the man has membership in the world in many other respects"; 2) the generally recognized feeling that a husband was "more deeply injured" by an adulterous wife than was a wife who showed patience with an adulterous husband, the wife being frequently the recipient of both sympathy and respect while the man was held in low esteem; 3) the uncertainty of paternity, "which endangered the core of the marriage and the natural relationship to the children in the highest degree."[35] Von Savigny's views mirrored prevailing attitudes in German society at mid-century, and, as Jürgen Kocka reminds us, rather than reducing in intensity, "the legal, political, and social inequality between the sexes during the nineteenth century in many respects increased."[36] These grossly doubled standards in sexual behavior were also undergirded by a very candid and preceptial male chauvinism that permeated the writings of philosophers and other cultural *distingués* of the period.

"They are *sexus sequior*, the inferior sex in every respect," groused the German philosopher Arthur Schopenhauer: "one should be indulgent towards their weaknesses, but to pay them honour is ridiculous beyond measure and demeans us even in their eyes. . . . we with our old French gallantry and insipid women-veneration, that highest flower of Christian-Germanic stupidity."[37] Though Schopenhauer was a caustic foeman of the duel, his later German epigoni drew the reverse conclusion from their forerunner's fundamental premise of *sexus sequior*: as the inferior sex, women needed protection and dueling was the means. It is no accident that the last two decades of the nineteenth century in Europe, when dueling was at its height in Germany, was also "the golden age of Schopenhauer's influence"[38] Schopenhauer's ethical admonition to repudiate the Will (our insatiable drives) as a chronic misfortune, found its practical correlate in the subjugation of women, who embodied torturesome libidinal energy. Schopenhauer's atheism undercut even paternalistic Christian notions of the woman's subservient yet respected role in a man's life, for he acceded her a purely biological function, existing "solely for the propagation of the race" and finding in this duty her "entire function."[39]

Schopenhauer's most illustrious intellectual heir Friedrich Nietzsche (1844–1900), whose thought exercised a tremendous force at the turn of the century, reiterated this same intolerant view in many of his writings and particularly in *Also Sprach Zarathustra* (1883), which, next to the Bible and Goethe's *Faust*, was said to be found in the satchels of more German soldiers during the First World War than any other book.[40] In his chapter entitled *"Von Alten und Jungen Weiblein"* ("Of Old and Young Women"), the gynophobic hyperbole scatters rich as he puts words like the following into the mouth of a withered crone: "Man should be trained for war and woman for the recreation of the warrior: all else is folly." "The happiness of the man is: I want. The happiness of the woman is: he wants." "The genuine man wants two things: danger and play. Therefore he wants woman, as the most dangerous plaything."[41] Nietzsche has been characterized as possessing an "old-fashioned sense of honor."[42] He once toyed with the idea of dueling for the sake of that very dangerous plaything, the bewitching Lou Salomé (he danced to the crack of *her* whip) and, while composing *Also Sprach Zarathustra*, sent sullen missives to his imagined rival Paul Rée, venting the wish to give him "a lesson in practical morals with a few bullets."[43] On another occasion he crowed, "The barrel of a pistol is for me at the moment a source of relatively agreeable thoughts."[44] Eric Bentley, in his book on nineteenth-century protofascist sources observed how "Nietzsche's sex life is a brief catalogue of *gaucheries*. He was always defeated and died dreaming of manly grandeur."[45]

In Friedrich Spielhagen's novel *Sturmflut* (*Stormtide*, 1877) a young lady remarks, "At this moment there are only three men whom one must study carefully: Bismarck, Hartmann, and Wagner: the politics of the present, the music of the future, reconciled by the philosophy of the unconscious—there you have the signature of the century!"[46] The Second Reich of Otto von Bismarck (Bismarck, a pistol duelist himself, was fond of characterizing Germany as a "manlier" nation than others) was undersigned by two spiritual disciples of Schopenhauer. Schopenhauer's chief work *Die Welt als Wille und Vorstellung* (*The World as Will and Representation*, 1819) had an enormous impact on composer Richard Wagner (1813–83), arguably the century's preeminent musical and cultural figure. He read and reread Schopenhauer's magnum opus throughout his life, especially during the periods of his greatest artistic productivity, and, according to a biographer, "the extent to which Wagner's philosophical outlook, as expressed in his later music dramas, was affected by Schopenhauer can scarcely be overstated."[47] It is therefore hardly startling that the operas of the artist whom Otto Weininger regarded as "the greatest man since Christ's time," would provide the late nineteenth century "with the narrative context for many of the details in its iconography of misogyny."[48]

Inspired largely by thirteenth-century sources and themes, Wagner's compositions—from *Tannhäuser* (1845) to his final opera *Parsifal* (1882)—contain some of the most vivid evocations of the nineteenth century's "chivalrous" ethos. His masterpiece *Der Ring des Nibelungen* (1876) is particularly sumptuous in depictions of lofty quests and the temptations of sensual, illicit love, and its sword-waving, dragon-slaying hero Siegfried is a youth afraid of nothing save women.[49] Most notable, however, is *Lohengrin* (1850), which has the Knight of the Holy Grail appearing in a swan-powered boat at the blast of a herald's trumpet. He offers to champion the cause of Elsa, the victim of false accusations, who in turn promises her hand in marriage should he save her honor. Lohengrin triumphs in single combat and proclaims his victory a tribute to her purity, then demands her eternal fealty, assurances she unhesitatingly gives so that she might be enveloped completely by his heroic presence and ever bask in his manly glow.[50] And why not? The nineteenth-century French historian Jules Michelet described Elsa as the personification of the German middle-class woman who "loves, and loves always. She is humble, obedient, and would like to obey still more. She is fitted for only one thing, love." Bram Dijkstra describes *Lohengrin*'s "Wedding March" as a bride's parade toward self-obliteration in the years to come.[51]

The German Empire's leading philosopher in its first decades was Eduard von Hartmann who helped popularize Schopenhauer's anti-Hegelian, proto-Freudian school in his *Philosophie des Unbewussten* (*Philosophy of the Unconscious*, 1869), which by 1879 had sailed through eight editions. In 1886, Hartmann published *Moderne Probleme*, containing a provocative section on women which had its clear point of departure in Schopenhauerian attitudes. Hartmann constructed a sexual dialectic between men and women whereby the man symbolized activity and desire and the woman stood for passivity and tractability (*Gewähren*). Renunciation was easier for women than it was for men, and for this reason women possessed a "secret supremacy" that had to be shrewdly compensated for in legal maintenance of male hegemony. Harking back to Friedrich Carl von Savigny's arguments, Hartmann asserted that the transgression of an adulterous wife was always more catastrophic to the family than that of the philandering husband, because of the prospect of bastards desecrating the familial hearth. Hartmann put forth the proposition that forgiveness in this regard was fully commensurate with the dignity of a woman, whereas "the divine gentleness of pardon" was unbecoming a man and only made him despicable.[52] In a later book entitled *Tagesfragen* (*Questions of the Day*), which appeared in 1896, the year of the first great public discourse on the dueling question, Hartmann affirmed the duel as a necessary deterrent for lack of compelling strictures against adultery and seduction in the German penal code.[53]

The widely read pedagogue and idealist philosopher Friedrich Paulsen also drew connections between the duel and issues of gender in his *System der Ethik* (1889). Echoing the previous statements of both Savigny and Hartmann, Paulsen specified a woman's constitutionally submissive character as forming one of the chief psychological differences between the sexes. Whereas the male of the species was an obdurate creature of "attack and defense," the female was more enduring, pliant, and suited for suffering; to sustain this view he cited the fact that male rates of suicide were four times those of women. As a corollary to her passive nature, a woman possessed no independent honor of her own, and was therefore reduced to a life lived vicariously, reaping any semblance of social distinction solely through the achievements of her husband.[54] Paulsen described the coercive fundament that underlay many bourgeois households and marriages at the time, when he described male honor as being "increased through the things which heighten the power and influence of an individual in relation to his environment; or, in other words, that which enhances his ability to be of use or of harm to others." Like Hartmann, Paulsen deplored the fact that "in no area is the legal protection of individual rights so inadequate as in matters of honor," yet he simultaneously resisted the idea that positive collation of honor violations was feasible since an offense always rested on the inchoate sensitivity of its object. The duel was a form of "regulated self-help," a declaration of self-sufficiency in an area where appeal to the law was an avowal of impotence in dispatching one's personal affairs. Such an appeal was particularly shameful, needless to say, when women were the spoil.[55]

Paulsen's a priori gender depictions, extrapolating from artificial social constraints placed on women in the late nineteenth century, were characteristic of almost dogmatic conceits endemic to the era. Because a virtuous woman was believed naturally feeble, her inborn "need for love"[56] made her naturally vulnerable to unscrupulous male advances, and so she required hale and robust sentries to guarantee the sexual purity she lacked not only sufficient physical resources to protect but the requisite moral discipline and self-control to preserve.

SEXUAL HONOR

All this chest-beating and breast-baring would seem to betoken an obsessive male concern with female sexual responses, and the duel was indeed viewed as a sort of chastity belt engirdling society. Various authors described it as "the indispensable final emergency measure against the running rampant of society"; as "this doubtlessly most effective antidote to the trivializing of the sense of . . . family honor"; as a bulwark against "the penetration of French views of married life and relations between the sexes."[57] It is instructive to note that all three of these remarks, including the last, were made in reference to the single major European power in which the duel had been all but abolished: Great Britain. German advocates were infuriated by the perception in England, even before the duel's banishment from Victoria's realm in the 1840s, that, according to V. G. Kiernan, "on the whole, marital fidelity seemed not worth fighting about."[58] And available evidence in this area does indicate that the vast majority of English duels in the first half of the nineteenth century were not instigated through conflicts of an erotic nature; the case also in nineteenth-century America where "actually very few duels anywhere in the country were fought about the fair sex."[59] At the turn of the century, one queasy German officer expressed alarm:

> Under English influences a certain modernization of views is beginning to occur, which I for my part am unable to acquire any taste for. I hold the conviction that only *the* cavalier who places his family honor so high that he is always prepared to enter the lists for its preservation, can demand unconditional respect for his rights from third parties.[60]

Aside from the arrogant feelings the duel engendered within the contexts of class and gender, a nationalistic component is notable in churlish references to wanton English morals and *"französische Liebe"* (actually, a French kiss of a racier variety), always darkly profiled against the sunburst radiance of vestal German womanhood, whose honor was held a "sacrosanct treasure."[61] From the time of the Napoleonic Wars and Fichte's *Reden an die Deutsche Nation* (*Addresses to the German Nation*, 1808), Germans had defined themselves as ethically superior over and against the morally reprobate French, but the enmity focused against Britannia may have been a more recent development that owed in part to the keen antagonism generated by the Anglo-German naval race after 1897. During a Berlin party ringing out the old century on New Year's Eve 1899, an Anglo-German cultural clash was ignited when one of the English guests, a Mr. Wheeler, stole a chaste kiss from "a charming young lady of German stock" who had innocently wandered beneath a garland of mistletoe hung to advantage from the ballroom chandelier by Wheeler's festive countrymen. The young woman did not seem to object but her bumptious sibling was unimpressed with the yuletide tradition. He demanded that either the crypto-rapist marry his sister, or meet him in a duel. The affair was smoothed over with the British subject's promise to do the decent thing and the maligned brother's dignity was salvaged. The sister's reaction to her shotgun wedding was not reported.[62]

In the all-time German classic *Faust* (1808), Valentin dies cursing his sister Gretchen after being mortally wounded by her demon-lover in a duel for her honor.[63] In lieu of virile husbands, brothers (followed by fathers, nephews, uncles, and fathers-in-law) might do in a bind, and could be equally vexatious with the Eternal Feminine to draw them on.[64] In 1897, a Bonn University student challenged another for keeping his back turned to his sister for what he considered an inordinate length of time.[65] In less silly affairs, challenges were imminent. Upon announcement of her pregnancy, the erstwhile mistress of Viennese playwright Arthur Schnitzler insisted that her brother would not bear the news amiably, "and with a tragic-comic effect . . . she kept repeating over and over again, 'a duel is inevitable.'"[66]

The duel, though hardly an impregnable shield, may indeed have been highly effective in preserving virginity among young ladies of good family and compelling a certain general continence in German gentlemen. The prospect of a duel must have greatly diminished—though, in some adventuresome cases, perhaps magnified—one's delight in an unconventional love affair. If, as one authority alleged, "the sexual-honor drive [*sexuelle Ehrtrieb*] of the woman protects society from complete derangement,"[67] the duel averted the pestilence of social anarchy by helping yearning hearts congeal. Premarital and extramarital concupiscence was probably accompanied by second thoughts and nagging doubts having their origin in the unsettling knowledge that fleshly indulgence could issue not only in babies and venereal diseases but in cadavers. One night under Venus might mean not only a lifetime under mercury, as the saying went, but a reckoning with Mars. "Where men duel," wrote Herbert Cysarz, "women are at least not seduced on caprice or for the sake of a parlor game."[68]

Who was seducing whom? In 1889, critic Alexander von Oettingen placed dueling's onus squarely on the slim shoulders of its supposedly prime beneficiaries. He saw swooning, palpitating women as being so decisive in nurturing stoic heroics that "one could write a fat book with the sole theme: *Women as the Cause of the Immoral Duel*":

> There exists among ladies a secret appreciation, indeed a feeling of adoration for the "chivalrous courage" of duelists, while one looks upon young men as hardly complete who dismiss the duel from reasons of conscience and religious-moral conviction. When it be said of a youth that he is disposed against the duel, it counts among many young ladies almost as a defect. They would rather converse and dance with a notorious duel enthusiast, and in the drawing room know how to excite with a certain *besoin d'emotion* every sparkling individual case. The ladies are mostly unsuspecting of what pernicious influence they consciously or unconsciously exercise upon male youth and their thoughtless judgment of the dueling question.

He went on to extol male Turks and Mongols for their solidarity against the "women's sect" (*Damentheil*) and their concomitant resistance to the dueling bug, and to decry the romantic plays and novels found in every "*Damenboudoir*" paying homage to the duel. He concluded predictably that the "*Damenwelt*" practiced a Circian sorcery over men of honor, turning them into swine, grunting and snorting for dominion through mortal combat.[69]

Cranks like von Oettingen may or may not be spurious guides with regard to actual female feelings, but they do help disclose male attitudes. The incantatory use of *Damen*-this and *Damen*-that, for example, conjures the Wilhelmine era's strict sexual divisions that helped foster the dueling ethos in the first place. And, as men swallow best their fear and rarely their pride when watched by women, any real or imaginable plaudits were certain to ellicit Childe-Haroldesque feats from not a few otherwise tepid souls. One caricature out of the German satirical magazine *Simplicissimus* entitled "From the Letter of a Young Wife" (1905) depicted a proud husband in bed titillating his dewy young miss with his most cherished physical asset: "Never marry a *Corpsstudent*, my dear Erna," writes the wife, "All night I have to admire the saber scars on his body."[70] Heinrich Mann's Diederich Hessling is miffed at his lady friend's failure to note some newly sustained beauty marks: "He looked discontentedly straight ahead. His

Schmisse, . . . all his well-acquired manliness: was that nothing to her? She didn't notice it at all?" Invariably he rejects the woman and is recognized for his true worth only by another male: "'*Schöne Schmisse,*' he said; and to the other gentleman: 'Don't you think so?'"[71] Though blamed on womanly pulchritude, dueling owed at least as much to a surplus of male testosterone: "For is it not precisely . . . the so desirable feminine beauty that inflames the love-crazed passion [*Liebesleidenschaft*] of the man and arouses him to a dangerous duel, to a life or death struggle, when another is favored? For what is life? Worthless without the sole possession of and made happy by the adored woman's love."[72]

But to whatever extent the duel for female honor was really a male affair, it was not a male monopoly. The distaff side assumed limited liability. Such was posited by the moral philosopher L. Jeudon and the sociologist Gabriel Tarde in connection with French damoiselles,[73] and Henry James burlesqued the perceived enthusiasm in *The American* (1876) when he makes his Parisian coquette squeal, "A duel—that would give me a push! . . . *C'est ça qui pose une femme!*"[74] German women can hardly be said to have gained an admired social reputation as the publicized object of a duel, but anti-duelists like Carl von Rüts were assuredly overstating their case in maintaining that "the truly pure and chaste-feeling maiden would rebel against the union with any such defender of his honor."[75] Women could not have been entirely insensitive to the poignant beauty of male sacrifice on their behalf. Indeed, a partisan of the German Anti-Dueling League found sufficient cause to reprimand women too soon made glad by the duel's Joe-college peacocking.[76] In the Reichstag in 1912, a special entreaty was made from the side of the Liberal Union to German mothers, for "when the proper feeling of honor is preserved strong and pure in our children, in ourselves and in our homes, then we will contribute a good deal to the duel's elimination."[77] Four hundred female adherents of the anti-dueling movement in the Habsburg Empire were impressed enough with the woman's role to make a direct plea to the ladies of Austria in 1907, beseeching them "to bring their influence to bear in the circle of family and friends so the conviction can finally emerge that true defense of honor is not to be found in the duel."[78] Women garnered much of their identities through their husbands and it is therefore not inconceivable that under appropriate circumstances they might occasionally urge their protectors to take forceful action on their account. Stood the man idly by, it could have been interpreted as a poor reflection on the esteem in which the wife was held by her companion. In an anonymous sketch with the relevant title "*Das Duell*" (1901), a mortal combat is interpreted as a betrayal of love by a woman stricken with jealousy for a rival on whose account her lover

will the next morning supposedly scuffle.[79] Describing a dashing relation of his, Arthur Schnitzler raved, "A duel wouldn't have meant
anything to him. . . . he would have been ready, naturally, and willing
to fight one at any time. Who could have doubted it. And how the
women adored him!"[80]

As defined by the dueling codes, a man abdicated his standing as a
gentleman through such "unchivalrous" behavior as compromising
"the honor of a woman through exposure of an intimate secret."[81]
Needless to say, a court of law was the last place a self-styled *Ehrenmann* would choose to air a whispered trust. Although many morals
crimes (*Sittlichkeitsverbrechen*) were prosecuted in quarantined trials,
other more peripheral cases slaked the public's prurient interest with
naughty accounts of sadism, lesbian love, and pederastic intercourse.[82]
For this reason, and because the courts were perceived as failing to
provide worthwhile reparation in the realm of sexual injury to one's
"family honor," gentlemen scorned the law and allowed a brace of
pistols to adjust their disputes.[83] But, having placed the delicate affair
beyond appeal, circumspection still remained crucial. As one dueling
manual stressed, "There can arise a case in which the grounds for a
duel concern a lady whose honor, reputation, or standing would suffer if it became known that for her sake and for this or that reason a
duel had taken place."[84] One's own reputation too. Not all "ladies"
may have been women. It was then possible to protect everyone's
good name either by camouflaging the affair's casus belli in some perfectly plausible row or pretextual exchange of words. If prevarication
were not to one's taste or absolute secrecy of paramount importance,
the duties usually assigned to confidential seconds could be provisionally assumed by the two partisans. In such an event the details of combat would be hammered out by the belligerent pair and the seconds
enjoined to show understanding and confirm the stipulations ignorant
of their contingent factors.[85]

The arrangement in Berlin in 1893 between Professor Fromhold and
Reserve Lieutenant Klein was far from unusual. The occasion for the
duel was a woman and was fought accordingly: with only two of the
usual four seconds in attendance, at the unholy hour of 4:00 a.m. in the
remote Zehlendorfer Forest, and at a hazardous five paces *à barrière*
with rifled pistols and three exchanges. Despite no casualties resulting
and precautions to keep the affair quiet, the story hit the newsstands
a week later.[86] Because of the severe conditions customarily agreed to
in duels over women, the danger did always exist of a grave wound or
an exhibit "A" body raising questions with the authorities that might
eventually arraign the case on a dueling charge. Judges paid particular
deference to the plight of women and one's "family honor" when im-
posing sentences, and so the affair's substantive origin was liable to

receive dishonorable mention in a trial that dug the dirt, thus jeopardizing, ironically, the reputation it had been fought to protect.

Such were the various facets incident to the case in 1893 of the Berlin
industrialist de la Croix, illustrative of the odd and elaborate dramas
a woman could spark while playing a virtually anonymous role. Some
time before, the married de la Croix had received a challenge from a
Dr. Röwer concerning a woman whom both men apparently prized.
Somehow de la Croix was able to refuse the challenge, and shortly
Röwer whisked off on an expedition to German East Africa, from
which he returned to Berlin in late 1892. During Röwer's absence the
chagrined de la Croix made daily visits to the shooting range. Hearing
the news of Röwer's safe return, de la Croix boldly approached his
rival, insulted him, and received another challenge, which it took no
arm-twisting for him to nonchalantly accept. Rifled pistols were
placed into service and twenty paces stepped off in Berlin's Tegeler
Forest, de la Croix presumably confident at relatively long range. But
round after round passed without result. Following every exchange,
an attempt at reconciliation was mediated by the attending seconds,
but in each instance it was waved off by de la Croix, intractable and
determined to profit from his long hours of target practice. The climax
came at the eighth volley, when a bullet stove in the right side of
Röwer's chest. He was dead on arrival at the hospital and his body
was relegated to an unconsecrated grave—unconsecrated, but
adorned with a flowery wreath from a mysterious donor. The ensuing
trial was sensational, but because of the airtight discretion exercised
by both combatants prior to their showdown (Röwer "had rarely even
mentioned the matter to his friends," and de la Croix "had taken scrupulous care to prevent the origins [of the conflict] from becoming public.") and that exercised by the post-mortem legal investigation, details
of the shadowy affair were hushed and the public screened from delib-
erations. The press was admitted for the verdict:

> Due to the severity of the conditions [of the duel], it might be questioned
> whether the allocation of punishment is commensurate with the mini-
> mum sentence. The court believed to answer this question in the negative
> because the accused had been insulted in his family honor in the most
> shamefaced way, and reached for the pistol in affliction and desperation.
> Under these circumstances it was necessary for him to impose serious
> conditions so as not to render the duel child's play.

The minimum sentence under Article 206 of the German penal code
for the felony of killing a man in a duel was two years. Several months
later de la Croix was munificently pardoned for his premeditated dev-
iltry by the Kaiser.[87]

Under Wilhelm II, pardons and light penalties were particularly bountiful for duelists who had jostled on behalf of their women. In 1901 in Mainz, *Oberleutnant* Richter was served a sentence of just three months after a duel with a fellow officer in a bicker over Richter's wife, from whom he later separated. His opponent was given two years, and after five weeks, Wilhelm interceded on Richter's behalf.[88] Two young men who had both suffered honorable wounds in a Berlin pistol duel for the sake of a "pretty salesgirl" in 1898, feigned blithe unconcern about possible legal repercussions as they both placed "confident hope in a pardon."[89] In 1896, the *Rittergutsbesitzer* Heinrich von Sprenger was so enraged by the *Rittmeister* von Hühnerbein's assertions that the former's wife had recently been "overcome with sensual love for him and had made improper suggestions" (*"und unzüchtige Anträge gemacht habe"*), that he infracted the dueling code by challenging his son-in-law.[90] The duel took place in early spring in Berlin's Jungfernheide at fifteen paces with rifled barrels and on the fourth pass von Hühnerbein had a zinger atomize his shin. Each duelist received six months honorable internment but, upon petition for pardon, von Sprenger's sentence was reduced by half because it was determined that, in view of having been "most violently assaulted in his family honor," his challenge was "not carelessly tendered." Von Hühnerbein's sentence stuck.[91]

A certain excess of chivalrous sentiment could be lavished on some women. A duel that was fought near the Schloss Ruheleben in the Grunewald in 1891 on account of a creature from the *"demi-monde"* was described in court as proceeding from "ignoble" motives and the duelists were slapped with stiff prison terms.[92] Distinguished members of society, for example two Leipzig doctors in 1892, might war and die over a humble café waitress,[93] but such "an unqualified indiscretion" was frowned upon and the dueling codes warned men of honor against wrangles spawned by "lascivious women or ladies of dubious reputation."[94] Husbands were counseled to reject challenges from the lovers of their estranged or divorced spouses.[95] Women not fitting certain immaculate conceptions did not merit the duel's implicit commendation, unlike in Third Republic France where they apparently did.[96] But the sexual purity of the otiose bourgeois wife—a purity that could be exonerated in clear conscience when menaced—was hypocritically funded by industrious prostitutes whose company a respectable *Ehrenmann* might enjoy so long as discretion was observed, but on account of whose raddled meat he could never so much as cross swords.[97]

Women of more venerated social standing, on the other hand, were regarded as precious objets d'art; though a random smudge on even their unalloyed virtue threatened to make social pariahs of them as well. For even retroactive calling to rights through the duel was considered a poor cleansing agent in seductions where "the spouse is robbed of his wife, her love and she herself are stolen from him," or where a young girl was deprived "of the single thing that makes her desirable, her innocence."[98] By extension of this masculine ideology, Eduard von Hartmann claimed a maiden bride as the right of every man, "any deception in this respect being a legal grounds for divorce, just like adultery," and labeled widows and divorcées "equivalent to a ware that has suffered damage and whose worth has dropped in price."[99]

A woman's value was apparently negotiable in monetary terms. "Eine Ehrenschuld" ("A Debt of Honor," 1912) by Wilhelm Heydrich recounts the story of a young man who falls for the attractive wife of his older friend but feels inhibited from consummating the affair with the anticipant Ehefrau because of an outstanding debt of six hundred Marks he has with her husband—as if sexual deception would set him yet further back in his financial obligations. He remonstrates with his prospective mistress that "the sum should remain outstanding so long as we still feel something for one another. It shall be the guardian of our virtue."[100] The steepest fine for a "simple insult" in Wilhelmine Germany was six hundred Marks and the dueling codes gave creditors the right to reject challenges from debtors who wished to pay back old IOUs with added interest.[101] It is no accident that the violation of one's "household honor" was regarded as an infringement commensurate with the breaking and entering of common burglary.[102] Clearly, the content of a sexual affront was unlawful theft or willful destruction of private property, and the allusions to "family honor" and "sexual honor" also proceeded from the male anxiety for his female possessions, which could be ineffaceably damaged or confiscated if vigilance were not exercised and a timely self-defense applied.

But because they were at bottom regarded as personal property, even women of easier virtue were jealously guarded by possessive bourgeois husbands and lovers, who, taking little pleasure themselves in the merchandise, were still determined to deprive another of its charms through assertion of their acquisitive urge, well-honed in the capitalist marketplace. The central action of Arthur Schnitzler's posthumous play Ritterlichkeit (Chivalry) pivots about the question of a woman's real worth as adjusted to the honor index. Karl, in a vain attempt to save his brother's life, envisages that disclosure of his sibling's lover's promiscuous past to the woman's husband will deflate the estimation in which he holds her—he who believes to be saving her spotless virtue through a duel. In a moment of frustration, Karl fulminates: "I see a person who wants to kill someone, who loathes another because he stole from him a string of pearls; and I will tell him that they are not pearls, that they are gravel . . . no, filthy dirt. . . ." His friend parries: "He will then reply to you: 'But the thief still thought this ornament was pearls, and that's why I will kill him.' "[103] The bourgeois breadwinner had invested a great deal of surplus-labor value into his commodity, and the fear of expropriation of his means of reproduction found a suitable scapegoat in the empire's Social Democrats. Such was tacitly admitted in 1896 when the *Norddeutsche Allgemeine Zeitung* accused the Marxist party of being an opponent of dueling so as to "undermine the chastity of the woman and the weapon honor [*Waffenehre*] of the man."[104]

But even socialists, sworn enemies of the duel and self-proclaimed feminists, could be brought to bow before the dictates of the hoary chivalrous ethos: "The man who would rob me of you," swore the founder of German socialism Ferdinand Lassalle (1825–64) to his beloved Helene von Dönniges, "I would shoot straight through the heart."[105] In the most famous German duel of the half-century, a woman and a socialist were at the hub of the fracas. Typical of so many of these affairs was the man's breakneck turnabout in attitude as soon as the scandal became public; at which point, Lassalle's pathetic declarations of suffering in disconsolate letters to his suddenly coy mistress were transformed into scathing accusations against the "reproachable prostitute." Prostitute or not, a challenge was promptly rendered at fifteen paces by Helene's fiancé, a Rumanian aristocrat and former *Corpsstudent* named Ranko von Rakowicz, and the next morning the bilked labor leader took a fatal ball in the lower stomach from a man he had never met, for a woman he pretended to despise.[106]

The indirect assault on a man's honor through a woman was sure to generate such impersonal encounters whose purported raison d'être may have been an object of derision or even disinterest to the men involved. In this sense, a woman truly was *"impropre au duel,"* for any "insults" hurled her way streaked past to smite the "natural protector."[107] In Hermann Sudermann's play *Der Gute Ruf* (*The Good Reputation*, 1913), the *geheime Kommerzienrat* Weisegger, whose wife is suspected of being untrue, avers indifference to his spouse's fate: "What happens to my marriage internally is momentarily wholly irrelevant. First the good reputation of my house must be secured."[108] To cite Schnitzler one last time—an author preoccupied with the bankruptcy of the nineteenth-century masculine ideal—in the drama *Das Weite Land* (*The Vast Land*, 1911) the neglected wife demands an explanation from her inconstant and usually apathetic husband for the sudden duel he will fight on account of her affair with a youthful officer:

GENIA: What in the world are you thinking of? How do you permit
  yourself . . .

FRIEDRICH: Oh, don't worry. I won't hurt him much, probably not at all.

GENIA: But why? If you cherished me in the slightest . . . if it was hate . . .
  rage . . . jealousy . . . love . . .

FRIEDRICH: Yes, well, of all that I feel damn little. I just refuse to play
  the fool.[109]

Refusal to "play the fool" was the result of an assiduously nurtured
self-image among German *Ehrenmänner* of the cavalier who could re-
sent an insult through red-blooded force. A general characteristic of
this type of hero, often consumed by egotism and engrossed in himself, is an infinite disregard for the feelings of others, and a duel was
rarely an effort to save a woman's honor or rescue a marriage. It was
certainly never a valentine.

EFFI BRIEST AND CÉCILE

By the late nineteenth century, the tyranny of ingrained peer group
expectations may have been the critical factor in convincing many to
duel who themselves had not been wholly successful at internalizing
the chivalrous creed. The dread of social humiliation always eclipsed
the fear of eternity. In two novels, *Effi Briest* (1896) and *Cécile* (1887),
Theodor Fontane (1819–98) illustrated to limpid effect the significant
bearing that such pressures, and accompanying male self-perceptions,
had on a husband's impulse to duel.

Effi Briest is the more renowned work. Thomas Mann clustered this
novel in a triumvirate with *Madame Bovary* (1857) and *Anna Karenina*
(1877) for its cogent psycho-social depiction of a woman crushed by
her environment. The story is easily told: The *"Naturkind"* Effi is married at the tender age of seventeen to an ambitious civil servant twenty
years her senior, Geert von Instetten, "bearer of all the manly virtues"
and, as Effi judges, "a man of principle, and I . . . I have none." The
names have allegorical significance: Geert is a word for stem and Effi
sounds like *Efeu*, meaning "ivy": ergo, Geert the stem and Effi the ivy
entwining herself upward about him, expressive of the allegedly dependent nature of women, of their clinging vine quality.[110] The match
is the perfect Wilhelmine union of sexual polarities: *"Weiber weiblich,
Männer männlich"* ("Women womanly, men manly") as Effi's father
dotes on saying. Bored and lonely in her staid, loveless marriage, in
her role as mistress of a doll's house, Effi falls to the persistent ad-

vances of Major Crampas, a friend of Instetten's, and enjoys a brief dalliance with him that is interrupted by her husband's promotion and transfer to Berlin, where Effi settles to the routine of a Frau *Ministerialrat*. Six years later, while Effi is away at a spa, Instetten discovers old love letters from Crampas, whom he challenges to a duel. The old friends are reacquainted at ten paces and Crampas dies. Instetten divorces Effi and retains their only child. Effi dies in disgrace a few years later, saying, "I would like to have my old name again on my gravestone; I did the other no honor." Her husband is condemned to a life of miserable regret.[111]

The duel for Effi's honor is not the immediate result of her fleeting indiscretion. Rather, it is the direct consequence of her husband's dire faux pas when he betrays the disagreeable secret of his wife's peccadillo. Before issuing a challenge, Instetten mulls over his dilemma with a man in whom he places absolute confidence, the *Geheimrat* Wüllersdorf. The offense to Instetten's honor is over half a dozen years old, and he voices the notion that a "statute of limitations" (*Verjährungstheorie*) might now be in effect that would beset a recrudescence of the affair. Wüllersdorf admits, "I must frankly confess, it appears to me that the question hinges here." He then asks Instetten: "Do you feel so injured, insulted, outraged, that it's either him or you? Is that how it is?" Instetten replies that he feels no trace of hatred or thirst for revenge, still loves his wife, and "despite myself, feel inclined toward forgiveness in the last corner of my heart." Wüllersdorf poses the reader's obvious question: "Then why all the fuss?" Instetten tells him why:

> Decide for yourself, Wüllersdorf. It is now ten o'clock. Six hours ago at the outset, I'll grant you I still had a free hand, there was still a way out. But not any more, now I am in a cul-de-sac. If you like, I'm the guilty one; I should have had more self-control, been more guarded, shut everything up inside of me and struggled it all out in my own heart. But it hit me too suddenly, too powerfully, and so I can hardly reproach myself for not having kept my nerve better. I called and left a note for you, and from that moment on the matter was out of my hands. From that moment on my unhappiness, and what is worse, the spot on my honor, had an accessory, and after the first words that we exchanged here it now has an accomplice. And because this accomplice exists, I cannot turn back.

Wüllersdorf assures Instetten that his confidence rests with him "as in a grave," but Instetten is adamant, prognosticating that even his good friend would eventually learn to despise him as "an object of your pity" (*ein Gegenstand Ihrer Teilnahme*) and that this is simply too much to bear. To have confided in one was confiding in one too many. Wüllersdorf is compelled to agree and in doleful resignation utters, "Our cult of honor is a form of idolatry, but we must submit to it so long as the idol holds sway."[112]

As in *Effi Briest*, the crucial factor in *Cécile* that brings the insulted husband to issue a challenge is the knowledge that his indirect humiliation—through his wife—has a witness. While vacationing in Saxony's Harz Mountains, Herr von Leslie-Gordon, former engineer in the Prussian army, meets the fetching Cécile and her retired officer husband, the distinguished von St. Arnaud. Gordon is immediately taken with Cécile, and she with him. After several months of friendship, he realizes that his attraction is of a deeper nature than at first suspected. In view of his feelings, both deem it wise to part, but after the separation Gordon spies Cécile one evening in Berlin at the opera chatting animatedly with a possible rival. Stabbed with jealousy, he storms into their balcony, later follows Cécile home, and is rewarded for his audacity the next day with a challenge from the furious St. Arnaud, a gentleman who has already destroyed a man in a duel on account of Cécile's extraordinary charms.

The morning after the opera box incident, at breakfast, St. Arnaud interrogates his wife: "What's all this about Gordon?" Cécile replies: "Nothing." St. Arnaud mentions the "eternal letters" of Gordon addressed to her, but when Cécile pointedly asks if he should care to read them, he pooh-poohs their significance. What concerns him is the fact that a third party had witnessed the affair of the night before:

> Nonsense. I know love letters; the best ones—those one never receives, and what remains is so good as nothing. And incidentally, his asservations and regrets are a matter of complete indifference to me, but not his manner in front of witnesses, not his behavior in the presence of others. He insulted you. I learned from the principal what happened; Hedemeyer told me about it yesterday in the club, and I just want confirmation from your own lips. I can overlook the loge matter, but to follow you back here: Outrageous! As if he had to play the avenger of your honor.

Cécile has little to say, especially since her husband's plans are clear. St. Arnaud rails against the brazen home-wrecking (*Hausfriedensbruch*) of Gordon and pronounces gravely: "Thus exists an insult that affects not only you but above all *me*. And I have not learned to tolerantly accept affronteries." Later anthropologists have described how "the essence of an affront is that another should dare to affront one,"[113] and, as Nietzsche pointed out, "Being moral means being highly accessible to fear."[114] Immorality in German society was a reproach against disobedience; it was not the deed itself—namely adultery—but one's lack of fear of reprisal for the deed that was the hateful thing, the source of resentment. And if morality was the equivalent of fearfulness, honor meant the power to inspire it:

> He was injured in his most sensitive if not only sensitive spot, in his pride. The amorous adventure as such did not awaken his resentment against Gordon, but rather the thought that the fear of *him*, the man of determination, was insufficient deterrence. To be feared, to intimidate, to make felt at any moment the superiority that courage gives, that was his true passion. And this nondescript Gordon, this former Prussian sapper-lieutenant, this cable layer and international wire-stringer, *he* had believed he could put his little game past him. The presumer.

In an antagonistic letter conferring the challenge, St. Arnaud reemphasizes his objection not to the content of Gordon's affront—his erotic intentions—but to its "how," the form it took before onlookers. That was the "unforgiveable sin." He adds: "Frau von St. Arnaud gave herself into your protection when she unqualifiedly disclosed her heart to you, and to deny a woman this protection is unchivalrous and *dishonorable*." Gordon falls in the ensuing duel. St. Arnaud's final judgment on him is that he "disregarded the social divisions that we on this side of the water still for the time being have." In a postscript, St. Arnaud writes Cécile that she should try not to take the matter so hard, for "the world is no hothouse for over-sensitive feelings."[115] At least not for wives. Their husbands afforded themselves this luxury.

There is nothing in the world that is not what it is merely by contrast. The sixth chapter looks at dueling in Third Republic France. As Germany's chief cultural and political rival after 1870, and with Paris as Europe's fin de siècle dueling capital, it would be idle to slight Marianne—and certainly no way to treat a lady.

28. "Duel in the Bois de Boulogne." Wood engraving by G. Durand, 1874. (Bildarchiv Preussischer Kulturbesitz, Berlin)

And Death Shall Have No Dominion

The Frenchman fights as he drinks, as he eats, as he sleeps,
as he accomplishes all the ordinary functions of life.
—Alfred d'Almbert, *Physiologie du duel* (1853)[1]

THE DUEL was like oxygen to nineteenth-century Frenchmen because of their persistent efforts to achieve a *juste milieu* between the glories of the ancien régime and the French Revolutionary bequest. The result of this unlikely fusion of privilege and democracy was retention of the aristocratic duel—for everybody. While dueling and populism were mutually exclusive in Germany, in France they cohabitated the same conceptual plane on relatively peaceable terms. Of course, French workers as a general rule were not duelists, but the French socialist icon Jean Jaurès once traded shots with nationalist Paul Déroulède. The mind refuses to function over the idea of the Social Democrat August Bebel ever having a duel with, say, the Minister of War General Heinrich von Gossler, with whom Bebel had so many verbal battles in the Reichstag. The former would have considered it beneath his dignity and inconsonant with his political principles, while the latter, one time responding to a direct put-down from Bebel, declared himself to be "completely impervious to such insults as are uttered against me from the social democratic side."[2] It took a certain M. Peyramont of Paris to issue labor leader Bebel a challenge in 1893.[3] Equal before the muzzle of a pistol or the glinting stainless of a filigreed épée, all Frenchmen were potential gentlemen. "Ah! Whatever is to be said against the duel," effused Nougarede de Fayet, "there is something about it which uplifts the soul of the citizen."[4] The German duel did not uplift the soul of the citizen; it exalted the prerogatives of the ruling class.

The French Revolution may have succeeded in formally abolishing highborn privilege and overthrowing the feudal order, but the duel refused to budge. This was the case partly because of the fervor with which dueling was taken up in bourgeois circles just before and immediately following the popular uprising of 1789. The right to duel, previously a sole privilege of French society's upper crust, was construed as an integral aspect of personal liberty by an ambitious middle class avid to assimilate the coveted habits of their betters. Thus revolutionary tribunals were hesitant to prosecute the activity.[5] There were feeble legislative attempts to discourage both Third Estate neophytes and Second Estate veterans, but they all failed. In 1791 the proposal to include a seven-article anti-dueling ordinance in the new penal code was rejected by the relevant authorities as impolitic and superfluous. The duel was no longer an exclusive possession of the old nobility, they contended, and the articles covering homicide were sufficient legal retaliation for anyone slain in a duel. Going a step further, on 17 September 1792 (five weeks after the "second French revolution," when the Parisian crowd sacked the Tuileries royal palace, driving the king from the throne), in a decree of the National Assembly, all those cases pending against duelists since the storming of the Bastille in July of 1789 were waived.[6] The legislature thus amnestied the past and gave a blank check to the future. Because a number of duelists since 1789 were themselves members of the Assembly, this last act came as no surprise.[7]

Under Napoleon (1799–1814), the dueling delict stayed submerged in the general law against murder and assault,[8] and early-nineteenth-century courts tended to excuse killer duelists on the very rationale that there existed no specific and definitive legislation forbidding the duel. Through the Restoration (1814–30) and the July Monarchy (1830–48) it became accepted practice to prosecute only those duels in which a fatality had been engendered through a breach of the established rules (e.g., Chatauvillard's *Essai sur le duel*, 1836) governing the combat. But still, courts were loath to convict.[9] During France's Second Empire (1852–70), the report of an 1859 governmental commission headed by the legal savant Valette held the duel to be an exonerable if not excusable offense, and concluded by recommending a "moderate repression," which imprecise guideline informed the erratic course of French jurisprudence thereafter.[10] In the Third Republic (1870–1940), an 1882 commission charged with revision of the *code pénal Vaudois* inserted a disposition that condemned the idea of the duel but conceded its legitimacy in select cases.[11] By 1890, one French dueling buff was able to state confidently that "when the duel takes place under conditions of irreproachable fairness, even though it should have a fatal issue, adversaries and witnesses escape most of the time unharmed from the tribunal."[12] Unlike in Germany, where dueling was regarded as a mark of civilized self-control, French jurisprudence tended to treat the duel as a "crime" of passion, and by the 1890s dueling rates had soared to between four and five hundred per year.[13] Third Republic France was a dueling-abolitionist's nightmare.

In 1908, the leader of the international Anti-Dueling League, the Infante of Spain Don Alfonso de Bourbon, lamented the fact that of all the European countries in which the duel still clung to life, France had put up by far the stiffest resistance to his movement. Its internal state of affairs had, in fact, "crippled the undertaking."[14]

Because of its miniscule rate of fatality, Don Alfonso also referred to French combat as a "comedy-duel."[15] As one is able to imbed the German duel in Wilhelmine society's authoritarian structure by investigating its lethality, so also can the peculiarly republican style of dueling in *belle époque* France emerge by posing the heuristic question as to its harmlessness. The French duel's dearth of tragedy owed to five dominant factors: the nature of French law, the choice of weaponry, the published dueling protocols, the prevalence of dueling among journalists and politicians, and the ascendant role enjoyed by the French bourgeoisie.

In liberal French law, because dueling itself was not a special crime, the fatal result of a duel was not accorded special penal treatment but rather became eligible for prosecution under the general articles defining homicide. Assuming they even made the police blotter, German duelists theoretically had a great deal less to fear from a court of law, receiving the bearable minimal sentence of two years (and often a pardon to boot) in many if not most fatal outcomes. Although these distinctions are obscured somewhat by the fact that both nations were hesitant to prosecute their duelists to the full extent of their respective laws, nominal legal guidelines must have had some effect in predisposing German and French duelists to carry out their affairs with varying degrees of malice. The freedom to master a situation oneself, foregoing all legal rights in the name of independent action, this was consummately suited to the fierce and jealously guarded individualism of the French republican. The French state's laissez-faire policy regarding the duel enabled such freedom, while simultaneously delimiting its tragic abuses—what might elsewhere be termed its logical issue.

The trihedral épée, or light sword, also seldom failed in its dual task of redeeming honor and sparing life. It boasted a long aristocratic tradition dating to the days of Valois kings when thousands of French nobles were skewered by straight blades. It was an inherently testing weapon. In Third Republic France, however, a reciprocal prudence between often well-trained combatants usually assured that a nick on the arm would satisfy honor. For this reason protective gauntlets were frequently discarded to ensure a brisk end to épée duels in which sharp, deft points played about opposing wrists. Duels were a dime a dozen in France because this custom was so widespread, making them hardly battles *à outrance*. Gustave Flaubert lampooned this tradition in *L'Education Sentimentale* (1869): Just before a duel is to commence, one of the swordsmen conks out from fright, scratching his thumb as he falls. When he is revived the "duel" is declared over and the wounded's arm commended to a sling.[16] In another sardonic piece, the humorist Grosculade designated a bloody nose incurred in the course of a match *"comme une satisfaction suffisante."*[17] The Italian composer Amilcare Ponchielli could not resist some low comedy in his opera *Marion de Lorme* (1885), based on a play by Victor Hugo, in which a French sword duel ends with one of the parties simulating death and thereafter skipping through society incognito.[18] It is no coincidence that Maupassant's panicky "coward" (*Un Lâche*), terrified of dying, commits suicide before a pistol duel. Bouts with épées usually guaranteed a long and healthy life, although the iodine in all those little cuts must have been quite painful.

The épée enjoyed most favored weapon status not only due to its utility in avoiding debilitating wounds but also because of the lilting grace it imparted to melodramatic showdowns. In the hand of an experienced duelist it was more elegant than the saber and less terminal than bullets. And épée duels were technicolor productions. Flashy flourishes and athletic vigor were practically authorized. In his *Essai*, Chatauvillard wrote that "stooping, stretching, springing to the right, to the left, and forward, and to vault about your adversary, are all within the rules of combat."[19] Flynn *would* have been in. At a Parisian duel between rival Italian fencing masters in 1904, the reporter for *L'Illustration* flew into a transport over "the vigor and elasticity of their muscles, the temper of their blades, the *maestria* and *furia* of their swordplay, their extraordinary endurance" in a feature-length bout of almost three hours and not a droplet of blood.[20] At these duels anything could happen, except a finishing stroke. In 1901, in another épéecurean epic, the critical point of interest was the ensemble of one of the combatants, who, gussied-up in a long fur-lined coat of Persian lamb and sporting a wide-brimmed black sombrero, "was hardly lacking in panache." His attitude was equally praiseworthy, evoking "a certain romantic allure, slightly theatrical perhaps, but *au fond*, not displeasing to many of us Latins, which is after all what we are."[21] In illustrations of the period, seconds look like jaded impresarios forced to watch the scenery get chewed up by third-rate actors. Duelists dabbed on greasepaint, not warpaint.

In 1890 the London *Times* forecast that "a special photographic apparatus will no doubt be added to the next special correspondent, and the newspaper press will have the means of criticising duels just as it criticises artistic, musical, or dramatic entertainment."[22] This prediction was realized in an 1896 report of a pistol duel between the Prince de Sagan and M. Abel Hermant, accompanied by a large black-and-white photo of the combat:

> One is able to confirm that the bearing of the combatants under fire was excellent: M. Hermant, a slender silhouette, frail, of a youthful virility; the Prince, strong broad shoulders, spryness thrown into relief by the silver head of hair and set off by the moustache, but his prestige as sovereign arbiter of elegance slightly spoiled by soiled linen and by the large spectacles in place of the legendary monocle. At 11:05 four balls were exchanged without result. Honor was satisfied.[23]

Honor was satisfied? That was one name for it. Even *au pistolet*, the duel exemplified the French aptitude for seizing the picturesqueness of things.

The épée, however, was unqualifiedly the glamour weapon of the French nation, and the gentlemanly art of fencing proved an irresistible discipline to men of wide and diverse stamp. One author even ascribed the Hungarian passion for swordplay to the 1849 wave of expatriate Magyars who flooded back to Budapest after the *Ausgleich* and amnesty of 1867, and who during their exile in Paris had acquired a taste for steel (if not exactly for the épée) and brought it home with them. A fencing hall in Budapest at the turn of the century claimed to have hosted some one thousand duels in the course of a single year; the term "duel" in this instance surely being used very loosely, which would figure when one considers the Hungarian combat's place of origin.[24] By the 1880s the passion for *l'escrime* in France had reached similar epidemic proportions, and fencing clubs began springing up throughout the country.[25] One contemporary asserted that "every young fellow who pretends to be stylish . . . must pass an hour or two every day in the fencing-rooms under the orders of his trainer."[26] But though stylish, in the fencing clubs "class diversity was the general rule," and trainers known as masters-at-arms (by 1890, there were one hundred in Paris alone) were "invariably of lower-class origins," which did not however prevent them from becoming significant public figures. According to Robert Nye, "The social integration, character formation, and refinement that were believed to take place in the *salles d'armes* were linked directly to the republican and democratic ideology that was sweeping simultaneously through France."[27] Fencing was also thought "a healthy activity that makes a supple and strong physique, imparting courage, resolution, and confidence in oneself." One famous octogenarian fencer swore by *l'escrime* for keeping him fit, and had the custom of training hard for thirty minutes every day.

At his funeral he wanted an épée placed in his casket, acclaiming, "Fencing is my last mistress and she always has smiles for me." The *salles d'armes*, flourishing in the Latin Quarter, could rival the boudoirs of any of its clientele's luxury-loving mistresses. They were posh clubs replete with amenities. One hall, belonging to a M. Lacoze, was decorated throughout in a Japanese motif, with parasols, divans, and armor from the land of the Samurai to induce blue-chip performances.[28]

In French fencing the emphasis was not exactly on standing your ground and taking your licks. One outstanding practitioner of the time was described in rhapsodic terms that evoked Nijinsky rather than Dempsey:

> His technique is composed of dexterity, softness, and elegance; his limbs are of infinite suppleness; it is impossible to see whether his feet are touching the ground. . . . [O]ne imagines that he is fencing with Balbiani, the ballet-master, if it were not for the fact that one feels a rude point, and at the end of the arm a devil of a sword that feints, retreats, advances, presses you and almost always ends up, while deceiving yours, in striking you full in the chest. . . . [E]verything is executed with such skill, a grace so elegant, so chic, if you will, sustained by a technique so sure and so excellent that one ends up by admiring: *cela est joli*.[29]

A great deal of classical ballet, in fact, was and is directly related to this tu-tued style of swordsmanship. Guy de Maupassant, in his novel *Bel-Ami* (1885), limned a *pas de deux* in which the requisite standards of beauty are met: "They feinted and recovered with an elastic grace, with a measured vigor, with part sureness of strength, part sobriety of gesture, part impeccable demeanor, part moderation of technique that surprised and charmed the novice crowd."[30] In the early nineteenth century, Madame de Staël submitted that the Germans dueled less than the French owing to the fact that her countrymen were more "*vive*."[31] That was not just one woman's opinion. In point of fact, D'Artagnan and Cyrano, not Old Heidelberg, were the French duelist's inspiration. A Gallic observer of German student fencing in 1893 concluded his article by saying that he had found the combats regimented and impersonal; implying that Germans' wits were as dull as their bladework, fencing "not like men, but like machines."[32] Another French journalist in 1910 compared the insensate *Mensur* with English boxing and Spanish bullfighting, disliking the clumsy protective padding, "inconceivable to our national spirit, in love with the spontaneous duel, elegant and risking all."[33]

Au contraire. "Risking all" was not the premise upon which most French rencontres were based. Epée duels habitually ceased at the

sight of blood, and while pistol duels were theoretically more dangerous, in French practice they were as safe if not safer than swords. Precisely opposite to Germany, in France the pistol was resorted to when
little was at stake, as a cautionary measure. How could this be? The
bets were off and the fix was on. A common French method of doctor-
ing the pistol duel was to use balls made out of quicksilver, which,
apart from a slightly silvery cast, had the same weight and resemblance of normal balls. When the fragile decoys were tamped down
into the barrel they would be automatically pulverized, and as the
guns were fired the mercury would fan out harmlessly and invisibly
into the air. These contrivances were expensive but were little marvels
of deception, leaving no perceptible trace of chicanery. A more meta-
phorical artifice was to use shrunken balls. These dinky beebees
would bounce along the inside of the barrel to be flung at random
through the atmosphere; even if the balls did inadvertently reach their
destination, they were too small and light to perforate the clothing of
the targeted duelist and would simply leave him with a baffling prick-
ling sensation. The only disadvantage to this trick was that the unsus-
pecting user could not assume the ready position with the barrel
pointing downward as was the custom preparatory to the command
to aim. In such a case the mini-ball would dribble apathetically out
onto the ground. In the third scheme, completely normal balls would
be used but the charge would be reduced. The "chargette" would de-
celerate the ball, which, though of regulation size, would be just as
ineffective against the sturdy material of linen shirtsleeves as the un-
dersized sort. Moreover, the shaved charge would impart a downward parabola to the sphere, which would usually fall short of its goal.
By contrast, an overcharge was counterproductive because such a ball
had the tendency to describe an upward trajectory. Hence, the unsus-
pecting duelist who had the intention of sparing his opponent by aiming at the ground just in front of him, was doing him no kindness.[34] But
if one had experienced and charitable seconds, a rendezvous with
gunpowder was rarely a *liaison dangereuse.*

It may have been to save their own skins that seconds concocted
damage-control encounters. As in Germany, seconds were responsible
for intercepting any stratagem that could possibly give one duelist an
unfair advantage over another. But in addition, French *témoins* were
also saddled with co-responsibility for deaths or injuries resulting
from irregularities of combat or any deviation from the codified
norms. In some circumstances they could be punished more severely
than the duelists themselves,[35] an item certain to take the blasé shrug
out of any boulevardier second's shoulders. Therefore, failing all other
intrigues, in pistol duels the two opponents would usually be placed

29. The 1904 Déroulède-Jaurès duel on the French-Spanish frontier. Not a contest for the agoraphobic. From "Le Duel Déroulède-Jaurès sur la Frontière Franco-Espagnole, le 6 Décembre," in *L'Illustration*, 10 December 1904. (Bildarchiv Preussischer Kultur-besitz, Berlin)

at such a wide, nay vast, interval from one another that there was very little chance, come its journey's end, of a wearied bullet finding a billet. All this, of course, assuming that shots were being fired in the general direction of an adversary. Mark Twain described the conditions of a duel at thirty-five paces between Léon Gambetta and former Minister of the Interior Marie-François de Fourtou in 1877:

> The police noticed that the public had massed themselves together on the right and left of the field: they therefore begged a delay, while they should put these poor people in a place of safety.
> The request was granted.
> The police having ordered the two multitudes to take positions behind the duelists, we were once more ready.[36]

French duels were not always exclusive functions—there was safety in numbers. At the turn of the century, *L'Illustration* noted: "The fashion of public duels has definitely established itself here, and it even seems that the more private the affair, the greater the publicity."[37] In a "secret" French duel between a conservative and a socialist parliamentary deputy in 1902, a crowd of 150 curious spectators crashed the

30. Parisian épée duel. From "Le Duel Pini-San Malato," in *L'Illustration*, 12 March 1904. (Bildarchiv Preussischer Kulturbesitz, Berlin)

strictly private gate.[38] The 1888 épée duel between General Georges Boulanger and Prime Minister Charles Floquet was a *fête champêtre* that took place behind a fashionable house, with young ladies serving cold drinks to journalists in the front garden.[39] The 1906 pistol duel between the Minister of War André and General de Négrier transpired in the garden of the Prince Joachim Murat's Paris mansion while waiters in white aprons tended the culinary needs of reporters waiting on the front sidewalk.[40] Ballyhooed matches between rival fencing masters were surefire box office, crowds of up to two hundred thrillseekers being not uncommon.[41] Mark Twain quipped that he "would rather be a hero of a French duel than a crowned and sceptered monarch."[42] At the end of bouts, if honor had been satisfied and nobody accidentally slaughtered, it was champagne wishes and caviar dreams, an elaborate celebratory breakfast of reconciliation normally taking place.[43] In an undoubted satire on the circus atmosphere that had grown up around the French duel in recent years, Guy de Teramond's "*Un Duel*" (1903) describes a droll fictional affair in which the men of honor are seconded by clowns and sword-swallowers.[44]

Unlike most German duels, which were furtive and surreptitious, French duels usually managed their way into the news chronicles. Fame, after all, was frequently the whole reason behind the commotion. The French duel was a well-orchestrated publicity stunt with every member of the cast hand-picked for his role. In Maupassant's

"*Un Lâche*," directly after the insult (a stare directed at a lady in an ice cream parlor) and the formal exchange of calling cards, the "coward" still possesses enough presence of mind to select his seconds on the basis of star power: "Whom would he choose? He sought out the most highly-regarded and celebrated men of his acquaintance. He was able finally to get the Marquis de la Tour and Colonel Bourden, a *grand seigneur* and a soldier, whose names would look good in the papers."[45] Even in those instances where there were no reporters on hand to immortalize the morning glories in the evening editions, there was the *procès-verbal*, or duel protocol, a form filled out by the four seconds prior to commencement and upon completion of the duel. It was, in fact, the duty of the seconds to publish in the papers a complete account of the combat and its attendant circumstances in the form of a *procès-verbal*, and it was a rare affair indeed that did not eventually make copy for all the world to read and appraise. The prolific duelist and journalist Henri Rochefort observed that the duel could be abolished straightaway in France "if there weren't always four gentleman available to draw up a duel-report, and fifty newspapers to print it. In ninety-one out of ninety-two cases, one duels for the gallery. Suppress the gallery and you exterminate the duel."[46]

Although there seems never to have been any proclivity among fervid men of honor to settle their highly personal disputes in court, in 1881 this reluctance was reinforced by the legislators. In that year a new press law was passed that redefined the slander and libel guidelines of its flinty Bonapartist forerunner, decreeing the softest of penalties for offenses. This new law triggered a rash of self-help duels, especially among the journalistic set whose stock-in-trade was a reputation for fearless reporting. It is no coincidence that "the boldest or most venomous journalists of the era were also the most frequent duelers."[47] Some of the more caustic Parisian newspapers, such as *Le Figaro* and *Le Gaulois*, set up private *salles d'armes* to keep their journalists in proper fighting trim.[48] Conditioning was vital. Sometimes panic would seize a mild-mannered reporter and he would have to make a run for it, as in one instance when the editor of *Evénement* took flight like Hektor, the pursuant Achilles right on his heels.[49] But the professional imperative to duel became more resounding than ever after 1881, and writer-journalist frays spattered the headlines.[50] Personal attacks in the press and the duel that would often result were delectable fare for a scandal-hungry public. Free-lancers catered to this demand by serving up their own histrionic bon-bons in the pages of the various dailies with pens mightier than their swords. Few reputations or careers could be enhanced through the death of an opponent, especially when attended by foul play or unchivalrous tactics. No public figure

31. A 1909 journalist duel in Paris's Parc des Princes velodrome in which only a single ball was discharged. The offending party in the original dispute—at far right, seen walking away—refused to return fire. This was unthinkable in Germany for two reasons. First, one always returned fire; and second, even had it been the case that a single shot were acceptable, it would then have had to be directed at the *offended* party, who needed to brave a bullet to give the duel any real meaning—namely, the proving of courage to belie an insult's implied aspersion on your manhood. From "Le Duel Bernstein-Chevasse," in *L'Illustration*, 30 October 1909. (Bildarchiv Preussischer Kulturbesitz, Berlin)

could afford such a risk. The journalist's goal was not to if necessary die so honor could live, but to live so as to better enjoy his honor: to get top billing and amass a following. In these duels, one way or another, you were never consigned to oblivion.

Perhaps legislators were disinclined to suppress dueling because it was a tool of their trade as well. Ever since the Revolution, French statesmen had resorted to swords and pistols for settling parliamentary debates and hashing out ideological differences, with the residual effect of promoting their own celebrity. Even Budapest, famous for its profusion of political duels at the fin de siècle, was only a "little Paris."[51] In the Third Republic, arguably the five preeminent politicos of the prewar era—Adolphe Thiers, Léon Gambetta, Paul Déroulède, Georges Clemenceau, and Jean Jaurès—all had their political records enhanced through duels. Georges Clemenceau, Mr. Third Republic, was credited with twenty-two of them; only one of his opponents was ever seriously injured.[52] For a politician, it was always safer to duel. Prime Minister Jules Ferry's (1882–85) final fall from political grace in 1887 owed to the public perception that he had chickened-out of a duel proposed by General Georges Boulanger.[53] As opposed to Germany, where certain political allegiances obviated participation in duels (namely, those *Reichsfeinde*, the Catholic Center and the Social Democrats) and where dueling itself was a divisive issue, France witnessed incessant combats across party lines. This was the obvious reason (aside from the fact that the French duel was literally not hurting anyone) why the international Anti-Dueling League was unable to get a political toehold there. Whether Orleanist, Opportunist, Bonapartist,

Radical Republican, or Socialist, the duel was the *lingua franca* of heated political exchange and was at its most piquant during periodic government crises such as the Panama Scandal and the Dreyfus Affair. "Your hand on your heart," asked the writer Walsh rhetorically, "would you be in a position to assert that the Chamber of Deputies would not have restored pugilism if the duel, civilization's master of ceremonies, had not been there to keep order?"[54] The English *Daily News* noted in 1891 that the French custom of *au premier sang* was less a trial of courage than was "a stand-up fight with fists,"[55] and so slug-fests would probably not have been to the Chamber's taste faute de mieux. Dueling would abide. But a black horror of black eyes was, at least, one point of consensus among French and Germans.

No hands across the Vosges when it came to army dueling. First off, in addition to officers, enlisted men and noncoms were permitted to duel in the French service. Duelists came from all walks of French life by the time of the Third Republic, and so it is not surprising that every military rank should have been likewise endowed with the gift of honor. The German duel was just as consistent, demarcating lines of class within society and order of rank within the military. Second, France had no courts of honor to arbitrate strife among army personnel. The French officer therefore remained free of the caste-conscious notions of collective honor which the German tribunals helped breed in the standing and reserve officer corps. Every French soldier was responsible for the defense of his honor without regard for imperious judgments handed down from a panel of magisterial colleagues, and the absence of special councils and courts to oversee the behavior of officers and supervise their duels precluded elitist conceits from mixing with disputes of a personal and private nature. And, as might be guessed, the French army duel's slogan was not *pro patria mori*—more like la-dee-dah. Army issue swords were fixed with screw threads a few centimeters from the tip, where a small plate would be mounted to practice safe dueling. This preventitive was dreamed up during the Napoleonic era when duels would take place both with and without the gadget, but by the Third Republic its use had become standard.[56] Sabers were generally employed by cavalry officers, and then mostly with blunted points to preclude deep ingress.[57]

From the eighteenth century until about 1880, the army set the tone for dueling in France. The majority of the undersigned in Chatauvillard's 1836 *Essai sur le Duel* were high-ranking officers, and in Flaubert's *L'Education Sentimentale* set in the 1840s, he has a foursome of seconds consult the military authorities on how to conduct the upcoming duel with which they have been entrusted.[58] In the 1860s during the reign of Napoleon III one commentator wrote: "There is hardly a regiment in the garrison of Paris which has not its professed duellist, officer or private."[59] But by the 1880s, when the incidence of civilian duels increased, the army resigned its leadership role and its duel began to stagnate. In fact, it was often the case that civilians would wound military personnel in duels, raising an uncomfortable question whether the defenders of French soil were receiving adequate instruction in sidearms.[60] With the ignominious defeat in 1888 of the dashing General Boulanger by the nearsighted sexagenarian M. Floquet in an épée duel,[61] and the introduction of universal three-year conscription that next year, the middle class conclusively superseded the army as the duel's primary social pillar. The French army duel was never distinguished by its mortal quality, but the French bourgeoisie, led by its columnists and lawmakers, and letting its self-respect ride, placed special emphasis on the duel's more stylish components.

Writing at the turn of the century, the American satirist Ambrose Bierce may have been making quite conscious allusion to the French style of monomachy when he defined the "Duel, [noun]" as, "A formal ceremony preliminary to the reconciliation of two enemies. Great skill is necessary to its satisfactory observance; if awkwardly performed the most unexpected and deplorable consequences sometimes ensue. A long time ago a man lost his life in a duel."[62]

In 1883, Guy de Maupassant wrote "*Un Duel.*" It is set in the year 1871, directly following the final surrender of France in the Franco-Prussian War. A freshly demobilized (and physically unprepossessing) Frenchman is traveling on the train to Switzerland where his family had taken refuge just before the invasion. At one whistlestop, a strapping Prussian officer enters the Frenchman's compartment, which he is sharing with two Englishmen. After a period of relentless bullying by the Prussian, the Frenchman finally snaps and leaps upon his tormenter to give him a savage beating. The officer attempts to draw his saber in an *Ehrennotwehr* riposte, but is helpless in the face of the Frenchman's emotional ferocity. The Englishmen look on with curiosity. After it is over, the officer demands satisfaction. At the next station, symbolic Strassburg, they all disembark. The Prussian requisitions a pair of pistols, whose owners, two comrades, serve as seconds. The Englishmen second the unpracticed Frenchman, who, in the "on cue" duel at twenty paces, blows the Prussian to kingdom come. The Englishmen hurry their charge back to the train before it chugs from the platform, and then let rip with a "Hip, hip, hip, hooray!"[1]

If Maupassant intended this story to be an act of literary vengeance for the Franco-Prussian "duel" of 1870–71, its denouement was also an accurate forecast of how the next "affair" between the two countries would conclude. The French did not fare badly against the Germans in September of 1914. The nation-in-arms displayed superb valor in repulsing von Moltke's Paris-bound juggernaut. Thereafter, countless Frenchmen sacrificed life and limb in the war to end all wars, until Germany sued for peace in November 1918.

For all their rococo swordplay, our squeamish French ably defended their honor against the bloodthirsty Hun.

One should not surmise overmuch from a nation's duel.

It is nonetheless difficult to deny correlations between the Wilhelmine affair of honor and what happened in the Third Reich. When cold-blooded killing is the subject, it seems coy, and not a little cowardly, to sidestep the question of what light dueling might shed on the phenomenon of National Socialism.

From a study of the German duel it is apparent that leaders of the German nation manifested certain attitudes about love and justice, war and peace, life and death, and displayed a *mentalité* divergent from that of other Western nations. Recognition of this fact recalls that certain matter which has transfixed German historians ever since the Second World War—the *Sonderweg* (Separate Path) debate, to wit: Was there something peculiar about German history? And, if so, was this peculiarity a significant factor in the later victory of Hitler and his policies? The question, more precisely posed, is: In comparison to other countries of the period, did Germany's middle class suffer from a "deficit of bourgeoisness,"[2] a deficit that played a primary role in the emergence of the Nazis? It may seem highly irregular to bother with German history's "sins of omission." Ranke's legendary dictum for history-writing was, after all, "as it actually happened," not "as it actually did *not* happen."[3] However, asking what did not happen is a perfectly sound line of investigation into the solution of, shall we say, a mystery. On his way to unraveling the mystery of "Silver Blaze," Mr. Sherlock Holmes cites a key piece of evidence. Thick-headed Inspector Gregory of Scotland Yard asks:

> "Is there any point to which you wish to draw my attention?"
> "To the curious incident of the dog in the night-time."
> "The dog did nothing in the night-time."
> "That was the curious incident," remarked Sherlock Holmes.[4]

In her otherwise admirable book *Ehrenmänner: Das Duell in der bürgerlichen Gesellschaft*, Ute Frevert conflates what has been called the "feudalization" of the German bourgeoisie with what she judges to be an *embourgeoisement* of the aristocratic duel, two different things.[5] In its social conformations, cultural content, and political reverberations, the case to be made for the German duel as even remotely bourgeois is rather underwhelming. Descended from medieval chivalry, it was innately antithetical to classical liberalism[6] with its cultural commitment to rational moral law and social justice. It was inimical to civic virtue and a spirit of compromise, tolerance, gradualism, and peaceful coexistence. The duel praised power and glorified war. Its validity was funded on tradition, authority, and a kind of dogma about the preeminence of valor, that most "ennobling" of qualities. An expression of liberal individualism? The ethos of *Standesehre* defies this theory, since dueling's mainspring was rarely a genuinely free, voluntaristic impulse. An articulation of middle-class *Bildung*? As an aesthetic recipe for "self-perfection" (*Selbstvervollkommnung*) culminating in self-annihilation, dueling has a certain offbeat Romantic or German metaphysical logic; but even from this standpoint it leaves ample room for doubts. Frevert's idea is basically that had the duel for honor not existed in nineteenth-century Germany, it would have been necessary for the German bourgeoisie to invent it, so congruent was it with their *Bildung*-derived notions of "self-perfection" and so neatly did it tally with general bourgeois concepts of self-identity. Accordingly, had the aristocracy been off, say, shooting croquet under the Linden instead of trading potshots in Potsdam, that would have been just ducky with the bourgeoisie who, though perchance not shunning croquet, would have dueled just the same. This croquet example is perhaps silly, but no more so than the logical conclusion one must needs draw from Frevert's argument.[7]

Or, let us recall Thomas Mann's *Der Zauberberg*. The duel coming at the novel's end is the immanent and culminating dialectical clash between two opposed *Weltanschauungen* whose running battle has carried the story along for its duration. On the one side is Italian-born humanist Ludovico Settembrini, representing the western neo-classical heritage of Enlightenment. He exemplifies the nineteenth-century liberal-bourgeois values of rationality, science, meliorism, republicanism, the legal state, equal rights, and individual liberties. He believes in civilization. His adversary in the duel, Leo Naphta, is medieval to the core. Naphta's inspiration is the preindustrial, predemocratic world of the Middle Ages, with its hierarchy, authority, and order. He is made happy by the thought of a world filled with spontaneous sacrifice and devotional suffering—a world of primeval nobility that has not forgotten how to pray. He believes in the redemptive power of the extravagant and the irrational, in the supreme efficacy of horror and bloodshed in adjusting modernity's leveling, undifferentiated effects. He possesses a wild Nietzschean streak that strives less for self-perfection than for self-overcoming. In sum, he is a romantic nihilist with a crown of thorns, a cultural pessimist of the first order, symbolizing everything for which Settembrini's mainline occidental principles pretend nothing but an undisguised contempt.

In the period between Naphta's challenge and the forthcoming duel, Settembrini, that ideal bourgeois mind-set, expounds forcefully on the necessity of dueling, ending his little speech on a rhetorical note to which our ears have lately become well attuned: "Whoever is incapable of standing up for his ideals with his person, his arm, his blood, is not worthy of them, and it is above all important to remain a man in all things spiritual." The novel's main figure, Hans Castorp, who has been the pedagogical object of both Naphta's and Settembrini's efforts at conversion to their respective points of view throughout the book, and who will later function poetically as the duel's *Unparteiische*—Castorp hears Settembrini's speech, and reflects:

> Herr Settembrini's words were clear and logical, yet coming from him they sounded alien and unnatural. His thoughts were not his thoughts—indeed, it were as if he had not even hit upon the idea of the duel himself,

but had instead borrowed [*übernommen*] it from the little terrorist Naphta—; they were an expression of the extent of shared inner forces to which Herr Settembrini's lovely Reason had become a slave and tool.[8]

If anything, the notion that death in a duel was somehow beautiful, in the words of V. G. Kiernan, "has the accent of an infantile inability to peer beyond the momentary burst of applause into the long silence of nothingness. There was indeed, joined to strong group consciousness, a childlike something in the cult of honor peculiar to a class like an aristocracy, which never truly grows up."[9] By embracing the inner child, bourgeoisie empowered the puffed-up aristocrat they had always hungered to become, or at least be like. And, abstractly considered, dueling was the perfect vehicle, representing a centrifugal aristocratic style of lavish and ostentatious dissolution that had little in common with the centripetal bourgeois hallmark of scrupulous amassment.[10] There was a world of difference between throwing away your life and saving for a rainy day. Frevert imputes far too much idealism and clearheaded self-determination to a blood-and-guts business primarily beholden to the gusts of human passion and the pitiless demands of social cachet. The crude fact is that dueling in Germany was the product of a basically retrograde and negative worldview, having more in common with the shallow nihilism of Max Stirner's *culte de moi* (experiencing a revival in the 1890s) than with idealistic personality-building. Its motives were frequently dark, often frivolous. As it deadened bodies, it deadened souls, although you quickly get the idea that men of honor were never much in the soul department to begin with. Their relation to *Geist* was more than a little tenuous. Caressed by philosophical euphemism, however, dueling became, variously, the mending of the subject-object split, an act of immanent transcendence, the negation of the negation of the progress of the consciousness of freedom. But despite all the niceties, it was still killing, icy and deliberate. This detail, often lost on duelists, should not be lost on the historian whose employment is to pierce just this sort of sham labeling.

But not to load our argument immoderately: Let us suppose for a moment that certain deep-seated, highly idiosyncratic middle-class conceptions of personal autonomy and self-realization did, in fact, find their consummate vehicle in the German variety of duel. This would be a curious expression of neo-Humanism, but let us suppose. Labeling these attitudes "German" liberalism would then not so much beg the question of a German *Sonderweg* as finally answer it. While endeavoring to show the extent to which the German bourgeoisie willingly dueled and were masters of and not mastered by the practice,

Frevert has thoroughly demonstrated the extent to which the bourgeoisie was in fact *dominated* by preindustrial forms. This is the unintentional paradox of her thesis, and precisely the point about the *Sonderweg* idea: that the German middle class assimilated certain values of the nobility in such an effortless fashion as to effect a sociological *trompe l'oeil* in which these values, to the historical observer, appear to have been adapted and not *adopted*. Those doing the adapting were the aristocrats. In his discussion of the durability of precapitalist attitudes and phenomena in nineteenth- and early-twentieth-century Europe, Arno J. Mayer notes that

> the old elites excelled at selectively ingesting, adapting, and assimilating new ideas and practices without seriously endangering their traditional status, temperament, and outlook. . . . This prudential and circumscribed adjustment was facilitated by the bourgeoisie's rage for co-optation and ennoblement. Whereas the nobility was skilled at adaptation, the bourgeoisie excelled at emulation. Throughout the nineteenth and early twentieth centuries the *grands bourgeois* kept denying themselves by imitating and appropriating the ways of the nobility in the hope of climbing into it.[11]

If such can be said of France and England—where Mayer acknowledges the political backseat occupied by those nations' nobilities—how much more true in the case of Junker-run Germany and its castebound duel.[12]

The turn to pistols in the nineteenth century certainly suited the untrained German *Bürger*, but it was the patrician officer corps that championed the changeover from swords. The one undeniably nonliberal, nonbourgeois institution in Germany—the army—was the duel's chief procurator. It was under the moral and political sway of the aristocratic officer corps that the bourgeois sector of the German Empire experienced a "social militarization."[13] And the other bourgeois dueling socializer *par excellence*, the university clubs, never made any secret of their desire to copy the army cult of honor in all its facets save weaponry, and that of course came later. The officer was the measure of all things. "In general those may be considered gentlemen," declared a dueling code written for civilians, "who, be it through birth, through self-acquired social position, or as a result of completed studies, raises himself above the level of the common honorable man and by dint of one of the aforementioned can be treated as an equal with the officer."[14] Moreover, the "standards of the officer corps were basically the standards of the nobility tightly focussed and made more explicit."[15] The idea of the duel's *embourgeoisement* and the consequences for a modification of the *Sonderweg* theory cannot be squared with the role of the army in perpetuating dueling in a country where, in the apt words of one Reichstag deputy in 1914, "it is not the honorable citizen that is the manifold, practicable life ideal for the middle class of the German people, but rather the dashing Herr 'von' with the upturned moustache."[16] How bourgeois could a convention be whose leading pillar regarded civilians as the "inner enemy"?[17] We have seen how the worst dueling offenders—reserve officers, students, and former students—were held spellbound by the honorific conceptions of the officer, and how, after 1897, when officers cut back on dueling, so also did civil society in general—and this certainly not because of any stricter enforcement of the law, or greater respect for it.

When not under the immediate tutelage of aristocratic conceptions of honor, however, regular officers of regular lineage seemed indifferent to dueling. The overwhelmingly bourgeois naval officer corps recorded only ten duels between 1870–1895, a small fraction of the army total.[18] Close shipboard quarters must have provided numerous occasions for strife among mariners that, in the army, would have obliged an instantaneous duel. Wilhelm II was repeatedly at pains to impress upon his bourgeois gentlemen the importance of energy and resoluteness in settling matters of honor,[19] which was diametrically opposite to his handling of the army after 1897. That was also the year of the First Naval Bill, when the fleet's growing stature and celebrity should have impelled sea officers to assert their collective honor at least as pushily as army counterparts who were saddled with an explicit restraining order.

"In all Germany," wrote Friedrich Meinecke, "one can detect something new around 1890 not only politically but also spiritually."[20] In 1890, cultural criticism such as Julius Langbehn's *Rembrandt als Erzieher* (*Rembrandt as Teacher*), born of ennui and disgust with the emptiness of modern life, sought "to condemn intellectualism and science, to denounce modern culture, to praise the 'free' individual and the true German aristocrat, to revive the German past."[21] It was during this decade that Nietzsche's high-keyed, amoral philosophy of aristocratic radicalism first gained converts, trumpeting the virtues of bravery and suffering, and vindicating remorseless instinct. It was a time when the poet Stefan George circulated through his verse "a philosophy of courage, austere, noble, anti-democratic, and somewhat perverse."[22] In music, particularly that of Richard Strauss (among his alluringly epic titles: *Death and Transfiguration*—1890, *Also Sprach Zarathustra*—1896, *Don Quixote*—1898, and the self-aggrandizing *A Hero's Life*—1899), Germany experienced "a hothouse lasciviousness which betrayed the first signs of morbidity in bourgeois culture."[23] An "undercurrent of morbidity" also existed in German theatre, where its tragedies by such playwrights as Wedekind and Hauptmann "were not so much curative, like Ibsen's, nor compassionate, like Chekov's, but obsessively focused on mankind's cruelty to man, on his bent toward self-destruction and on death. Death by murder, suicide, or some more esoteric form resolved nearly all German drama of the nineties and early 1900s."[24] While Oscar Wilde was busy plumping art for art's sake, the bourgeois Pan-German League was established in 1890 to spread the inspired gospel of war for war's sake. Wilhelmine Germany wanted to make war, not love. It was not the prototype for a kinder, gentler society, but rather a world of natural selection and class struggle in which one had to be strong because there was no pity to waste on the weak. What was "new around 1890" was not really new at all: Hobbesian anthropology was simply making an electrifying comeback.

One of its guises was neo-chivalry. Writing in 1896, one enthusiast was so caught up in the joy of battle that he forgot the code of honor:

> Now to the duel itself! Installation of the combatants, seconds, umpire, doctor, rules, and everywhere the code! My fellow students! I will repeat myself yet again, when two people want to fight with lethal weapons, then it should also be serious—life or death, and on such occasions forms are ludicrous! Away with doctor, seconds, or any sort of code! When two are resolved to risk their lives against one another, one leaves them alone to settle the matter, without any kind of hindrance.—It will be more savage and brutal than customary, and a bloodless and easy engagement is out of the question—but what harm is done? At least it is bloodily serious and the purpose of such a battle (the purpose that gives it its sense) is fulfilled: either the offender is killed (then atonement is achieved) or the offended (then he has fallen in defense of his "honor," what for a sensitive man must always be preferable to letting fly with a pair of inconsequential bullets).—If they want to duel, then let them do it under natural conditions, then let them make it serious and not act out a comedy that only now and then will perchance emerge a tragedy![25]

As Arno Mayer reminds us, "This cult of war was an elite, not a plebeian affair":

> Between 1890 and 1914 social Darwinist and Nietzschean formulas permeated the upper reaches of polity and society. Because of their antidemocratic, elitist, and combative inflection they were ideally suited to help the refractory elements of the ruling and governing classes raise up and intellectualize their deep-seated and ever watchful illiberalism. They provided the ideational ingredients for the transformation of unreflective traditionalism into a conscious and deliberate aristocratic reaction.[26]

Along with the Zeitgeist, the character of the German middle classes also changed. In one of the several recent studies on German middle-class formation sponsored by the historian Jürgen Kocka, he delineates three phases in the development of nineteenth-century *Bürgertum* which can be borrowed as an interpretive model to posit a special "aristocratic" style of duel among this class in the decades immediately preceding the Great War. The first phase, briefly noted, stretched from the late eighteenth to the mid-nineteenth century and encompassed the emergence of the so-called *Bildungsbürgertum*, which acquired learning at the *Gymnasium* and the university to achieve a degree of social equality with aristocrats.

The second phase extended from the rise of industrial capitalism in the middle part of the century to the advent of the *Wirtschaftsbürgertum*, or economic bourgeoisie (1840s to the 1870s). The *Bildung* component in the bourgeoisie now became diluted and emerged less as an "ideology of attack" enabling assimilation with the aristocracy, than as an "exclusionary mechanism" to screen off the proletariat and the petty bourgeoisie.[27] Priorities shifted and an inner restructuring of the bourgeoisie took place. Instead of continuing to challenge the nobility and identify itself in opposition to it, the upper-middle class made its peace with these traditional elites and turned volte-face to engage a new rival from below, the Fourth Estate of urban workers. This threat not only helped consolidate disparate elements within the upper bourgeoisie but created a relative community of interest between middle class and nobility, a budding marriage engaged in the 1860s with the flood of upper-middle-class men into the traditionally aristocratic officer corps and the newly created reserve forces, and later consecrated by the conservative nationalism of iron and rye and *Weltpolitik*.[28] It was during the 1860s and early 1870s that the liberal influence was at its height in Germany, but from the mid-1870s with the promulgation of the anti-Catholic *Kulturkampf* and the anti-socialist laws, a general "deliberalization"[29] of public and political life took place, thus making this second phase both a culmination and a watershed of Germany's bourgeois epoch.

In the third phase from the 1880s until the First World War, *Bildung* faded yet further as a defining tenet of upper bourgeois identity and the *Bildungsbürgertum* correspondingly faltered as a social and political force. Through it all, particularly in Prussia where dueling was most firmly entrenched, the nobility maintained its undisputed grip on power and in tests of strength generally saw its own interests prevail. It should be recalled that even those fundamentally middle-class planks of universal manhood suffrage, parliamentary representation and constitutionalism, had been granted and secured from *above*. In the final decades of the *Kaiserreich*, therefore, the lopsided social alliance of *Geburtsadel* and *Bürgertum* was cemented not only through the latter's buying up of noble estates, through systematic intermarriage and ennoblement,[30] but through armed defense of their personal honor under the aristocratic banner of *Standesehre*. While impatient bourgeoisie paced back and forth in an upper-middle-class "'antechamber to the nobility,'" they meanwhile simulated "a society of rank among themselves. . . . with such officious titles as *Kommerzienrat, Justizrat, Baurat, Medizinalrat*, and *Regierungsrat*—first and second grade."[31] All this was symptomatic of a flight into preliberal traditions in which *Bildung* proved to be a "self-important, petty, demanding right of exclusivity."[32] What was taking place—to use Hans-Ulrich Wehler's term—was an "aristocratization" of the upper middle class:

> From this time on, the neo-humanistic idea of *Bildung* was rapidly watered-down, incalculably so; it degenerated into diplomas from the *Gymnasium* and the university or state exams that were a mark of legitimacy expedient to one's career, into the right to bear titles in order to be taken up into "good society." Therewith went a fatal weakening of the humanistic, civilizing impulse that had once distinguished the original neo-Humanism. . . . Under the new conditions, extreme nationalism and the radical Right found their point of entry, illiberalism was rampant, xenophobia grew. . . . New emerging ideologies such as social-Darwinism offered a pseudo-scientific legitimation of the right of the strongest nation, of the right of the socially strongest that clearly embodied the consequences of the selection of the "fittest."[33]

Here one can clearly see the ahistoricist pitfalls of such chronologically wide-ranging studies as Frevert's, extending from the late eighteenth to the early twentieth century, that treat large spans of time as thematically cohesive chunks. Wolfram Siemann warns against falling prey to the temptation of attributing the social predicament of the late-Wilhelmian bourgeoisie to the relatively liberal period of the 1860s and 1870s in discussion of the *Sonderweg*.[34] We should beware of the reverse tendency.

In the pathbreaking *The Peculiarities of German History* (1984),[35] which helped to kindle the aforementioned work of Kocka, Wehler, and intellectually related German historians, David Blackbourn attempts to correct the crooked German road. Attributing "a strong sense of honour and duty" to the German bourgeoisie, he then contends that this "had little to do with any aristocratic model," alluding to a certain South German *Ehrenschutzverein* (Society for the Protection of Honor) "which explicitly rejected duelling as part of its code of honour." He concludes therefrom that, "There is little need to invoke the theory of feudalization."[36] In one of his more recent efforts, in which figures a piece by Ute Frevert on dueling, Blackbourn revises his opinion, saying that Ute Frevert "shows that those German bourgeois who engaged in duels were not simply imitating aristocratic norms; the meaning of the duel for middle-class Germans was shaped by the place it occupied within a specifically bourgeois code of honour."[37] There seems here an unnatural willingness to promote the same supposition about the *Sonderweg* through contrary conclusions about the duel, what I believe is called heads I win, tails you lose.

Attempting to prove the *Feudalisierungstheorie*'s opposite is a tricky proposition when you have the duel as spoiler. Blackbourn makes a great deal of that "crucial sphere," that "necessary foundation of a fully bourgeois society"—the establishment of the "rule of law" within the framework of the *Rechtsstaat*. He cites the example of the Prussian Law Code of 1794, signaling "a major break with the corporate state," which, as we have seen in the context of honor and the duel, did not offer formal equality before the law by any stretch of the imagination. He adduces the example of the imperial penal code of 1871, which, if it "was based squarely on property rights," also gave tacit legitimacy to the inequitable code of honor through implicit recognition of the duel. He mentions the "legal accountability of the bureaucracy, finally achieved in Prussia in the 1870s," which, as concerned dueling, did not exist even in principle. Germany's university elite were duelists all, and alumni of student dueling societies serving in official state capacities were, by virtue of their continued allegiance to the *Comment*, placed on an illegal footing with respect to Article 129 of the penal code forbidding membership in a fraternity whose pursuits undermined state authority. The army and its duel was also a permanent and irritating thorn in the side of legal order. In all its various permutations, the cult of honor scorned the legal order while backing to the hilt the historic prevailing one. "Legal 'certainty,'"— what the constitution supposedly guaranteed—was a fiction when it came to the baroque duel, which gave the *Rechtsstaat* a smart cuff on the ear.[38]

Blackbourn would have us believe:

[T]he bourgeois assumption of a quasi-aristocratic lifestyle was something conscious, cultivated, purposely nurtured. Bourgeois country seats and hunting zeal should not be interpreted one-sidedly as proof of aristocratization, but also as a sign of bourgeois strength, as expression of a bourgeois feeling of self-worth: it was to show that one now was an important part of the social elite. This behavior speaks rather for bourgeois confidence than for bourgeois resignation.[39]

But then he also writes that the German bourgeoisie undertook a "silent revolution" in civil society. This consisted in, among other things, princely menageries giving way to public zoos, opera lovers displaying bourgeois propriety by saving up all their applause for the end of an act or performance, and noble breeches and stockings being cast off for frock coats and trousers.[40] Again, Blackbourn is trying to pull the fast one of heads I win, tails you lose: bourgeois assumption of prevailing aristocratic styles as a sign of growing bourgeois confidence and social influence, and bourgeois trendsetting as a mark of growing bourgeois confidence and social influence.

Surely the point is *these men dueled*—and not because they were overbrimming with bourgeois high spirits (although granted they shot each other in bourgeois pants). The code of honor—bounding a middle class whose definitive essence was *Satisfaktionsfähigkeit*—implied a fundamental acceptance of a feudal ethos in matters of ultimate importance, and not where one ogled baboons or whether the lyric stage crowd suffered a collective case of premature congratulation. The bourgeoisie realized that in Wilhelmine society, sixteen noble quarters was nine-tenths of the law, and their dueling was a capitulation to the aristocratic game and its rules, an acknowledgment of aristocratic ascendancy. Daily social intercourse among the German upper middle class was regulated not by the law of the bourgeois *Rechtsstaat*, but by a chivalrous code that buttressed an autocratic system of government and reinforced a hierarchical world of basic social inequalities. Any ritual whose duly convicted acolytes were practically offered the keys to the city on a silver platter by the despotic throwback Wilhelm II—giving his name to the era—must a fortiori be approached with a great deal of suspicion. And, in fact, as Friedhelm Guttandin has shown in his book on the European duel's role in preserving the centralized monarchical state, the exercise of pardon in these cases was not only an expression of the monarch's sovereign status in relation to the law, but made "the *Ehrenmann* into the king's man, into his vassal" by making him dependent on the royal grace and putting him in the royal debt.[41] In *Rethinking German History: Nineteenth-Century Germany and the Origins of the Third Reich*, Richard Evans asserts that "nearly all the examples cited by Blackbourn in support of his thesis are open to one kind of objection or another," thus underlining their deductive nature, and then cites approvingly Blackbourn and Eley's own suggestion that "careful empirical research is needed before the real areas of difference [e.g., between Germany, France, and England] can be properly delineated."[42]

At the fin de siècle, while Germans perished with alarming regularity to preindustrial conceptions of manhood, the English and the French bourgeoisie perished the thought, having long outgrown their infatuation with this illiberal habit. The French gave feudalization the lie through a nonelitist, nonlethal bowdlerization that allows us in this instance, yes, to discuss the duel's *embourgeoisement*. Blackbourn stresses that in the bourgeois-aristocratic debate, "What matters is the terms on which this symbiosis of old and new took place."[43] Unlike the German bourgeoisie, the French did duel on their own terms—for fame, fortune, and fun, the privilege theoretically and practicably open to all those with any fencing savoir faire. Robert Nye has noted that in France,

> Fencing and the duel served to dramatize and symbolically represent the principal ideological components of republican ideology—individual liberty and equality—and therefore helped universalize and popularize the civic value system of the Third Republic. In principle, any man, no matter what his origins, could cultivate the art of fencing and engage in duels because the new regime recognized all men as free agents responsible for their actions. On the other hand, fencing and the duel helped promote equality because no man could refuse to cross swords with a legitimate opponent at the risk of personal shame and public ridicule. A world that recognized, at least in theory, no social boundaries in an activity once reserved for a narrow elite was a male social universe of perfect individualism and equality. Male societies governed by honor codes have always possessed this egalitarian potential.[44]

Unfortunately in Germany where *Standesehre* reigned supreme, this potential was never tapped. The duel as an institution never yielded new social meanings *à la française*.

By the 1840s, real dueling in France was a spent bullet. In 1844, the duel was abolished in Britain altogether.[45] In Germany, however, it was during this very period that dueling gained a new lease on life— through Friedrich Wilhelm IV's army decree of 1843 (effectively negating his reformist father's attempt to constitute an inward honor of conscience) and the exploitable Prussian Code of 1851—and that bourgeois inhibitions atrophied. As its neighbors were withdrawing, German duelists were just gathering momentum. Whether or not what I, with my inordinate gift for the obvious, hold to be self-evident is true—that a "deficit of bourgeoisness" was responsible—the German story does indeed stand out as "peculiar." Maybe no one is really disputing this, but its fact needs to be reemphasized among all the recent attempts to modify it, and therefore it is *this* study which should be considered that "much-needed corrective"[46] from the perspective of dueling. While some historians have seemingly dedicated their entire careers to driving nails into the coffin of the *Sonderweg* "myth," it is my modest wish to prize out just a few of these nails with a little conceptual hammer of my own in the hope that those fashionable rumors of the *Sonderweg*'s demise may be seen as greatly exaggerated.

If we slant the question of *Sonderweg* in the manner of Ralf Dahrendorf, "Why is it that so few in Germany embraced the principle of liberal democracy?" the duel may assist us in answering it. This is a less daunting formulation than "How was the Holocaust possible?" or even "How was National Socialism possible?" though it may intimate replies to each. Considering Dahrendorf's four social bases for liberal democracy, we see that in no way did the duel help to create "equal citizenship rights." Conflicts were obviously not "regulated rationally." Men of honor did not represent an elite that reflected "the color and diversity of social interests." And because of the highly private and exclusive nature of honorific sensibility, "public virtues" were decidedly not "the predominant value orientation."[47] Dahrendorf's own sociological treatise explains German shortcomings in these four areas, but one need look no further than the duel as an index attesting to these failures. Indeed, the duel in Imperial Germany was not only a major impediment to the development of a strong bourgeois social identity, but it was also a significant barrier to German success in the democratic sphere. One speaks of "the democratic functions of dueling in post-unitary Italy,"[48] and in democratic France, innocuous dueling was a normalized solution to private discord entirely compatible with the bourgeois state, thus not really "dueling" at all, as such is by historical definition an illegal activity (see chapter I, "Origins"). But in Germany, where dueling was both criminal and deadly, a code of honor permitted the aristocratized elite to place itself *above* the law. This situation would spawn highly regrettable political consequences when German officers and doctors, judges and lawyers, civil servants and other high state functionaries whose reactionary tempers had been molded during the duel's prewar heyday and in student dueling societies, remained in place after the revolution of 1918–19 to flout the statutes of the despised Weimar Republic, thus facilitating the Nazi conquest of power in 1933. As German President Richard von Weizsäcker reminded his country in the autumn of 1992, during the rash of radical Rightist violence against foreigners: "We must never forget why the first German republic failed. It was not because there were too many Nazis too early, but because for too long there were too few democrats."[49]

National Socialist thinkers, according to Robert Koehl, "quite consciously tried to model the New Order along feudal lines."[50] And they were largely inspired by the quixotic conception of the knight. Witness Hubert Lanzinger's famous painting depicting Adolf Hitler decked in the raiment of Lohengrin, astride a black steed, a swastika-covered banner clutched in his mailed fist.[51] A generation after the duel's decline the chivalrous ethos still served as a defining tenet of German identity, exercising a profound influence over the Nazi imagination. It is highly questionable whether such attitudinizing could have been so vividly revived across the millenial stream of time had not the Wilhelmine duel functioned as stepping-stone. The dueling codes of the last quarter century before the Great War repeatedly stressed that it was proper observance of the courtly, aristocratic rules that alone made an encounter "chivalrous." After all, "he who disregards the chivalrous practices is not a gentleman."[52] Dueling manuals portrayed the ritual as a latter-day joust and men of honor as coeval Galahads. The cover of Gustav Hergsell's *Duell-Codex* (1891) was adorned with a genuflecting knight resplendent in armor, trusty sword in hand, receiving a laurel wreath from a comely maid, while in the background two beplumed champions broke lances from the backs of spirited chargers.[53] In discussions of the duel, *ritterlich* was employed as a modifier to describe everything from one's "chivalrous responsibility" and "chivalrous duty" to one's "chivalrous conduct," "chivalrous thinking," and "chivalrous feelings." Great attention was paid to fighting a duel "in a chivalrous manner," according to "the rules of chivalry" and the "chivalrous ethos," all so as to acquire "chivalrous satisfaction." The man of honor's worldview, at least in the context of dueling, was defined "from the standpoint of chivalry."[54] In 1912, to celebrate the centennial of the Krupp armaments, Kaiser Wilhelm, Chancellor von Bethmann-Hollweg and his cabinet, the general staff, and the navy's admirals all appeared at the Krupp's Villa Hügel for a staged medieval tournament of mounted knights.[55] Mark Girouard, in his study of the revival of chivalry in nineteenth-century England, posits the existence of a yet more powerful cult of neo-chivalry in Germany before the First World War.[56] The German duel, particularly for a woman's honor, bears this out.

Whatever one conceives National Socialism to be, its quintessence was the SS.[57] By decree of its leader Heinrich Himmler (1900–1945), every SS man had "the right and duty to defend his honor by force of arms," and in a letter to the SS Legal Service in 1938 he outlined the conventional Wilhelmine guidelines for doing so.[58] What is more, Himmler patterned his own cult of honor, like that of his Wilhelmine

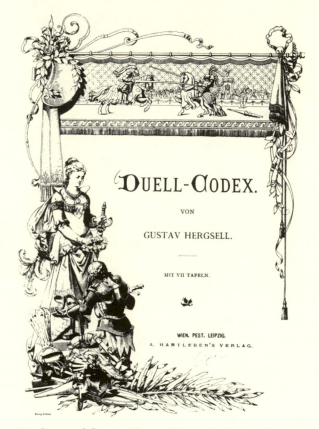

32. Cover of Gustav Hergsell's *Duell-Codex* (Vienna, Pest, Leipzig, 1891). (Bayerische Staatsbibliothek, Munich)

predecessors, on medieval archetypes. He modeled his "new knighthood," his "sworn liege men," on the "brutalized chivalry" of the Teutonic Knights, conquerors of the barbarous East in the fourteenth century.[59] The *Reichsführer-SS*, "who lived as much in the past as in the present," desired that special prestige "comparable to that of the medieval order of chivalry" be attached to his Order of the Death's Head, and so he festooned it with oaths and rites of a bygone era.[60] He held court at the castle of Wewelsburg, near the Teutoburger forest in western Germany, typifying "what Camelot had been to King Arthur and the Knights of the Round Table, Monsalvat to Perceval and the Knights of the Holy Grail, a mystical seat hidden from the gaze of the uninitiated, the towered sanctum of the higher orders of SS chivalry."[61] Wewelsburg was equipped with a vast dining hall where stood an oaken Round Table about which clustered, like Arthur's dozen bravest knights, Himmler's twelve most distinguished *Obergruppenführer*. Beneath the dining hall dwelled a stone crypt dubbed "the realm of the dead," in the middle of which was a well where the arms of slain *Obergruppenführer* would be consumed by ritual fire.[62] "Never forget," Himmler once reminded an assembly of SS chieftains, "we are a knightly order."[63]

As history has sadly shown, Himmler's obsession with castles and knights was not the play-acting of an elaborate costume drama. He wished to reanimate a Dark Age embodying true Germanness, a racial sense of which informed his execution squads as they parceled out death in wholesale lots. The combination of this eugenic chivalry, the Black Order's "terrific cult of manliness," its "heroic code of morals," and its elite claims as "Germany's New Aristocracy," indicate an unwholesome bequest.[64] SS formations wore belt buckles bearing the slogan "My Honor is Loyalty" as they put their unpleasant brand of honor into effect with a calculated murderousness and efficiency reminiscent of an elite that had likewise "sought the heroic victory over the self as the victory over all moral and religious scruples."[65] Wilhelmine *Ehrenmänner*, through open confrontation with the obscene and horrible, and unconcerned with legal justice or moral repercussions, were guided by a similar desire to prove nothing beyond their disdain for death. According to Hans Buchheim, this ethos could spawn certain disagreeable outgrowths:

> If a man believes that any cause is justified provided the war is a good one, if he is concerned not with what he is fighting for but only with how he fights, he is conditioned to heroic action in a criminal cause. Although such an heroic fighter imagines that he must rely on himself alone, the whole basis of his existence is in fact so unstable that he can be swept up into the service of an organization claiming totalitarian authority—and he will perceive that this has happened not at all or too late.[66]

It is true that whereas duelists met on a level killing field, victims of the SS had little choice in the matter. But given the cruel concatenation of events over time, it is not unimaginable that disdain for death might materialize as a disregard for life, that dueling's social, ethnic, and other prejudices could reduce to biological ones, and that its idealistic veneer would finally peel away to expose the reckless plunge into morbid pseudo-heroics. In tandem with certain systemic deficiencies in the German nation-state, the duelist psychology—owing infinitely more to the spirit of Potsdam than to that of Weimar—could have ripened into something like tragic malignancy and lent itself to the tidy and unruffled execution of National Socialism's extremer measures, or, in Ralf Dahrendorf's blunter language, "turned doctors and judges and officers into murderers."[67]

But let he who is without sin cast the first stone. As Heinrich Himmler knew, and once said, "It is the curse of greatness that it must step over dead bodies."[68]

Abbreviations Used in Notes

BHSA	Bayerisches Hauptstaatsarchiv, Munich
DKJ	*Das Kleine Journal*
GLA	Generallandesarchiv, Karlsruhe
GSA	Geheimes Staatsarchiv, Berlin
HSA	Hauptstaatsarchiv, Stuttgart
SPdH	Stenographische Protokolle des Herrenhauses
SPdR	Stenographische Protokolle des Reichstags

Notes

Introduction

1. Timothy Mitchell, *Blood Sport: A Social History of Spanish Bullfighting* (Philadelphia, 1991), XIV.

2. Inazo Nitobe, *Bushido: The Warrior's Code* (Santa Clarita, Calif.: 1979), no pagination for page of quote.

3. Robert A. Nye, *Masculinity and Male Codes of Honor in Modern France* (Oxford, 1993), 11–12.

4. See *SPdR*, 72d Session, 20 April 1896, 1811; and Theodor Fontane, *Effi Briest: mit Materialien* (Stuttgart, 1984), chapter 29: 250. *Das Kleine Journal* was my time tunnel to the duel, although I had a most difficult time tracking it down, and when I finally uncovered it in the East Berlin *Staatsbibliothek*, the East German secret police put a *Spitzel*, an informer, on my tail in order to discover what I found so intriguing about this obscure little gazette I was spending two months going back and forth across the border every day to read and surrender twenty-five robust Deutschmarks for twenty-five miserable Ostmarks every time in the process too. In other words, they thought I must have had an ulterior motive; they could not believe this thing was so important to me. But it was. In brief, *Das Kleine Journal* was to all appearances a politically neutral paper that specialized in local Berlin news and entertainment such as sporting events and theater, and reported with great relish episodes of violent death, like suicides, murders, accidents, and duels. It gave very detailed and factual accounts of the duels. The paper was reputable and survived into the Weimar Republic. Although its audience would probably have been very wide-ranging, I do not imagine that the kind of people who were doing most of the dueling were reading it (i.e., that it was in this sense the "official organ of the duelists," August Bebel's words not mine), except for maybe second lieutenants who wanted the racing form. Unafraid of alienating its readership, *DKJ*'s (our footnote abbreviation) dueling accounts were notably uninhibited and often indiscreet, so one got all the attendant facts of a case, relevant or not. The slander and libel laws in Germany were very tough, a fact which probably kept the otherwise freewheeling reporting honest. I frequently cross-referenced *DKJ*'s dueling articles with available juridical records, and I found its journalism to be quite reliable. I cannot recall who published it. I will have to look that up some day—as I will also have to someday petition to read my *Stasi* file.

5. Lionel Trilling, *The Liberal Imagination* (New York, 1978), "The Sense of the Past": 175.

6. Fritz Stern, *The Politics of Cultural Despair: A Study in the Rise of Germanic Ideology* (Berkeley, 1961), XXVII.

7. Albert von Boguslawski, *Die Ehre und das Duell* (Berlin, 1896), IV.

8. From Arthur Schnitzler, "Der Sekundant," in *Traumnovelle und andere Erzählungen: Das erzählerische Werk*, vol. 6 (Frankfurt am Main, 1961), 254.

9. Blaise Pascal, *Pensées* (1670), section VI, no. 358.

Chapter I

1. Sir Thomas Malory, *Le Morte d'Arthur*, prose rendition by Keith Barnes (New York, 1962), "The Tournament at Surluse": 287.

2. See *SPdR*, 61st Session, 12 May 1912, 1942, according to Mertin; and *SPdR*, 20th Session, 15 January 1906, 569.

3. Albert von Boguslawski, *Die Ehre und das Duell* (Berlin, 1896), 3.

4. See Pierre Lacaze, *En Garde: Du duel à l'escrime* (Paris, 1991), 12.

5. Ibid., 13.

6. V. G. Kiernan, *The Duel in European History: Honour and Reign of the Aristocracy* (Oxford, 1988), 37.

7. See Egon Eis, *Duell* (Munich, 1971), 251.

8. See Robert Baldick, *The Duel* (Great Britain, 1965), 12–13.

9. See Eis, *Duell*, 251.

10. Henry Charles Lea, *The Duel and the Oath* (Philadelphia, 1974), 177.

11. Ibid.

12. See Lea, *Oath*, 177; Eis, *Duell*, 252; and Baldick, *Duel*, 14.

13. See J. G. Millingen, *The History of Duelling*, vol. 1 (London, 1841), 31–32.

14. From Lacaze, *En Garde*, 17.

15. See Baldick, *Duel*, 17.

16. See Eis, *Duell*, 254.

17. Lea, *Oath*, 8.

18. See von Boguslawski, *Die Ehre*, 17, 21.

19. See Baldick, *Duel*, 17.

20. Carl von Rüts, *Die Duellgegnerschaft* (Berlin, 1903), 11.

21. Conrad Thümmel, *Der gerichtliche Zweikampf und das heutige Duell* (Hamburg, 1887), 134.

22. Von Boguslawski, *Die Ehre*, 30.

23. See Major Ben C. Truman, *The Field of Honor: Being a Complete and Comprehensive History of Duelling in all Countries* (New York, 1884), 11.

24. This battle resulted from the murder of the dog's aristocratic master. Sole witness to the episode had been the dog, whose outraged testimony manifested itself in repeated attacks on one Chevalier Maquer. Upon the king's command, the Chevalier was buried up to his waist in the soil of the isle of Notre Dame with only a shield and a stick by which to defend himself against the plaintiff. The dog was pulled from Maquer's throat only after he confessed the crime, and his neck was yet further abused when later strangled at the gibbet. For this account, see Baldick, *Duel*, 20–21.

25. See Dieter Prokowsky, *Die Geschichte der Duellbekämpfung* (Bonn, 1965), 23–27. Prokowsky also points out that any causal relationship ascribed to the cessation of the German medieval *Fehderecht* (the right to private warfare be-

tween vassal lords) in Emperor Maximilian II's decree of 1495, and the onset of dueling in Germany late in the sixteenth century, is, in view of the time span separating the two events, improbable (p. 29).

26. Joachim Bumke, *The Concept of Knighthood in the Middle Ages*, trans. W.T.H. and Erika Jackson (New York, 1982), 78.

27. See Raymond Rudorff, *Knights and the Age of Chivalry* (New York, 1974), 109.

28. See Friedhelm Guttandin, *Das Paradoxe Schicksal der Ehre: Zum Wandel der adligen Ehre und zur Bedeutung von Duell und Ehre für den monarchischen Zentralstaat* (Berlin, 1993), 93–106.

29. See Richard Barber, *The Knight and Chivalry* (New York, 1970), 165, 168; and Leon Gautier, *Chivalry*, ed. Jacques Levron, trans. D. C. Dunning (London, 1965), 268–69.

30. Barber, *The Knight and Chivalry*, 173–77.

31. See Prokowsky, *Duellbekämpfung*, 1–2.

32. See François Billacois, *Le Duel dans la société française des XVIe–XVIIe siècles: Essais de psychosociologie historique* (Paris, 1986), 83–94, for a slightly different interpretation of this incident but the author nevertheless recognizes its significance as a watershed.

33. See Lacaze, *En Garde*, 38.

34. Ibid.

35. See Eis, *Duell*, 257; von Boguslawski, *Die Ehre*, 34; and Dr. Adolph Kohut, *Das Buch berühmter Duelle* (Berlin, 1888), 27.

36. See Henner Huhle and Helma Brunck, *500 Jahre Fechtmeister in Deutschland: Ältester privilegierter Berufsstand* (Frankfurt am Main, 1987), 56; and Prokowsky, *Duellbekämpfung*, 22. Charles once challenged Francis to a duel, who rejected it for reasons of his own.

37. Dr. Georg von Below, *Das Duell und der germanische Ehrbegriff* (Kassel, 1896), 32, 40; and id., *Das Duell in Deutschland: Geschichte und Gegenwart* (Kassel, 1896), 11.

38. See Eis, *Duell*, 258; Kohut, *Das Buch*, 23; and Lacaze, *En Garde*, 23–25.

39. See Huhle and Brunck, *500 Jahre Fechtmeister*, 54–55.

40. Ibid., 46–50, 58; and Lacaze, *En Garde*, 28.

41. See Eis, *Duell*, 254–55.

42. From Millingen, *The History of Duelling*, 311–12.

43. See Karl Demeter, *Das Deutsche Offizierkorps in Gesellschaft und Staat, 1650–1945* (Frankfurt am Main, 1962), 113.

44. Ibid., 114–15.

45. Guttandin, *Paradoxe Schicksal*, 352.

46. *DKJ*, no. 242, 9 April 1895.

47. See von Boguslawski, *Die Ehre*, 41.

48. See Demeter, *Deutsche Offizierkorps*, 117.

49. *SPdR*, 61st Session, 13 May 1912, 1941, Heyn of the German Liberal People's Party (*Deutsche freisinnige Volkspartei*) quoting from Friedrich Wilhelm's decree.

50. Lorenzo Sabine, *Notes on Duels and Duelling* (Boston, 1855), 14.

51. See von Boguslawski, *Die Ehre*, 43.

52. See von Below, *Germanische Ehrbegriff*, 30.

53. See Demeter, *Deutsche Offizierkorps*, 117–18.

54. See von Boguslawski, *Die Ehre*, 44–45.

55. See Prokowsky, *Duellbekämpfung*, 124–25.

56. See von Boguslawski, *Die Ehre*, 56.

57. See Ute Frevert, "Bürgerlichkeit und Ehre: Zur Geschichte des Duells in England und Deutschland," in *Bürgertum im 19. Jahrhundert: Deutschland im europäischen Vergleich*, vol. 3, ed. Jürgen Kocka (Munich, 1988), 114; id., "Die Ehre der Bürger im Spiegel ihrer Duelle: Ansichten des 19. Jahrhunderts," in *Historische Zeitschrift* 249 (1989): 549–50, 564; and id., *Ehrenmänner: Das Duell in der bürgerlichen Gesellschaft* (Munich, 1991), 65–88.

58. See Prokowsky, *Duellbekämpfung*, 130–34; and also Frevert, *Ehrenmänner*, 71 ff., for the rather particular case of Bavaria.

59. See Breslauer [Rechtsanwalt], *Duellstrafen: Materialien gesammelt von Breslauer* (Berlin, 1890).

60. See Millingen, *The History of Duelling*, 32.

61. *SPdR*, 41st Session, 15 February 1896, 1009.

62. For a comparison of European penal codes addressing the crime of dueling, see Breslauer, *Duellstrafen*, up to the year 1890; and see Carl Rohte, *Das Zweikampfdelikt in den geltenden Strafgesetzen der Staaten Europas* (Leipzig, 1908) to take into account the last two decades before the First World War.

63. As cited in Dr. M. Liepmann, *Duell und Ehre* (Berlin, 1904), 33.

64. *SPdR*, 140th Session, 11 February 1902, 4127, according to Dr. Nieberding of the Social Democrats.

65. See *SPdR*, 138th Session, 8 February 1902, 4070, for the story as told by Bassermann of the National Liberals.

66. Alan Bullock, *Hitler: A Study in Tyranny* (New York, 1971), 64.

67. See *SPdR*, 126th Session, 17 November 1896, 3305, according to August Bebel.

68. See *SPdR*, 138th Session, 2 February 1902, 4059, according to Schrader of the Liberal Union (*Freisinnige Vereinigung*).

69. *SPdR*, 278th Session, 9 March 1903, 1897.

70. *DKJ*, no. 31, 31 January 1892; and *DKJ*, no. 192, 15 July 1892.

71. *GSA*, Rep. 84a 8035 (23 May 1885).

72. *SPdR*, 10th Session, 13 December 1886, 187, according to Dr. Rosshirt, affiliation not denoted.

73. See the *Pall Mall Gazette*, 12 March 1890, in *A Complete Bibliography of Fencing and Duelling*, ed. Carl Thimm (London, 1896), 442.

74. *SPdR*, 61st Session, 13 May 1912, 1925.

73. In 1891, an expatriate German named Richard Goerdler, safely ensconced as a professor of music at the Pennington Seminary in New Jersey, took the unprecedented step of issuing a challenge to Wilhelm II: "If the Emperor kills me I will die shouting 'The German Republic for ever;' and if I die, my death will be a signal for an uprising of the German people in favour

of free government such as the world has rarely witnessed." From the *New York Herald*, 2 June 1891, in *A Complete Bibliography*, 474–77.

76. See Albert von Öthalom, *Ehre und Ehrenschutz* (Vienna, Leipzig, 1908), 105.

77. See Rudolf Graf Czernin, *Die Duellfrage* (Vienna, 1904), 45.

78. From Rohte, *Das Zweikampfdelikt*, 3–6. Most European penal codes also failed to offer precise dueling definitions.

79. *DKJ*, no. 33, 3 February 1895.

80. *GSA*, Rep. 84a 8036, no. 286 (March 1885).

81. Jürgen Kocka, "Bürgertum und Bürgerlichkeit als Probleme der deutschen Geschichte vom späten 18. zum frühen 20. Jahrhundert," in *Bürger und Bürgerlichkeit im 19. Jahrhundert*, ed. Jürgen Kocka (Göttingen, 1987), 53.

82. *SPdR*, 10th Session, 13 December 1886, 186.

83. Hildegard Baronin Spitzemberg, from her diary dated 9 April 1894, in *Am Hof der Hohenzollern*, ed. Rudolf Vierhaus (n.p., 1965), 165.

84. The sole exception were the debates carried on throughout the year 1896, which excited a greater public and governmental awareness of the dueling problem and helped produce Wilhelm II's cabinet order of 1 January 1897 discouraging dueling among his army officers. See chapter III.

85. *SPdR*, 127th Session, 19 November 1896, 3339–40, Dr. Conrad.

86. *SPdR*, 138th Session, 8 February 1902, 4030, Dr. Esche.

87. *SPdR*, 20th Session, 15 January 1906, 565, Herr Träger.

88. *SPdR*, 278th Session, 9 March 1903, 8496.

89. *GSA*, Rep. 84a 8037, "Erlass Num. 78, Allgemeine Verfügung vom 16. November 1897,—betreffend die strafrechtliche Behandlung der Duellvergehen und der Beleidigungen."

90. For discussion of these and related themes, see Stadthagen of the SPD's statements in *SPdR*, 138th Session, 8 March 1902, 4705; Dr. Herzfeld of the SPD's statements in *SPdR*, 140th Session, 11 March 1902, 4104; and Lebedour of the SPD's statements in *SPdR*, 61st Session, 13 May 1912, 1926–27.

91. "The rather mild punishment for slander contained in the law was made weaker still by the exemption from punishment of any statement made in parliament, judicial tribunals, or, by implication, administrative councils. A public official, in other words, could not be legally construed to have slandered a colleague, no matter how personal the nature of the affront. . . . Worse, even if a judgment was brought against the *fact* of the slander, the slander itself was not refuted; a man was obliged to drag it around with him thereafter like a ball and chain." See Robert A. Nye, *Masculinity and Male Codes of Honor in Modern France* (Oxford, 1993), 175–76.

92. See *GSA*, Rep. 84a 8037 (ca. 1912), "Anträge der Deutschen Anti-Duell-Liga betr. Änderungen des Strafgesetzbuchs, der Gerichtsverfassung und der Strafprozessordnung zwecks Bekämpfung des Duellwesens."

93. Gustav Ristow, *Ehrenkodex* (Vienna, 1909), XXIV.

94. From Comte de Chatauvillard, *Duell-Codex*, translated from the French with notations by C.v.L. (Karlsruhe, 1888; originally published in 1864), "Vorwort des Übersetzers."

95. *SPdR*, 20th Session, 15 January 1906, 551–52, according to the Ministry of War.

96. *GSA*, Rep. 84a 8037, "Denkschrift zu dem Reichsjustizamt, Nr. 2023" (3 April 1914).

97. See *SPdR*, 235th Session, 13 March 1914, 8067, as summarized by Gröber of the Center Party.

98. In late-nineteenth-century Germany, duelists usually went before a *Schwurgericht*, a court composed of professional and lay judges. See Anthony E. Simpson, "Dandelions on the Field of Honor: Dueling, the Middle Classes, and the Law in Nineteenth-Century England," in *Criminal Justice History* 9 (1988): 121–25; and Gabriel Letainturier-Fradin, *Le Duel à travers les Ages, Histoire et Législation, Duels Célèbres—Code du Duel* (Nice, 1890), 74–75.

99. See, for example, August Bebel's statement in *SPdR*, 20th Session, 15 January 1906, 561.

100. *SPdR*, 72d Session, 20 April 1896, 1808.

101. See, for example, *SPdR*, 241st Session, 26 March 1914, 8258, according to Stadthagen of the Social Democrats.

102. For two of those incidents, see *SPdR*, 73d Session, 4 April 1896, 1824–25, according to Gröber of the Center Party; and *SPdR*, 241st Session, 26 March 1914, 8264, according to Liesching of the People's Party.

103. *SPdR*, 73d Session, 21 April 1896, 1818.

104. As cited in *GSA*, Rep. 84a 8040, 10th Session, 170 (8 May 1907).

105. *SPdR*, 235th Session, 3 March 1914, 8089, according to Wendel of the SPD.

106. Alexander von Oettingen, *Zur Duellfrage* (Dorpat, 1889), 82.

107. The article was entitled "A Fourth at Skat," 24 October 1893, and also encompassed criticism of Philip Eulenberg, a court favorite of the Kaiser. It attacked the anti-Bismarckian clique that had ensconced itself in the political division of the Foreign Ministry after the Iron Chancellor's ouster in 1890. See Gordon Craig, *Germany, 1866–1945* (New York, 1978), 234.

108. *DKJ*, no. 345, 2 October 1894.

109. See Gordon Craig, *From Bismarck to Adenauer: Aspects of German Statecraft* (New York, 1965).

110. Frances Gies, *The Knight in History* (New York, 1984), 4; and Bumke, *Knighthood*, 155.

111. Von Oettingen, *Zur Duellfrage*, 71.

112. Von einem Praktiker, *Unser Ehren- und Waffen-Comment* (Thorn, 1893), 11.

113. See *SPdR*, 72d Session, 20 April 1896, 1808, according to August Bebel; and *SPdR*, 73d Session, 21 April 1896, 1815–17, according to Graf Bernstorff.

114. See Arno J. Mayer, *The Persistence of the Old Regime: Europe to the Great War* (New York, 1981), 158.

115. The upper middle class about this time, according to Jürgen Kocka, was composed of 3 to 4 percent of the gainfully employed population. Adding students, officers, landed aristocracy, and miscellaneous others, August Bebel's estimate of 5 percent of the German (male) population being *satisfaktionsfähig* would appear accurate. Contemporary estimates usually are.

For discussion of these and related themes, see Jürgen Kocka, "Bürgertum und bürgerliche Gesellschaft im 19. Jahrhundert: Europäische Entwicklungen und deutsche Eigenarten," in *Bürgertum im 19. Jahrhundert: Deutschland im europäischen Vergleich*, vol. 1, ed. Jürgen Kocka (Munich, 1988); and also id., "Bürgertum und Bürgerlichkeit als Probleme der deutschen Geschichte vom späten 18. zum frühen 20. Jahrhundert," in *Bürger und Bürgerlichkeit im 19. Jahrhundert*, ed. Jürgen Kocka (Göttingen, 1987).

116. Dr. Emil Dangelmaier, *Der Kampf um die Ehre* (Vienna, Leipzig, 1896), 6.

117. Goethe, in 1768, in a sword duel with a fellow Leipzig student, who injured him on the arm. See Peter Krause, *"O du alte schöne Burschenherrlichkeit": Die Studenten und ihr Brauchtum* (Graz, Vienna, Cologne, 1979), 137. Heine, in 1841, at pistols, "with Salomon Strauss from the Jewish gutter of Frankfurt"—in Heine's words. Heine was grazed on the hip. See Kohut, *Das Buch*, 69–77, for an account.

118. *DKJ*, no. 105, 16 September 1896.

119. See *SPdR*, 72d Session, 20 April 1896, 1802, as cited by Bachem of the Center. Kaiser Wilhelm was kept apprised of the affair throughout its development and was notified by telegraph of the duel's final issue by Schrader's opponent's second. See *DKJ*, no. 100, 11 April 1896.

120. Heinrich von Treitschke, *Aufsätze, Reden und Briefe*, vol. 1, ed. Dr. Karl Martin Schiller (Meersburg, 1929), 752.

121. The first to eventually stop clapping and sit down was the director of the local paper factory. That same night he was arrested and given a ten-year sentence. See Alexander Solzhenitsyn, *The Gulag Archipelago* (New York, 1973), 69–70.

122. In *Honour and Shame: The Values of Mediterranean Society*, ed. J. G. Peristiany (Chicago, 1966), 197–98.

123. Eduard von Hartmann, *Tagesfragen* (Leipzig, 1896), 135.

124. Hans Hell, *Das Duell: ein Problem* (Berlin, 1904), 30.

125. Marion Gräfin Dönhoff, *Kindheit in Ostpreussen* (Berlin, 1990), 57–58.

126. Julian Pitt-Rivers, "The Concept of Honor," in *Honour and Shame*, 22.

127. Friedrich Paulsen, *System der Ethik* (Berlin, 1889), 446.

128. Von Rüts, *Die Duellgegnerschaft*, 22.

129. Marc J. Swartz, "Shame, Culture, and Status among the Swahili of Mombasa," in *Ethos* 16, no. 1 (March 1988): 23.

130. Von einem Praktiker, *Waffen-Comment*, 7.

131. See *SPdR*, 61st Session, 13 May 1912, 1935.

132. B. Wyatt-Brown, *Southern Honor: Ethics and Behavior in the Old South* (Oxford, 1982), 154–55.

133. Erving Goffmann, *Interaction Rituals: Essays in Face to Face Behavior* (Chicago, 1967), 232.

134. Dr. Karl Binding, *Die Ehre. Der Zweikampf* (Leipzig, 1909), 36–37.

135. *SPdR*, 235th Session, 13 March 1914, 8070–71.

136. *DKJ*, no. 305, 4 November 1896; and *DKJ*, no. 15, 15 January 1901.

137. From Arthur Schnitzler, *Reigen und andere Dramen: Das dramatische Werk*, vol. 2 (Frankfurt am Main, 1962), 40–45.

Chapter II

1. Arthur Schnitzler, *Ritterlichkeit*, ed. Rena R. Schlein (Bonn, 1975), 41.
2. *SPdH*, 10th Session, 8 May 1907, 173.
3. *GSA*, Rep. 84a 8037, "Der Vorentwurf zu einem Deutschen Strafgesetzbuch und der Zwkpf. Eine kritische Untersuchung: Anlage E."
4. Hermann Graf Keyserling, *Erörterungen über das Duell nebst einem Vorschlag* (Dorpat, 1883), 20.
5. Thomas Mann, *Der Zauberberg* (Frankfurt am Main, 1952), 140.
6. Lionel Trilling, *The Liberal Imagination* (New York, 1978), 121.
7. See von einem älteren aktiven Offizier, *Die conventionellen Gebräuche beim Zweikampf, unter besonderer Berücksichtigung des Offizierstandes* (Berlin, 1890; first published in 1882), 6; and Franz von Bolgar, *Die Regeln des Duells* (Vienna, 1891), IV.
8. See Gustav Ristow (Vienna, 1909), *Ehrenkodex*, XV.
9. See R. Sebetic, *Duell-Regeln* (Graz, 1879); Franz von Bolgar, *Die Regeln des Duells* (Vienna, 1891; first published in 1881); von einem älteren aktiven Offizier, *Gebräuche*; R. Wild-Queisner, *Das Duell: Ein Wort zur Beleuchtung desselben nach Ursprung, Form, Zweck und Nothwendigkeit für den Civil- und Militairstand* (Berlin, 1887); Gustav Hergsell, *Duell-Codex* (Vienna, Pest, Leipzig, 1891); Luigi Barbasetti, *Ehren-Codex*, translated and adapted to the Austro-Hungarian conventions by Gustav Ristow (Vienna, 1898); and Gustav Ristow, *Ehrenkodex*. In addition to direct quotations, I have footnoted those paragraphs where a unique and/or specific piece of information has been of particular help in formulating my general statement. In most instances, however, the information cited was already of so fundamental a nature that I regarded a footnote as a superfluity. To have cited just one or two of the sources would have been arbitrary. Where important contradictions occur between the codes, I note the fact.
10. See von einem älteren aktiven Offizier, *Gebräuche*, 5.
11. Comte de Chatauvillard, *Essai sur le duel* (Paris, 1836).
12. Von Bolgar, *Die Regeln*, V.
13. A. Croabbon, *Le Science du point d'honneur: Commentaire raisonné sur l'offense* (Paris, 1894), 393. For other French codes see Adolphe Tavernier, *L'Art du duel* (Paris, 1885); Comte de Duverger de St. Thomas, *Nouveau Code du Duel* (Paris, 1887); and Gabriel LeTainturier-Fradin, *Le Duel à travers les Ages, Histoires et Législation, Duels Célèbres—Code du Duel* (Nice, 1890).
14. Albert von Boguslawski, *Die Ehre und das Duell* (Berlin, 1896), 93.
15. *GSA*, Rep. 84a 8040, "Justiz-Ministeriums Zusammenstellungen und Nachweisungen über Verurtheilungen, Freisprechungen und Begnadigungen wegen Zweikämpfe" (1897): case #4.
16. Hergsell, *Duell-Codex*, 17.
17. Ristow, *Ehrenkodex*, 88.
18. An offended party could only accept an apology at the first level and still keep face—second- and third-level insults were deemed too severe for forgiveness. If, on the other hand, he rejected an apology at the first level, his right to choice of weaponry was forfeited. See *Gebräuche*, 11.

19. Hergsell, *Duell-Codex*, 17–18.

20. Friedhelm Guttandin, *Das Paradoxe Schicksal der Ehre: Zum Wandel der adligen Ehre und zur Bedeutung von Duell und Ehre für den monarchischen Zentralstaat* (Berlin, 1993), 27, 248–61.

21 Dr. Emil Dangelmaier, *Der Kampf um die Ehre* (Vienna, Leipzig, 1896), 20.

22. Ibid., 11.

23. Chatauvillard, *Essai*, 10.

24. Von Bolgar, *Die Regeln*, 9.

25. Hergsell, *Duell-Codex*, 29. This was the case in most countries where the duel persisted into the late nineteenth century. Montenegro was an exotic exception in which the opposite was true: duels were expressly allowed, but only when they took place without seconds. See Carl Rohte, *Zweikampfdelikt in den geltenden Strafgesetzen der Staaten Europas* (Leipzig, 1908), 122; and Breslauer [Rechtsanwalt], *Duellstrafen: Materialien gesammelt von Breslauer* (Berlin, 1890).

26. The term "seconds" was actually an anachronism from the sixteenth and seventeenth centuries when both the duelist and his retainers would do battle. The French properly labeled their quartet of helpmates *témoins*, or witnesses. The Germans often confused the two terms, calling their witnesses *Sekundanten* but on occasion correctly naming them *Zeugen*. I use the term "seconds" because it is customary and its connotations vibrate more than those of "witnesses," which hint of matrimony, even if seconds did exude a Best Man quality.

27. See the duel from Alexander Pushkin, *Eugene Onegin*, trans. Walter Arndt (New York, 1963), chapter 6, stanza 4: 140.

28. Chatauvillard, *Essai*, 97.

29. As cited in Robert Baldick, *The Duel* (Great Britain, 1965), 38.

30. Hergsell, *Duell-Codex*, 29, 30, 41.

31. Von Boguslawski, *Die Ehre*, 78.

32. See Comte de Chatauvillard, *Duell-Codex*, translated from the French with notations by C.v.L. (Karlsruhe, 1888; first published in 1864), chapter 4, article 1. In his introduction, the commentator mused, "I am surprised that a German translation has not earlier appeared."

33. See V. G. Kiernan, *The Duel in European History: Honour and Reign of the Aristocracy* (Oxford, 1988), 266–67.

34. *DKJ*, no. 224, 16 August 1892. In England and in early-nineteenth-century America this custom was known by the term "posting."

35. Von Bolgar, *Die Regeln*, 15.

36. *GSA*, Rep. 84a 8037, Prussian Ministry of Justice, no. 141.

37. Mann, *Der Zauberberg*, 962.

38. *DKJ*, no. 305, 4 November 1902.

39. *DKJ*, no. 292, 22 October 1896.

40. For examples of duels between officers taking place immediately after an insult, see *DKJ*, no. 171, 23 June 1896; and *DKJ*, no. 177, 29 June 1896.

41. Hergsell, *Duell-Codex*, 53. Likewise, "The mouth may not utter more than the arm is capable of upholding." Ristow, *Ehrenkodex*, 61.

42. Von Bolgar, *Die Regeln*, 20.

43. There are no reliable data for the incidence of fatalities and overall casualties. Extrapolating from Hans Hell, *Das Duell: ein Problem* (Berlin, 1904), 43–44, and based on my own estimations, approximately one in five German duels (whether pistol or saber) at this time was fatal, an extraordinarily high percentage when compared with available French, Italian, and Austrian statistics of the same period. As for overall casualty rates, Hell estimates that about two-thirds of all German duels ended in bloodshed, a figure with with which I am inclined to agree. See Ute Frevert, *Ehrenmänner: Das Duell in der bürgerlichen Gesellschaft* (Munich, 1991), 270, for patchy judicial statistics covering the larger period from 1800 to 1914 in Prussia and 1821 to 1912 in Bavaria (no breakdown into smaller increments of time), in which official fatality rates were 28.9 percent and 22.9 percent, respectively. For Italy, see Jacopo Gelli, *Die tödlichen Zweikämpfe des 19. Jahrhunderts* (a German translation from the Italian as excerpted in *DKJ*, no. 134, 27 December 1906; otherwise no place or date of publication); of 3,914 duels from 1879 to 1899 only 20 ended in death. For Austria, see Albert Wiesinger, *Das Duell vor dem Richterstuhle der Religion, der Moral, des Rechtes und der Geschichte* (Graz, 1895), as cited in István Deák, *Beyond Nationalism: A Social and Political History of the Habsburg Officer Corps, 1848–1918* (Oxford, 1990), 137, and compare with Heinrich Graf Coudenhove, *Der Minotaur der „Ehre"* (Berlin, 1902), 38; approximately one in every hundred duels was fatal. For France, see Robert A. Nye, "Dueling and Republican Manhood in the Third Republic" (unpublished paper, 1989); and id., *Masculinity and Male Codes of Honor in Modern France* (Oxford, 1993), 183–87, 190, 198, 200; at the fin de siècle, about 1 to 3 percent of all duels ended fatally. For England of the early nineteenth century, see Antony E. Simpson, "Dandelions on the Field of Honor: Dueling, the Middle Classes, and the Law in Nineteenth-Century England," in *Criminal Justice History* 9 (1988): 106–7. I know of no statistics for Spain or for Russia, but in the years before the First World War, no European penal code was softer on dueling than the Russian. Challenges, their acceptance, and bloodless duels were generally not punished, and the death or wounding of an opponent earned a maximum of four years honorable detention. As in Germany, these penalties were frequently commuted or pardoned away altogether, and, as in Germany, officers were obliged to challenge when insulted. These were fertile conditions for dueling, and of all the countries in Europe, Russia seems to have been closest to the German dueling paradigm. See Rohte, *Das Zweikampfdelikt*, 117–18.

44. Hergsell, *Duell-Codex*, 40.

45. Guy de Maupassant, *"Un Lâche,"* in *Contes et Nouvelles* (Paris, 1957).

46. Hergsell, *Duell-Codex*, 98.

47. See, for example, von Bolgar, *Die Regeln*, 25.

48. *DKJ*, no. 276, 6 October 1896.

49. *DKJ*, no. 12, 18 March 1907.

50. See von einem älteren aktiven Offizier, *Gebräuche*, 16–17.

51. *DKJ*, no. 194, 19 July 1883.

52. *DKJ*, no. 277, 11 October 1883.

53. *DKJ*, no. 210, 2 August 1898.

54. *DKJ*, no. 139, 27 December 1906.

55. *DKJ*, no. 94, 3 April 1896.

56. *DKJ*, no. 175, 28 June 1892.

57. *SPdR*, 98th Session, 27 November 1901, 2779–81.

58. *GSA*, Rep. 84a 8040. Here exist official records of 120 convictions from 1901 to 1905 under Articles 201–3, 205–8, and 210 of the penal code, as collated by the Prussian Ministry of Justice. Berlin and Cologne account for a combined total of 45 of these convictions, or 37.5 percent. The administrative districts of Stettin and Celle account for a combined total of 27 convictions, or 22.5 percent. These are the four conspicuous leaders. Therefore, from a total of thirteen Prussian administrative districts, those of Berlin, Cologne, Stettin, and Celle claimed an even 60 percent of the convictions under the aforementioned dueling articles from 1901 to 1905.

59. Notwithstanding, the administrative district of Cologne was three-quarters Catholic. The high rate of dueling in Cologne was, I think, primarily a function of the city and its environs being situated in that most densely populated industrial region of the Rhine.

60. See Barbasetti, *Ehren-Codex*, 81.

61. *DKJ*, no. 155, 28 March 1894.

62. *DKJ*, no. 161, 13 June 1899.

63. See Dr. Adolph Kohut, *Das Buch berühmter Duelle* (Berlin, 1888), 141.

64. See Ristow, *Ehrenkodex*, 140.

65. *DKJ*, no. 74, 16 March 1898.

66. See Charles Trench, *A History of Marksmanship* (Great Britain, 1972), 226–37.

67. For quote, see Hergsell, *Duell-Codex*, 147. According to Ristow, *Ehrenkodex*, 172–73, this creepy gaffe was committed quite often.

68. Barbasetti, *Ehren-Codex*, 111–12.

69. Ristow, *Ehrenkodex*, 83.

70. *DKJ*, no. 115, 26 April 1896.

71. Von Boguslawski, *Die Ehre*, 90.

72. See Ristow, *Ehrenkodex*, 177–78.

73. Ibid.

74. Hergsell, *Duell-Codex*, 97.

75. *Illustrierte Zeitung*, no. 2704, 27 April 1895.

76. See Pierre Lacaze, *En Garde: du duel à l'escrime* (Paris, 1991), 62, 120.

77. *SPdR*, 140th Session, 11 February 1902, 4090, according to Beckh of the German Liberal People's Party.

78. *SPdR*, 138th Session, 8 February 1902, 4070.

79. Hergsell, *Duell-Codex*, 35.

80. See Ristow, *Ehrenkodex*, 182; Barbasetti, *Ehren-Codex*, 83–84; and Hergsell, *Duell-Codex*, 89.

81. *GSA*, Rep. 84a, 8036 (23 April 1896).

82. See Heinrich Müller, *Gewehre, Pistolen, Revolver* (Leipzig, 1978), 190.

83. See Warren F. Schwartz, Keith Baxter, and David Ryan, "The Duel: Can These Gentleman be Acting Efficiently?" in *The Journal of Legal Studies* 13 (1984): 324.

84. See Frevert, *Ehrenmänner*, 202: "Standing perfectly still and having to

await the shot of the opponent, after having missed oneself, demanded an almost superhuman self-mastery." German pistol duelists remind me less of Nietzsche's *Übermenschen* than they do of Dante's rooted saplings in his seventh circle of Hell, to which he consigned all suicides: "We were men, and now are turned to wood." Dante Alighieri, *The Divine Comedy*, trans. H. R. Huse (U.S.A., 1954), canto 13: 64.

85. See *SPdR*, 127th Session, 19 November 1896, 3326.

86. See Simpson, "Dandelions," 110–16. Simpson also cites the fact that "resort to the pistol reflected the abandonment of fencing and swordplay in the education of the English Gentleman" (114).

87. Mann, *Der Zauberberg*, 953–67.

88. *DKJ*, no. 166, 19 June 1892.

89. Hergsell, *Duell-Codex*, 97.

90. Barbasetti, *Ehren-Codex*, 83–84.

91. From *The Standard*, 22 October 1890, in *A Complete Bibliography of Fencing and Duelling*, ed. Carl Thimm (London, 1896), 460.

92. The legitimacy of grabbing or deflecting an opponent's blade with the left hand was a matter of debate in France during the Third Republic. This situation may have arisen from the fact that in sixteenth- and early-seventeenth-century French rapier duels a misericord in the left hand was a common way of augmenting one's defense.

93. Hergsell, *Duell-Codex*, 80.

94. Von Bolgar, *Die Regeln*, 36.

95. Ibid., 38.

96. Ristow, *Ehrenkodex*, 129; see also Barbasetti, *Ehren-Codex*, 77–78.

97. Chatauvillard, *Essai*, 120.

98. See von Bolgar, *Die Regeln*, 41.

99. See Lacaze, *En Garde*, 79. Saber duels *mit Stich* bore little resemblance to modern fencing matches in which physical conditioning is more important than technique. Neither is modern competitive fencing very representative of how men dueled *ohne Stich* in which the defensive was still relatively important, for *touché* in such contests naturally meant more than just one of five points scored against you.

100. Arthur Schnitzler, *Erzählende Schriften von Arthur Schnitzler*, vol. 1 (Berlin, 1916), 265; see von Bolgar *Die Regeln*, 33, for the *ohne Stich* information.

101. *DKJ*, no. 30, 30 January 1893.

102. See Ristow, *Ehrencodex*, 128.

103. Kiernan, *The Duel*, 145, suggests that the advent in popularity of pistol dueling made a pause between the insult and the combat habitual because gentlemen did not carry pistols around with them, like they did swords, this fact stimulating the publication of formalized rules of combat etiquette that could be observed after a sufficient cooling-off period.

104. See David Harding, ed., *Weapons* (London, 1980), 115.

105. See Schwartz et al., "Acting Efficiently," 323. Prior agreement among seconds could stipulate a renewed shot, though this seems to have been a rare arrangement.

106. See Simpson, "Dandelions," 112.

107. Hergsell, *Duell-Codex*, 193.

108. See Dr. Hugo Schramm, *Ein Pereat den Duellen* (Leipzig, 1869), 20–24.

109. See Müller, *Gewehre*, 190–91; and Jaroslav Lugs, *Handfeuerwaffen* (German Democratic Republic, 1976), 48–49, 68–69.

110. *GSA*, Rep. 84a 8040, "Justiz-Ministeriums Zusammenstellungen und Nachweisungen über Verurtheilungen, Freisprechungen und Begnadigungen wegen Zweikämpfe, 1897–1906" (1897): case #3.

111. Mann, *Der Zauberberg*, 961.

112. See Hergsell, *Duell-Codex*, 170–71.

113. *DKJ*, no. 152, 6 June 1895.

114. Ristow, *Ehrenkodex*, 188–89.

115. In 1883 *Oberleutnant* von Schleyer was struck between the eyes by the first shot of Franz von Bolgar (selfsame author of *Die Regeln des Duells*?) at thirty-five paces. See *DKJ*, no. 140, 26 May 1883; and see also Kohut, *Das Buch* for corroboration. In 1884, over a disputed glass of schnaps, another unfortunate duelist suffered a similar fate when he was supposedly dropped by an opponent's first try at sixty paces. See *DKJ*, no. 136, 18 May 1884.

116. *DKJ*, no. 262, 11 July 1894.

117. See Stuart O. Landry, *Duelling in Old New Orleans* (New Orleans, 1950), 13.

118. *DKJ*, no. 262, 11 July 1894.

119. See Charles T. Harvey, *Shooting Muzzle Loading Hand Guns* (N.p., 1947), as cited in Schwartz et al., *Acting Efficiently*, 324.

120. See David Wallechinsky, *The Complete Book of the Olympics* (Boston, 1991), 456.

121. *DKJ*, no. 192, 15 July 1892. The actual duel was toned down to ten paces with only a bead, which made little difference to his dead opponent.

122. See *SPdR*, 235th Session, 13 March 1914, 8062, and the example of an officer duel overseen by a court of honor executed at twenty-five "*Sprungschritte*." Regardless of the distance, a death still resulted at the second exchange; according to Gröber of the Center.

123. In duels where shots were alternately exchanged by first one opponent then the other, there was no need to defend against oncoming fire as in other styles. Duelists would then stretch out their arms to shoot, the idea being that with the gun barrel as an extension of the arm one could sight better along a more distended axis.

124. From the *Pall Mall Gazette*, 30 August 1890, in *A Complete Bibliography*, 452.

125. *SPdR*, 10th Session, 13 December 1886, 174, according to Reichensperger of the Center.

126. See Hergsell, *Duell-Codex*, 170.

127. See Kohut, *Das Buch*, 162.

128. Chatauvillard, *Duell-Codex*, "Pistolenduelle mit Vorrücken; über Barrieren," chapter VI, article 18.

129. *DKJ*, no. 215, 8 August 1895.

130. *DKJ*, no. 255, 16 September 1892.

131. *GSA*, Rep. 84a 8037, Prussian Ministry of Justice, no. 141.

132. *DKJ*, no. 202, 25 July 1893.

133. *DKJ*, no. 27, 27 January 1893.

134. Simpson, "Dandelions," 113. The English would raise, point, and fire all in one smooth motion.

135. Mann, *Der Zauberberg*, 967.

136. See Jeffrey Meyers, "The Duel in Fiction," in *The North Dakota Quarterly* 51, no. 4 (1983). Pushkin fell in his fourth duel to the bullet of a Frenchman in 1837 in St. Petersburg. Another great Russian writer, Lermontov, died in a duel with a fellow countryman in the Caucasus in 1841.

137. Von Bolgar, *Die Regeln*, 47.

138. Ibid., 56.

139. Chatauvillard, *Essai*, 114.

140. Hergsell, *Duell-Codex*, 163; and von einem älteren aktiven Offizier, *Gebräuche*, 25.

141 See *Gebräuche*, 24.

142. See *DKJ*, no. 350, 20 December 1892; and *DKJ*, no. 100, 11 April 1896, for "on cue" duels at both these respective distances. Had the "on cue" duel been more hazardous and testing, it might have become the German duel *par excellence*, for it was the most impartial of the legitimate styles of combat. It was particularly suitable for mismatches in which one opponent held a distinct advantage in skill and experience, because this duel was based on the premise that less than optimal conditions might hurt the sharpshooter but would hardly impair the chances of a complete neophyte. Ute Frevert mentions how during the brief resuscitation of dueling under the Nazis, the *Reichskriegsminister* issued guidelines for *Wehrmacht* officers recommending the "on cue" duel to *Kampfunfähigkeit* as the "most chivalrous" form. See Frevert, *Ehrenmänner*, 260–61.

143. *DKJ*, no. 168, 20 June 1901.

144. See Robert A. Nye, "Dueling and Republican Manhood in the Third Republic" (unpublished paper, 1989); and also Nye, *Male Codes of Honor*, 183–87.

145. *DKJ*, no. 168, 20 June 1901.

146. Kohut, *Das Buch*, 171.

147. W. von Fürich, "Das Duell kritisch beleuchtet," in *Frankfurter Zeitgemässe Broschuren*, vol. 7, ed. Dr. Paul von Haffner (Frankfurt am Main, 1886), 199–200.

148. See Nye, *Male Codes of Honor*, 217–18; and see generally pp. 216–28.

149. Von Boguslawski, *Die Ehre*, 87.

150. See Simpson, *Dandelions*; and Donna T. Andrews, "The code of honor and its critics: the opposition to duelling in England, 1700–1850," in *Social History* 5, no. 3 (1980).

151. The fact that England was free of dueling is not to assert that subjects did not sometimes cross the Channel to the continent, usually Calais, to settle their quarrels. Outside of Europe, duels between Englishmen occasionally still took place on the Indian subcontinent. By the end of the century, officers expressly forbidden to duel could sometimes invent bizarre alternatives to circumvent the restriction, as in the strange case reported in 1894 of two British colonial officers stationed in India, a Captain Phillips and a Lieutenant

Shepherd, who resolved their difference in the following slithery manner: A poisonous snake was placed in a darkened room. After an hour, Phillips entered the chamber from one side and Shepherd from the other. Ten minutes after making their respective entrances, a scream came from Lieutenant Shepherd, who had been bitten. Phillips hurried frantically from the room, his hair turned supposedly white. Shepherd died in agony a few hours later. See *DKJ*, no. 255, 7 April 1894.

152. Heinrich von Treitschke, *Deutsche Geschichte im Neunzehnten Jahrhundert*, vol. 5 (Berlin, 1894), 480.

153. For example, see Alexander von Oettingen, *Zur Duellfrage* (Dorpat, 1889), 52; and Josef Bartunek, *Die Austragung von Ehrenangelegenheiten* (Vienna, 1912), 32–34.

154. Von Fürich, "Das Duell," 199.

155. See Ben C. Truman, *The Field of Honor* (New York, 1884), 158–59.

156. Von Boguslawski, *Die Ehre*, 88–89.

157. Jerome K. Jerome, *Three Men on the Bummel* (Leipzig, 1900), chapter 13.

158. Arthur Schnitzler, "Der Sekundant," in *Traumnovelle und andere Erzählungen: Das erzählerische Werk*, vol. 6 (Frankfurt am Main, 1961), 255.

159. Germaine de Staël, *De L'Allemagne*, vol. 1 (Paris, 1958), 83.

160. See Erving Goffmann, *Interaction Rituals: Essays in Face to Face Behavior* (Chicago, 1967), 207–39.

161. Albert von Öthalom, *Ehre und Ehrenschutz* (Vienna, Leipzig, 1908), 112.

162. James R. Webb, "Pistols for Two . . . Coffee for One," in *American Heritage* 26, no. 2 (February 1975): 67.

163. B. Wyatt-Brown, *Southern Honor: Ethics and Behavior in the Old South* (Oxford, 1982), 350.

164. Von Öthalom, *Ehrenschutz*, 112.

165. See Fritz Stern, *The Politics of Cultural Despair: A Study in the Rise of Germanic Ideology* (Berkeley, 1961), 130–31.

166. Kohut, *Das Buch*, 51, 47–48.

167. Ibid., 135. The "American duel," however, does not appear to have survived into the American century. In a 1902 Reichstag discussion of the 1886 proposal to outlaw the "American duel," deputy Gröber of the Center Party could casually remark, "I believe that we have no occasion to go any further into this question." See *SPdR*, 138th Session, 8 February 1902, 4028–29.

168. The "American duel's" more likely origin was European: the so-called "over-the-hanky-duel." The procedures assigned to this unique form were described at length by Chatauvillard in his *Essai sur le duel* (1836), listed under the heading *"Des Duels exceptionnels."* While duelists were attended by two adversarial seconds, the remaining pair would station themselves at least fifty paces from the site of coming combat, charging one of two smoothbore pistols and priming the other as if it too were loaded. At a signal from the pair, one of the waiting seconds would fetch the pistols and without a word remit them to the fourth second, who would then place the guns behind his back and have one of the duelists (chosen by lot) select either the left or right hand. The weapons would be distributed accordingly, in complete silence. The duelists would each then grasp a corner of a handkerchief and, at the signal clap from one of the seconds, fire point-blank into each other's chest. It was vital to fire

at the signal. A premature squeeze of the trigger was viewed as a chicanerous ploy to place your opponent—in case he had the loaded weapon—in the unenviable position of killing an unarmed man, thus pressuring him to a munificent forfeiture of his shot. Chatauvillard warned against this tactic: "If one of the two should fire before the signal, the other can, in clear conscience, blow his brains out [*lui brûler la cervelle à bout portant*]." See Chatauvillard, *Essai*, 81. Another influence leading to the "American duel" may have been the nerve-wracking "rope duel" or duel with a "single barrier," in which adversaries would align themselves opposite one another, each twenty or thirty paces on either side of a stretched-out rope or a stake driven into the ground. At the signal they would walk toward each other, discharging their sole bullet at leisure. Having missed, one would remain standing to await the fire of an opponent, who was then allowed to continue his forward progress until toeing the line of demarcation for some undisturbed target shooting. What set this barrier duel apart from more conventional styles was the fact that if the first to shoot had made a rapid advance and arrived flush with the rope or stake, and then had been feckless enough to miss, his life was not worth a red farthing: his opponent had the right to advance in turn, place the muzzle of his pistol against his antagonist's chest, and pull the trigger. All that remained the mark was to pray hard for a misfire. See Hergsell, *Duell-Codex*, 180.

169. *DKJ*, no. 203, 28 July 1883.

170. *DKJ*, no. 36, 6 February 1898.

171. *DKJ*, no. 207, 1 August 1883.

172. Von einem älteren aktiven Offizier, *Gebräuche*, 25.

173. Von Bolgar, *Die Regeln*, 71.

174. Hergsell, *Ehren-Codex*, 192.

175. Stern, *Despair*, XIV, XIX.

176. Brown, *Southern Honor*, 35.

177. See Roger Chickering, "Die Alldeutschen erwarten den Krieg," in *Bereit zum Krieg: Kriegsmentalität im wilhelminischen Deutschland, 1890–1914*, ed. Jost Dülffer and Karl Holl (Göttingen, 1986), 20–37.

178. Alexander Pushkin, "Der Schuss," in *Erzählungen* (Dessau, 1954).

179. See Schwartz et al., "Acting Efficiently," 346–49.

180. See, for example, von Bolgar, *Die Regeln*, 5.

181. See Josef Bartunek, *Die Austragung von Ehrenangelegenheiten* (Vienna, 1912), 19.

182. *DKJ*, no. 322, 21 November 1902.

183. Hauptmann Ernst von Dewitz, *Der Zweikampf: Vortrag gehalten am 1. Dezember 1880* (Berlin, 1892), 8, 32.

Chapter III

1. C. Balan, *Duell und Ehre: Ein Beitrag zur praktischen Lösung der Duellfrage unter besonderer Berücksichtigung der Verhältnisse des Deutschen Offizierkorps* (Berlin, 1890), 28.

2. Michael Geyer, "The Stigma of Violence, Nationalism, and War in Twentieth-Century Germany," in *German Studies Review: Special Issue—German Identity* 15, no. 4 (Winter 1992): 78.

3. As cited in Karl Demeter, *Das deutsche Offizierkorps in Gesellschaft und Staat, 1650–1945* (Frankfurt am Main, 1962), 121.

4. See V. G. Kiernan, *The Duel in European History: Honour and the Reign of the Aristocracy* (Oxford, 1988), 196; and Lorenzo Sabine, *Notes on Duels and Duelling* (Boston, 1855), 14.

5. See Alfred Vagts, *A History of Militarism* (New York, 1959), 177.

6. See J. G. Millingen, *The History of Duelling*, vol. 1 (London, 1841), 265.

7. Demeter, *Deutsche Offizierkorps*, Document no. 10: 265, as proposed by General Karl von Borstell.

8. Ibid., 122.

9. *SPdR*, 56th Session, 26 February 1902, 1522, as quoted by the Prussian Minister of War Heinrich von Gossler.

10. Demeter, *Deutsche Offizierkorps*, 123.

11. Ibid., 123–24, 136.

12. Millingen, *The History of Duelling*, 350.

13. *Universal: Chronik unserer Zeit* (Frankfurt am Main, 1832), 321.

14. Demeter, *Deutsche Offizierkorps*, 124–25.

15. Friedrich Meinecke, *Boyen*, vol. 2, 515 ff., as cited in Demeter, *Deutsche Offizierkorps*, 125.

16. Vagts, *Militarism*, 177.

17. *Allerhöchste Verordnungen über die Ehrengerichte und über das Verfahren bei Untersuchungen der zwischen Offizieren vorfallenden Streitigkeiten und Beleidigungen, sowie über die Bestrafung des Zweikampfes unter Offizieren* (Berlin, 1843).

18. See Dieter Prokowsky, *Die Geschichte der Duellbekämpfung* (Bonn, 1965), 134.

19. See Henri Brunschwig, *Enlightenment and Romanticism in Eighteenth-Century Prussia*, trans. Frank Jellinek (Chicago, 1974); and Hans Rosenberg, *Bureaucracy, Aristocracy and Autocracy: The Prussian Experience, 1660–1815* (Cambridge, Mass.: 1958).

20. Demeter, *Deutsche Offizierkorps*, 126.

21. Vagts, *Militarism*, 127.

22. Demeter, *Deutsche Offizierkorps*, 127.

23. See Albert von Boguslawski, *Die Ehre und das Duell* (Berlin, 1896), 62.

24. See *SPdR*, 56th Session, 26 February 1902, 1522–23. Prussian Minister of War von Gossler cited forty officer duels between 1832 and 1843, and sixty-four between 1843 and 1856.

25. General Edwin von Manteuffel shot up the hand of the *Stadtgerichtsrat* Karl von Twesten in 1861 after Twesten had attacked his policy of stacking the Prussian officer corps with nobility. See Adolph Kohut, *Das Buch berühmter Duelle* (Berlin, 1888), 96–104.

26. Millingen, *The History of Duelling*, 347.

27. These citations are taken from the introductory paragraphs to the *Verordnung über die Ehrengerichte der Offiziere im Preussischen Heere* (2 May 1874), as reprinted in von einem älteren aktiven Offizier, *Die conventionellen Gebräuche beim Zweikampf, unter besonderer Berücksichtigung des Offizierstandes* (Berlin, 1890).

28. Ibid.

29. Ibid.

30. *SPdR*, 46th Session, 25 April 1912, 1403, according to Haubsmann of the German Liberal People's Party.

31. See Martin Kitchen, *The German Officer Corps* (Oxford, 1968), 54.

32. *DKJ*, no. 352, 7 November 1893.

33. See Hermann Rumschöttel, *Das bayerische Offizierkorps, 1866–1914* (Munich, 1972), 156–57.

34. See *SPdR*, 56th Session, 26 February 1901, 1523, as cited by Minister of War von Gossler; *SPdR*, 138th Session, 8 February 1902, 4069–70, as cited by Bassermann quoting statistics of the War Minister; and Jonathan Steinberg, "The Kaiser's Navy and German Society," in *Past and Present*, no. 28 (July 1964).

35. *BHSA*, Abt. IV, Mkr. 11224, Introduction to *Bestimmungen zur Ergänzung der Einführungsordre zu der Verordnung über die Ehrengerichte der Offiziere im Preussischen Heere*.

36. *BHSA*, Abt. IV, Mkr. 1855, a secret dispatch from Wilhelm II to the Bavarian Minister of War, dated 5 July 1888.

37. See *SPdR*, 98th Session, 17 November 1901, 2783, as cited by Minister of War von Gossler; and *SPdR*, 278th Session, 9 March 1903, 8506, as cited by von Gossler.

38. See *SPdR*, 56th Session, 26 February 1901, 1523, extrapolating from statistics of von Gossler.

39. *SPdR*, 56th Session, 26 February 1901, 1523.

40. Antony Simpson, "Dandelions on the Field of Honor: Dueling, the Middle Classes, and the Law in Nineteenth-Century England," in *Criminal Justice History* 9 (1988): 138–39.

41. Ibid.

42. See Donna T. Andrews, "The code of honor and its critics: the opposition to duelling in England, 1700–1850," in *Social History* 5, no. 3 (1980).

43. *SPdR*, 278th Session, 9 March 1903, 8509, according to Heig.

44. See the statement by Dr. Bachem of the Center in *SPdR*, 26th Session, 15 January 1901, 698–700, and 56th Session, 26 February 1901, 1541–44; and the statements of Gröber of the Center in the 61st Session, 13 May 1912, 1931, and 235th Session, 13 March 1914, 8062–70.

45. *SPdR*, 73d Session, 21 April 1896, 1829–34. For other SPD discussions of this issue, see the statement of Vollmar in the 26th Session, 15 January 1901, 704; the statements of Bebel in the 56th Session, 26 February 1901, 1523–25, and 98th Session, 27 November 1901, 2793–97; and the statement of Haase in the 98th Session, 13 March 1914, 8073.

46. *SPdR*, 126th Session, 17 November 1896, 3300, according to Dr. Graf zu Stolberg-Wernigerode.

47. *SPdR*, 126th Session, 17 November 1896, 3299; and 127th Session, 19 November 1896, 3336, respectively.

48. Available statistical information would appear to belie such an assertion. Rates of civilian convictions for dueling remained relatively constant through 1897 and beyond, but this is probably due to the fact that violations were simply being more frequently prosecuted than before the 1897 order. The exact numbers for individuals convicted of dueling in given years are the following: 1886—79; 1887—90; 1888—99; 1889—75; 1890—66; 1891—60;

1892—77; 1893—63; 1894—83; 1895—107; 1896—110; 1897—140; 1898—154; 1899—99; 1900—88; 1901—91; 1902—74; 1903—101; 1904—73. See *SPdR*, 141st Session, 12 February 1902, 4134, as cited by Gröber of the Center; and *SPdR* 20th Session, 15 January 1906, 555, as cited by Bassermann of the National Liberals.

49. See Demeter, *Deutsche Offizierkorps*, 138–42.

50. R. Gädke, formerly colonel and commander of the Field Artillery Regiment 11, "Ehrengerichte," in *DKJ*, no. 25, 3 June 1912.

51. See Prussian Minister of War von Gossler's statement in *SPdR*, 98th Session, 27 November 1901, 2798; and *GLA*, Bestand 456 F9, Bestellnummer 461.

52. The compilations from Württemburg and Baden are based on original research, while the Bavarian information has been taken from Rumschöttel, *Bayerische Offizierkorps*, 150–205.

53. *SPdR*, 235th Session, 13 March 1914, 8080, according to Dr. Blunck of the Liberal Union.

54. *SPdR*, 235th Session, 13 March 1914, 8080.

55. *SPdR*, 235th Session, 13 March 1914, 8062, according to Gröber of the Center.

56. *SPdR*, 98th Session, 27 November 1901, 2788, as told by Haase of the SPD; and *SPdR*, 98th Session, 27 November 1901, 2790, as described by Major Krug von Nidda of the Saxon Army.

57. This account was taken from Rumschöttel, *Bayerische Offizierkorps*, 174–80.

58. *SPdR*, 278th Session, 9 March 1903, 8497–98, according to August Bebel of the SPD.

59. *SPdR*, 98th Session, 27 November 1901, 2788, as told by Haase of the SPD.

60. *GLA*, Bestand 456 F9, Bestellnummer 454.

61. *DKJ*, no. 12, 18 March 1907.

62. Major von Krafft, *Dienst und Leben des jungen Infanterie-Offiziers: Ein Lern und Lesebuch* (Berlin, 1914), 219–35.

63. Based on Hermann Rumschöttel's analysis of some thousand Bavarian honor court procedures, and my own analysis of half that many from the archives of Baden and Württemberg.

64. See Isabel V. Hull, *The Entourage of Kaiser Wilhelm II, 1888–1918* (Cambridge, 1982), 202.

65. *GLA*, Bestand 456 F9, Bestellnummern 439 and 462.

66. Rumschöttel, *Bayerische Offizierkorps*, 167.

67. For elaboration of this notion, see ibid., 183.

68. *GLA*, Bestand 456 F9, Bestellnummern 489, 450, 446.

69. Rumschöttel, *Bayerische Offizierkorps*, 182, 184.

70. See Rumschöttel, *Bayerische Offizierkorps*, 184, and for an entertaining rundown of the Bavarian honor court proceedings during this period, see 150–206. See also (if ambitious enough) *GLA*, "Verzeichnis der Ehrengerichtlichen-Akten bezw. Urteile des XIV. Armee-Korps, Bemerkung: Schriftwechsel L. 597/28 R.I.1 b., Blatt 215/216"; and *SHS*, "Zusammenstellung der im XIII. Armee-Korps behandelten ehrengerichtlichen Fälle vom Jahre 1871 an," Verzeichnis Nummer M 1/7 Bu 35.

71. From Albert von Öthalom, *Ehre und Ehrenschutz* (Vienna, Leipzig, 1908), 121.

72. See Jost Dülffer, "Einleitung: Dispositionen zum Krieg im wilhelmischen Deutschland," in *Bereit zum Krieg: Kriegsmentalität im wilhelmischen Deutschland*, ed. Jost Dülffer and Karl Holl (Göttingen, 1985), 15–16.

73. See Stolberg-Wernigerode, *Die Unentschiedene*, 327.

74. See August Bebel, *SPdR*, 72d Session, 20 April 1896, 1809; and Freiherr von Manteuffel, *SPdR*, 73d Session, 21 April 1896, 1826–27.

75. "Politische Korrespondenz," in *Preussische Jahrbücher* 84 (May 1896): 378.

76. *SPdR*, 145th Session, 17 February 1902, 4233, according to Lenzmann of the German Liberal Union.

77. Von Krafft, *Dienst und Leben*, 328.

78. R. Gädke, "Die Infamie des Duellzwangs," in *DKJ*, no. 35, 12 August 1912.

79. Clemens von Spohn, *Beurteilung der verschiedensten Ehrenfragen, die zu Ehrenhändeln und Ehrengerichten Anlass geben* (Berlin, 1911), 3.

80. See *SPdR*, 12th Session, 17 November 1896, 3305–6, according to Bebel of the SPD.

81. *SPdR*, 20th Session, 15 January 1906, 547–51, as described by Roeren of the Center.

82. See *SPdR*, 127th Session, 19 November 1896, 3343, as told by Schultze, Social Democrat from Königsberg.

83. See *SPdR*, 61st Session, 13 May 1912, 1939, as told by Schiffer of the National Liberals.

84. See *SPdR*, 127th Session, 19 November 1896, 3330–31, according to Lenzmann of the German Liberal People's Party.

85. See *SPdR*, 235th Session, 13 March 1914, 8089, according to Wendel of the SPD.

86. *DKJ*, no. 197, 20 July 1893.

87. *SPdR*, 72d Session, 20 April 1896, 1809.

88. *SPdR*, 98th Session, 27 November 1901, 2788, and 2786, according to Schrader.

89. *SPdR*, 20th Session, 15 January 1906, 552.

90. Von Spohn, *Ehrenhändeln*, 83.

91. Hull, *The Entourage*, 201.

92. Henry M. Pachter, *Modern Germany: A Social, Cultural, and Political History* (Boulder, Colorado: 1978), 39.

93. Quote from Stig Förster, "Alter und neuer Militarismus im Kaiserreich: Heeresrüstungspolitik und Dispositionen zum Krieg zwischen Status-quo-Sicherung und imperialistischer Expansion, 1890–1913," in *Bereit zum Krieg*, 137.

94. Carl von Clausewitz, *On War*, edited with an introduction by Anatol Rapoport (New York, 1968), 101.

95. Josef Bartunek, *Die Austragung von Ehrenangelegenheiten* (Vienna, 1912), 8.

96. Von Öthalom, *Ehre und Ehrenschutz*, 120.

97. Von Boguslawski, *Die Ehre*, 91.

98. Von Berchem, "Ehrenhändel," 22.

99. Dr. Emil Dangelmaier, *Kampf um die Ehre* (Vienna, Leipzig, 1896), 3–4.

100. Hull, *The Entourage*, 201.

101. Heinrich von Treitschke, *Politik: Vorlesungen gehalten an der Universität zu Berlin*, vol. 1 (Leipzig, 1918), 76–77.

102. Kiernan, *The Duel*, 274.

103. As cited in Detlef Bald, "Zum Kriegsbild der militärischen Führung im Kaiserreich," in *Bereit zum Krieg*, 150.

104. *DKJ*, no. 134, 17 May 1898.

105. *SPdR*, 20th Session, 15 January 1906, 555, 552, according to Himburg of the Conservatives, and 550.

106. *GSA*, Rep. 84a 8037, "Äusserung des Kriegsministers betreffend den Gesetzentwurf zur Abänderung der Bestrafung der Zweikämpfe, dem Königlichen Staatsministerium zu Schreiben des Herrn Reichskanzlers vom 3. April 1914. R.J.A. Nr. 2023 vorzulegen."

107. Von Falkenhayn, "Äusserung des Kriegministers," 5, 7–8.

108. *SPdR*, 138th Session, 8 February 1902, 4046, according to Heine.

109. Von einem älteren aktiven Offizier, *Gebräuche*, 3.

110. *SPdR*, 235th Session, 13 March 1914, 8074, according to Haase.

111. As quoted in *DKJ*, no. 5, 5 January 1897.

112. See Friedhelm Guttandin, *Das Paradoxe Schicksal der Ehre: Zum Wandel der adligen Ehre und zur Bedeutung von Duell und Ehre für den monarchischen Zentralstaat* (Berlin, 1993), 350–74.

113. Von Falkenhayn, "Äusserung des Kriegministers," 8.

114. Von Krafft, *Dienst und Leben*, 217.

115. Kitchen, *The German Officer Corps*, 50.

116. Hauptmann Ernst von Dewitz, *Der Zweikampf: Vortrag gehalten am 1. Dezember 1880* (Berlin, 1892), 13.

117. As cited in Heinrich Graf Coudenhove, *Der Minotaur der „Ehre": Studie zur Antiduellbewegung und Duelllüge* (Berlin, 1902), 44–45.

118. See Stolberg-Wernigerode, *Die Unentschiedene*, 322.

119. For quote, see von Krafft, *Dienst und Leben*, 217.

120. *SPdR*, 98th Session, 27 November 1901, 2792, according to Munckel.

121. *DKJ*, no. 352, 7 November 1893.

122. See the introduction to the order.

123. See *BHSA* IV, Bestand Mkr. 1855 and Beilage, Munich, 10 February 1914.

124. Von Krafft, *Dienst und Leben*, 221.

125. Friedrich Paulsen, *System der Ethik* (Berlin, 1889), 509–11.

126. See *SPdR*, 235th Session, 13 March 1914, 8070, according to von Falkenhayn.

127. *SPdR*, 235th Session, 13 March 1914, 8071.

128. Von Berchem, "Ehrenhändel," 9.

129. See Guttandin, *Paradoxe Schicksal*, 7–43, for a sustained treatment of this aristocratic/bourgeois binary from the perspective of a theory-based sociological inquiry.

130. Von Berchem, "Ehrenhändel," 10.

131. Ibid., 9.

132. Ibid., 23.

133. Von Dewitz, *Der Zweikampf*, 33.

134. Von Krafft, *Dienst und Leben*, 261.

135. Ibid., 259–60.

136. *DKJ*, no. 139, 21 May 1892.

137. *DKJ*, no. 41, 11 February 1895.

138. *SPdR*, 127th Session, 19 November 1896, 3342–43, as told by Schultze of the SPD.

139. For a general discussion of this case, see *SPdR*, 126th Session, 17 November 1896; and *SPdR*, 127th Session, 19 November 1896.

140. Arthur Schnitzler, *Erzählende Schriften von Arthur Schnitzler*, vol. 1 (Berlin, 1916).

Chapter IV

1. Mark Twain, *A Tramp Abroad* (New York, 1879), 40.

2. *DKJ*, no. 67, 9 March 1898.

3. "Le Duel dans les Universités Allemandes," in *L'Illustration*, 30 September 1893.

4. Jerome K. Jerome, *Three Men on the Bummel* (Leipzig, 1900), chapter 13.

5. This historical synopsis of the *Mensur* up to 1871 is largely taken from Henner Huhle and Helma Brunck, *500 Jahre Fechtmeister in Deutschland: Ältester privilegierter Berufsstand* (Frankfurt am Main, 1987), 54–87; and Peter Krause, *"O du alte schöne Burschenherrlichkeit": Die Studenten und ihr Brauchtum* (Graz, Vienna, Cologne, 1979), 133–35. Interpretive aspects are mine.

6. Huhle and Brunck, *500 Jahre Fechtmeister*, 54–87; and Krause, *Burschenherrlichkeit*, 133–35.

7. *GSA*, Rep. 84a 8035, "Erkenntnis des Königlichen Ober-Tribunals vom 6. Juni 1877."

8. Krause, *Burschenherrlichkeit*, 103.

9. "Urteil der vereinigten Strafsenate des Reichsgerichts, Plenarbeschluss," as cited in *DKJ*, no. 162, 17 June 1883.

10. *GSA*, Rep. 84a 8038, "Studentische Schlägermensuren" (6 April 1933).

11. *GSA*, Rep. 84a 8039, "Die Mensur wieder Straffrei," no. 96 (6 April 1933).

12. See Krause, *Burschenherrlichkeit*, 193–95.

13. See Huhle and Brunck, *500 Jahre Fechtmeister*, 91; and Dr. M. Liepmann, *Duell und Ehre* (Berlin, 1904), 21.

14. *GSA*, Rep. 84a 8040; and see also *GSA*, Rep. 84a, for Dr. Hamm's speech in a 1912 plenary session of the upper chamber of the Prussian Landtag, 8th Session, 14 May 1912.

15. *GSA*, Rep. 84a 8040, "Justiz-Ministeriums Zusammenstellungen und Nachweisungen über Verurtheilungen, Freisprechungen und Begnadigungen wegen Zweikämpfe, 1897–1906."

16. *GSA*, Rep. 84a, 8040 (1904): case #1.

17. Not all undergraduate caprice was obliged though, because the original sentences levied for dueling proper among students, albeit light, generally adhered. See *GSA*, Rep. 84a 8040.

18. From C. W. Allers, with introductory text by Professor Fr. Molden-hauen, *Das Deutsche Corpsleben* (Stuttgart, Berlin, Leipzig, ca. 1902), XIII.

19. *SPdR*, 127th Session, 19 November 1896, 3328, as told by Lenzmann of the Liberal Union.

20. *GSA*, Rep. 84a 8037, "Haus der Abgeordneten," 29th Session, 17 February 1902, 1906, according to Dr. Barth.

21. Carl Rohte, *Das Zweikampfdelikt in den geltenden Strafgesetzen der Staaten Europas* (Leipzig, 1908), 13.

22. See Hugo Schramm, *Ein Pereat den Duellen* (Leipzig, 1869), 14; and *GSA*, Rep. 84a 8038, "Bericht des Oberstaatsanwaltes bei dem Landgericht II" (4 September 1926); and *DKJ*, no. 169, 22 June 1884.

23. See Ben C. Truman, *The Field of Honor* (New York, 1884), 61.

24. For an example, see Schramm, *Ein Pereat*, 14.

25. *SPdR*, 10th Session, 13 December 1886, 193, according to the Freiherr Langwerth von Simmern, unaffiliated.

26. *GSA*, Rep. 84a 8037, "Petition um Änderung der Gesetzbestimmung, nach denen studentische Schlägermensuren als Zweikampf mit tödlichen Waffen angesehen und verurteilt werden."

27. *GSA*, Rep. 84a 8038, "Merkblatt zur Strafgesetzgebung gegen Mensur und Duell (Entwurf zum Abschnitt 18, Artikeln 270–274 eines Allgemeinen Deutschen Strafgesetzbuches)."

28. From *Vorwärts*, no. 299, 29 June 1930, in *GSA*, Rep. 84a 8038.

29. "Stenographischer Bericht über die Verhandlungen der bayerischen Kammer der Abgeordneten," 64th Session, no. 64, 24 January 1894, 566.

30. *SPdR*, 72d Session, 20 April 1896, 1798.

31. Hans Delbrück, "Politische Korrespondenz," in *Preussische Jahrbücher* 84 (May 1896): 378.

32. See, for example, *SPdR*, 26th Session, 15 January 1901, 696, the statement by Dr. Pachnicke of the Liberal Union.

33. *DKJ*, no. 178, 30 June 1896.

34. *DKJ*, no. 77, 19 March 1898; and *DKJ*, no. 170, 23 June 1898.

35. Dr. Paul von Salvisberg, *Das Duell und die Academische Jugend* (Munich, 1896), 29.

36. Friedrich Meinecke, *Erlebtes: 1862–1901* (Leipzig, 1941), 112–13.

37. Arthur Schnitzler, *Traumnovelle und andere Erzählungen: Das erzählerische Werk*, vol. 6 (Frankfurt am Main, 1979), 72–73. The unassuming physician of this story considers the possibility of a duel in two other cases, and all in the space of a single night. This story, unlike other Schnitzler offerings, has nothing remotely to do with dueling, which is merely a common aspect of the social landscape at the time, not to be commented on in any particular way by the author.

38. See Konrad H. Jarausch, *Deutsche Studenten, 1800–1970* (Frankfurt am Main, 1984), 61; and Josef Bartunek, *Die Austragung von Ehrenangelegenheiten* (Vienna, 1912), 27–28.

39. See von Salvisberg, *Academische Jugend*, 26–27.

40. See R.G.S. Weber, *The German Student Corps in the Third Reich* (London, 1986), 34.

41. Professor Theobald Ziegler, *Über Universitäten und Universitätsstudium* (Leipzig, Berlin, 1913), 126.

42. "Stenographischer Bericht über die Verhandlungen der bayerischen Kammer der Abgeordneten," 64th Session, 24 January 1894, 566, according to Dr. von Stauffenberg.

43. See Krause, *Burschenherrlichkeit*, 135.

44. For a couple examples of fatal student pistol duels with officers at this time, see *SPdR*, 98th Session, 27 November 1901, 2788; and *DKJ*, no. 5, 5 January 1902.

45. *DKJ*, no. 322, 21 November 1902.

46. See Huhle and Brunck, *500 Jahre Fechtmeister*, 89.

47. István Deák, *Beyond Nationalism: A Social and Political History of the Habsburg Officer Corps, 1848–1918* (Oxford, 1990), 134.

48. Meinecke, *Erlebtes*, 102.

49. Allers, *Das Deutsche Corpsleben*, XI.

50. Wilhelm Raabe, *Sämtlich Werke*, Series 1 (Leipzig, 1925), 371–72, 375.

51. Von einem Corpsstudenten, *Verfolgte Unschuld?* (Erlangen, 1896), 12.

52. Ziegler, *Über Universitäten*, 62.

53. Von einem Corpsstudenten, *Verfolgte Unschuld?*, 8–9.

54. See Jürgen Wolf, ed., *Materialien: Heinrich Mann, „Der Untertan"* (Stuttgart, 1979), 32.

55. Heinrich Mann, *Der Untertan* (Berlin, 1964), 22–23, 36–37.

56. Allers, *Das Deutsche Corpsleben*, XVI.

57. Mann, *Der Untertan*, 24.

58. Ibid.

59. Ziegler, *Über Universitäten*, 62.

60. See "Le Duel"; and Allers, *Das Deutsche Corpsleben*, VIII–IX.

61. See Erich Marks, *Bismarcks Jugend* (Berlin, 1915), 91.

62. See Jarausch, *Deutsche Studenten*, 60.

63. Cited in Salvisberg, *Academische Jugend*, 19.

64. Allers, *Das Deutsche Corpsleben*, XIII.

65. *GSA*, Rep. 84a 8037, Aachen Petition of 1912.

66. Von einem Praktiker, *Unser Ehren- und Waffen-Comment* (Thorn, 1893), 19.

67. *GSA*, Rep. 84a 8037, Aachen Petition of 1912.

68. *SPdR*, 10th Session, 13 December 1886, 193–94.

69. Von einem Praktiker, *Waffen-Comment*, 5.

70. See Weber, *Student Corps*, 34, 38.

71. Huhne and Brunck, *500 Jahre Fechtmeister*, 70.

72. Ziegler, *Über Universitäten*, 125.

73. "Le Duel."

74. Herbert Hoerner, *Die letzte Kugel* (Stuttgart, 1939), 6–7.

75. See von einem Praktiker, *Waffen-Comment*, 16.

76. See Major Ben C. Truman, *The Field of Honor: Being a Complete and Comprehensive History of Duelling in all Countries* (New York, 1884), 62.

77. See Richard A. Woeltz, "Sport, Culture, and Society in Late Imperial and Weimar Germany: Some Suggestions for Future Research," in *Journal of Sport History* 4 (1977).

78. Von einem Praktiker, *Waffen-Comment*, 18.

79. Cited in Salvisberg, *Academische Jugend*, 19–20.

80. Von einem Praktiker, *Waffen-Comment*, 19.

81. Heinrich Graf Coudenhove, *Der Minotaur der „Ehre": Studie zur Anti-duellbewegung und Duelllüge* (Berlin, 1904), 72.

82. Professor Theobald Ziegler, *Der deutsche Student* (Berlin, Leipzig, 1902), 118.

83. Allers, *Das Deutsche Corpsleben*, X.

84. Woeltz, "Sport, Culture, and Society," 297.

85. Heinrich von Treitschke, *Deutsche Geschichte im Neunzehnten Jahrhundert*, vol. 5 (Berlin, 1894), 480.

86. See Ute Frevert, *Ehrenmänner: Das Duell in der bürgerlichen Gesellschaft* (Munich, 1991), 151.

87. Truman, *The Field of Honor*, 62.

88. "Le Duel."

89. Ibid.

90. *DKJ*, no. 323, 9 September 1894; and *DKJ*, no. 179, 1 July 1902.

91. *DKJ*, no. 47, 17 February 1895.

92. "Stenographischer Bericht über die Verhandlungen der bayerischen Kammer der Abgeordneten," 64th Session, 24 January 1894, 564.

93. Jerome, *Three Men*, chapter 13.

94. Arthur Schnitzler, *My Youth in Vienna*, trans. Catherine Hutter (New York, 1970), 96.

95. See Twain, *A Tramp*, 43; and von Salvisberg, *Academische Jugend*, 25.

96. "Stenogramm des Reichstags," 41st Session, 19 April 1912, 1244, according to Heine of the SPD.

97. See Krause, *Burschenherrlichkeit*, 106.

98. Jarausch, *Deutsche Studenten*, 62.

99. In Bavaria, because less prestige was associated with the career of a bureaucrat, more incorporated students entered the professoriate than was the case in Prussia. See Krause, *Burschenherrlichkeit*, 106.

100. Ibid.

101. See Jarausch, *Deutsche Studenten*, 68.

102. Ibid., 66–67.

103. See Helen Lefkowitz Horowitz, *Campus Life: Undergraduate Culture from the End of the Eighteenth Century to the Present* (New York, 1987).

104. Krause, *Burschenherrlichkeit*, 106, in reference to the *Corps*.

105. Thomas Mann, *Der Zauberberg* (Frankfurt am Main, 1952), 701–2.

106. Ibid., 103–4.

107. See Jarausch, *Deutsche Studenten*, 66–67.

108. See Krause, *Burschenherrlichkeit*, 102; and Jarausch, *Deutsche Studenten*, 76.

109. See Krause, *Burschenherrlichkeit*, 104.

110. See Jarausch, *Deutsche Studenten*, 65–67.

111. Ibid., 63.

112. *SPdR*, 108th Session, 18 June 1896, 2713. See also *SPdR*, 127th Session, 19 November 1896, 3337, for that loose cannon Mirbach doing some more *Ehrenmann* posturing.

113. *SPdR*, 98th Session, 27 November 1901, 2796–97.

114. For the precise wording of the ban, which included both seconds and other onlookers, see W. von Fürich, "Das Duell kritisch beleuchtet," in *Frankfurter Zeitgemässe Broschuren*, vol. 7, ed. Dr. Paul von Haffner (Frankfurt am Main, 1886), 194–96.

115. *SPdR*, 126th Session, 17 November 1896, 3303, as cited by Bachem of the Center from the *Constitutio Apostolicae Sedis Moderatoni.*

116. See Jarausch, *Deutsche Studenten*, 63. Despite the ban, it was still possible not only to remain in good graces with the papal see, but to make a career in the Church hierarchy: the German Cardinal Diepenbrock was a duelist as a youngster. See "Stenographischer Bericht über die Verhandlungen der bayerischen Kammer der Abgeordneten," 64th Session, 24 January 1894, 571.

117. See Weber, *Student Corps*, 17.

118. See "Le Duel."

119. *SPdR*, 26th Session, 15 January 1901, 691–94, according to Trimborn of the Center.

120. *DKJ*, no. 202, 25 July 1893.

121. See Krause, *Burschenherrlichkeit*, 137.

122. Ibid., 105.

123. See Hans-Ulrich Wehler, *The German Empire, 1871–1918* (Dover, NH: 1985), 126.

124. Jarausch, *Deutsche Studenten*, 89.

125. *SPdR*, 235th Session, 13 March 1914, 8091, according to Wendel of the Social Democrats.

126. See Adrian Clive Roberts, "Arthur Schnitzler as a Pacifist Writer: The Critique of War and Militarism in Selected Works" (Ph.D. dissertation, University of California at San Diego: 1986), 52–53.

127. "Herzl contemplated taking the field himself as knightly champion of Jewish honor. He would challenge the leaders of Austrian anti-Semitism—Schönerer, Lueger, Prince Alois Liechtenstein—to a duel. If he should lose his life in the encounter, he would leave a letter signalizing his death as martyr-victim of 'the world's most unjust movement.' If he should win, Herzl envisaged . . . a stirring role in the courtroom in which he would be prosecuted for the death of his adversary. After extolling the personal honor of his victim, Herzl would give a great oration against anti-Semitism. The court, compelled to respect his nobility, would proclaim his innocence, the Jews would wish to send him to the Reichsrat as their representative, but Herzl would nobly refuse 'because I could not go to the House of Representatives over the body of a human being.' The palliative for anti-Semitism thus took the form of an affair of honor." See Carl Schorske, *Fin-de-Siècle Vienna* (New York, 1981), 160–61.

128. See Deák, *Beyond Nationalism*, 132–34; and Robert A. Nye, *Masculinity and Male Codes of Honor in Modern France* (Oxford, 1993), 205–10.

129. See Dr. Adolph Kohut, *Das Buch berühmter Duelle* (Berlin, 1888) for his Hungarian chapter; and see Steven Hughes, "Honor in Modern Italy and the *Codice Cavalleresco* of Iacopo Gelli," a paper prepared for the American Historical Association Annual Meeting (San Francisco, January 6–9, 1994), 2.

130. From the English periodical *The Hawk*, 2 February 1892, in *A Complete Bibliography*, 479.

131. See Jarausch, *Deutsche Studenten*, 64.

132. See Jürgen Kocka, "Bürgertum und bürgerliche Gesellschaft im 19. Jahrhundert," in *Bürgertum im 19. Jahrhundert: Deutschland im europäischen Vergleich*, vol. 1, ed. Jürgen Kocka (Munich, 1988), 70.

133. *SPdR*, 72d Session, 20 April 1896, 1805–7, 1903, according to Schall.

134. Von Fürich, *Das Duell*, 196–98.

135. *DKJ*, no. 31, 21 July 1913.

136. See von Fürich, *Das Duell*, 198.

137. Part 2, section 1, stanza 1, 26–27.

138. John Murder Ross, "Beyond the Phallic Illusion: Notes on Man's Heterosexuality," in *The Psychology of Men: New Psychoanalytic Perspectives*, ed. Gerald I. Fogel, Frederick M. Lane, and Robert S. Liebert (New York, 1986).

139. Ethel S. Person, "The Omni Available Woman and Lesbian Sex," in *The Psychology of Men*, 69.

140. By C. M. von Weber.

141. *Simplicissimus, Der Student: Kulturbilder aus dem Simplicissimus*, vol. 1 (Albert Langen Verlag, 1905), 38.

142. Mann, *Der Untertan*, 24.

143. *DKJ*, no. 258, 19 September 1898.

144. Rosa Mayreder, *A Survey of the Woman Problem*, a translation of *Zur Kritik der Weiblichkeit* (New York, 1913), 104.

145. Ibid., 132–33.

Chapter V

1. According to legend, after the performance of some brave and worthy deed, it was the medieval knight's sole wish to be granted *merci* as a sign of his Lady's favor. This might be merely a peck on the neck or perhaps a more explicit embrace. But above all, he desired only to please his Lady.

2. See Joachim Bumke, *The Concept of Knighthood in the Middle Ages*, translated from the German by W.T.H. and Erika Jackson (New York, 1982), 73, 77, 79–81, 87, 160.

3. *GSA*, Rep. 84a 8037, "Der Vorentwurf zu einem Deutschen Strafgesetzbuch und der Zweikampf. Eine kritische Untersuchung, Anlage E" (1912).

4. For a discussion of "The Cult of Invalidism" in late-nineteenth and early-twentieth-century Europe, see Bram Dijkstra, *Idols of Perversity: Fantasies of Feminine Evil in Fin-de-Siècle Culture* (New York, 1986), 25–63.

5. Alexander von Oettingen, *Zur Duellfrage* (Dorpat, 1889), 88–89.

6. *GSA*, Rep. 84a 8037, "Anträge der Deutschen Anti-Duell-Liga betr. Änderungen des Strafgesetzbuchs, der Gerichtsverfassung und der Strafprozessordnung zwecks Bekämpfung des Duellwesens" (March 1912), 8.

7. It is not clear if the War Minister meant relations with undesirable elements, varying degrees of "seduction," adultery, or all three. *DKJ*, no. 31, 21 July 1913.

8. See Luigi Barbasetti, *Ehren-Codex* (Vienna, 1898), 35–36, 41; and Gustav Ristow, *Ehrenkodex* (Vienna, 1909), 56.

9. See Clemens von Spohn, *Beurteilung der verschiedensten Ehrenfragen, die zu Ehrenhändeln und Ehrengerichten Anlass geben* (Berlin, 1911), 27.

10. Hermann Rumschöttel, *Das bayerische Offizierkorps, 1866–1914* (Munich, 1972), 166.

11. For quote, see Dr. Hugo Schramm, *Ein Pereat den Duellen* (Leipzig, 1869), 24.

12. See Dr. M. Liepmann, *Duell und Ehre* (Berlin, 1904), 41.

13. *SPdR*, 127th Session, 19 November 1896, 3337.

14. From an article entitled "Das Duell," in *SPdR*, 73d Session, 21 April 1896, 1834, as cited by the Conservative Schall.

15. See *SPdR*, 235th Session, 13 March 1914, 8091, according to Wendel of the SPD. See also *GSA*, Rep. 84a 8037, "Sonderdruck aus 'Der Salon' (Österreichisches Adelsblatt), Wien, 20.1.07, XV. Jahrgang, Nr. 3: 'Zur Frage der Duellbekämpfung' von Dr. Eduard Ritter von Liszt, Mitglied der Allgem. Anti-Duell-Liga für Österreich," 7, for a similar point of view as represented by the Austrian chapter of the League.

16. Von einem älteren aktiven Offizier, *Die conventionelle Gebräuche beim Zweikampf, unter besonderer Berücksichtigung des Offizierstandes* (Berlin, 1890), 9.

17. See Comte de Chatauvillard, *Duell-Codex*, translated from the French with notations by C.v.L. (Karlsruhe, 1888), chapter 1, article 2.

18. Ristow, *Ehrenkodex*, 30.

19. Franz von Bolgar, *Die Regeln des Duells* (Vienna, 1891), 8.

20. *BHSA*, Mkr. 11097, Lieutnant Freiherr von Berchem, "Ehrenhändel zwischen Offizieren und Zivilpersonen" (ca. 1904), 24.

21. Ristow, *Ehrenkodex* (Vienna, 1909), 30.

22. In 1991 there were a spate of "family honor" slayings of this kind among Muslims in Israel. See Joel Greenberg, "Honor Thy Sister," in *The Jerusalem Post Magazine* (3 January 1992).

23. *SPdR*, 145th Session, 17 February 1902, 4233, as expressed by Lenzmann of the Liberal Union.

24. See Dr. A. Reder, *Der Zweikampf im Deutschen Reichstag, 1896* (Munich, 1896), 5; and *DKJ*, no. 87, 27 March 1896.

25. *SPdH*, 10th Session, 8 May 1907, 173, from a statement by Graf von der Schulenberg-Günthal.

26. *SPdR*, 61st Session, 13 May 1912, 1942, according to Mertin of the *Reichspartei*. See also Albert von Boguslawski, *Die Ehre und das Duell* (Berlin, 1896), 83–84.

27. Dr. M. Liepmann, *Duell und Ehre* (Berlin, 1904), 24–25.

28. *GSA*, Rep. 84a 8037, Geh. Sanitätsrath Dr. Konrad Küster, "Das Duell," in *Beilage zur Allgemeinen Zeitung* 51 (3 March 1902).

29. *SPdR*, 235th Session, 13 March 1914, 8070–71.

30. See *DKJ*, no. 253, 15 September 1895.

31. Ristow, *Ehrenkodex*, 119; see also Barbasetti, *Ehren-Codex*, 64.

32. *SPdR*, 10th Session, 13 December 1886, 188, according to Rheinhaben of the *Reichspartei*.

33. For examples, see *DKJ*, no. 155, 28 March 1894; and *DKJ*, no. 201, 23 July 1896.

34. As discussed in the "Anträge der Deutschen Anti-Duell-Liga betr. Änderungen des Strafgesetzbuchs, der Gerichtsverfassung und der Strafpro-

zessordnung zwecks Bekämpfung des Duellwesens," *GSA*, Rep. 84a 8037. See also *SPdR*, 140th Session, 11 February 1902, 4112, for a brief discussion of the Falkenhagen-Bennigsen case, illustrating the last of these roadblocks to prosecution of adultery as a punitive insult. In military circles, court of honor proceedings for *Ehebruch* followed the guidelines elaborated above. As an example see *GLA*, Bestand 456 F9, Bestellnummer 472.

35. "Verhandlungen des im Jahre 1848 zusammenberufenen Vereinigten ständischen Ausschusses," vol. 3, compiled by Eduard Bleich (Berlin, 1848), 411–14, as cited in Theodor Fontane, *Effi Briest: mit Materialien*, ed. Hans-Peter Reisner and Rainer Siegle (Berlin, 1984), 332–33.

36. Jürgen Kocka, "Bürgertum und bürgerliche Gesellschaft im 19. Jahrhundert: Europäische Entwicklungen und deutsche Eigenarten," in *Bürgertum im 19. Jahrhundert: Deutschland im europäischen Vergleich*, vol. 1, ed. Jürgen Kocka (Munich, 1988), 44–45.

37. Arthur Schopenhauer, *Essays and Aphorisms*, ed. and trans. R. J. Hollingdale (Penguin Books, 1970), 86.

38. For quote, see David Luft, "Schopenhauer, Austria, and the Generation of 1905," in *Journal of Central European History* (March 1982): 54–55.

39. Schopenhauer, *Essays*, 86.

40. See Steven E. Aschheim, "Zarathustra in the Trenches: The Nietzsche Myth and World War I," in *Religion, Ideology and Nationalism in Europe* (Festschrift Yehoshua Arieli, Jerusalem, 1986), for a discussion of *Zarathustra*'s popularity among German soldiers during the war.

41. Friedrich Nietzsche, *Also Sprach Zarathustra: Ein Buch für Alle und Keinen* (Stockholm, 1948), Book 1, "Von Alten und Jungen Weiblein": 67–69.

42. Walter Kaufmann, ed. and trans., *The Portable Nietzsche* (New York, 1968), 105.

43. From H. A. Reyburn et al., *Nietzsche* (London, 1948), 293 ff., as cited in V. G. Kiernan, *The Duel in European History: Honour and Reign of the Aristocracy* (Oxford, 1988), 277.

44. From Kaufmann, *The Portable Nietzsche*, 105.

45. Eric Bentley, *A Century of Hero Worship* (Boston, 1957), 86–87. Bentley's name for these sources is "Heroic Vitalism."

46. Book 2, chapter 12, as cited in Gordon Craig, *Germany, 1866–1945* (Oxford, 1978), 194.

47. Barry Millington, *Wagner* (New York, 1984), 55–56. According to Millington, Wagner never dueled, but as a student in the 1830s he more than once "received the summons to an appointed place and faced the prospect of serious injury or worse. On one occasion he was saved by the fact that his opponent cut an artery in a previous contest; on another, his would-be adversary was killed in a duel shortly before they were to meet." (p. 8)

48. Dijkstra, *Idols*, 228.

49. Eric Bentley, *Hero Worship*, 182, calls Siegfried "manifestly and *par excellence*, the hero of Heroic Vitalism."

50. See *The Simon and Schuster Book of Opera* (New York, 1978), 218, for a summary of the action from *Lohengrin*.

51. Michelet quote as cited in Dijkstra, *Idols*, 20.

52. Eduard von Hartmann, *Moderne Probleme* (Leipzig, 1886), 37–43.

53. Eduard von Hartmann, *Tagesfragen* (Leipzig, 1896), 135–37.

54. See also Schopenhauer, *Essays*, 86: "Man strives in everything for a *direct* domination over things, either by comprehending or by subduing them. but woman is everywhere and always relegated to a merely *indirect* domination, which is achieved by means of man, who is consequently the only thing she has to dominate directly. Thus it lies in the nature of women to regard everything simply as a means of capturing a man, and their interest in anything else is only simulated, is no more than a detour, i.e., amounts to coquetry and mimicry."

55. Friedrich Paulsen, *System der Ethik* (Berlin, 1889), 387–88, 448, 507–8.

56. Albert von Öthalom, *Ehre und Ehrenschutz* (Vienna, Leipzig, 1908), 127.

57. See Heinrich von Treitschke, *Deutsche Geschichte im Neunzehnten Jahrhundert*, vol. 5 (Berlin, 1894), 480; von Öthalom, *Ehrenschutz*, 109–10; and von Boguslawski, *Die Ehre*, 24.

58. Kiernan, *The Duel*, 129.

59. See Antony Simpson, "Dandelions on the Field of Honor: Dueling, the Middle Classes, and the Law in Nineteenth-Century England," in *Criminal Justice History* 9 (1988): 116; and Stuart O. Landry, *Duelling in Old New Orleans* (New Orleans, 1950), 23, as corroborated by W. O. Stevens, *Pistols at Ten Paces* (n.p., n.d.).

60. Von Berchem, "Ehrenhändel," 24.

61. Von Spohn, *Ehrenfragen*, 31.

62. *DKJ*, no. 5, 6 January 1900.

63. See Johann Wolfgang von Goethe, *Faust* (Stuttgart, 1986), pt. 1, 3770–75: 110.

64. For a complete roster of the male pecking order in duels for women's honor, see Ristow, *Ehrenkodex*, 118–19; and Barbasetti, *Ehren-Codex*, 63–64.

65. *GSA*, Rep. 84a 8040 (1897): case # 9.

66. A duel never took place. It is not even clear if she was actually with child. What is clear is that, in Schnitzler's words, "basically I couldn't stand her." See Arthur Schnitzler, *My Youth in Vienna*, trans. Catherine Hutter (New York, 1970), 220.

67. Dr. Emil Dangelmaier, *Der Kampf um die Ehre* (Vienna, Leipzig, 1896), 9.

68. Herbert Cysarz, "Vom Diesseits und Jenseits der Ehre," in *Dichtung und Volkstum* 2 (1942): 83, as cited in Franz Haider, *Die Ehre als menschliches Problem* (Munich, 1972), 106.

69. Von Oettingen, *Duellfrage*, 88–101.

70. *Simplicissimus, Der Student: Kulturbilder aus dem Simplicissimus*, vol. 1 (Albert Langen Verlag, 1905), 36.

71. Heinrich Mann, *Der Untertan* (Berlin, 1964), 50, 92.

72. Von Öthalom, *Ehre und Ehrenschutz* (Vienna, Leipzig, 1908), 118.

73. See Gabriel Tarde, "Le Duel," in *Etudes pénales et sociales*, pt. 1 (Paris, 1892), 61; and L. Jeudon, *Le Morale de l'honneur* (Paris, 1911), 124, as cited in Edward Berenson, "The Affaire Caillaux: Honor, Masculinity, and the Duel in France of the Belle Epoque," in *Proceedings of the Western Society for French History* (New Orleans, 1990).

74. For episode, see Henry James, *The American* (New American Library, 1980), 210–14.

75. Carl von Rüts, *Die Duellgegnerschaft* (Berlin, 1903), 26.

76. See Heinrich Graf Coudenhove, *Der Minotaur der „Ehre": Studie zur Anti-duellbewegung und Duelllüge* (Berlin, 1902), 36.

77. *SPdR*, 61st Session, 13 May 1912, 1942, according to Heyn.

78. Von Öthalom, *Ehrenschutz*, 117.

79. *DKJ*, no. 279, 9 October 1901.

80. Schnitzler, *My Youth*, 209. As for Schnitzler's Vienna, in an 1894 report of a Viennese pistol duel, Berlin's *Das Kleine Journal* expressed surprise at the revelation that a woman for once had not been ascertained as the immediate causal factor. See *DKJ*, no. 247, 26 June 1894.

81. Barbasetti, *Ehren-Codex*, 2, 4.

82. *GSA*, Rep. 84a 8037, "Beleidigungsprozess und Duell."

83. See von Boguslawski, *Die Ehre*, 83.

84. Von einem älteren aktiven Offizier, *Gebräuche*, 14.

85. Ibid.

86. *DKJ*, no. 197, 20 July 1893.

87. For coverage of this case, see *DKJ*, no. 27, 16 January 1894; *DKJ*, no. 28, 16 January 1894; *DKJ*, no. 34, 19 January 1894; *DKJ*, no. 36, 20 January 1894; *DKJ*, no. 43, 24 January 1894; *DKJ*, no. 233, 12 June 1894; and *DKJ*, no. 245, 24 June 1894.

88. His opponent *Leutnant* Vogt was pardoned after a year of his sentence had been served. See *DKJ*, no. 207, 29 July 1902.

89. *DKJ*, no. 247, 8 September 1898.

90. See Ristow, *Ehrenkodex*, 123, for the proscription of duels between in-laws.

91. *GSA*, Rep. 84a 8040 (1897): case # 17.

92. *DKJ*, no. 204, 27 July 1892.

93. *DKJ*, no. 345, 15 December 1892.

94. Ristow, *Ehrenkodex*, 119.

95. See von Bolgar, *Die Regeln*, 57.

96. In those rare duels when a woman was at obvious issue. See Robert A. Nye, *Masculinity and Male Codes of Honor in Modern France* (Oxford, 1993), 203.

97. See von Spohn, *Ehrenfragen*, 27, for the first part of this advice which was tendered officers, but which I have freely interpolated as general counsel since what applied to the officer in matters of honor was in almost every instance a guideline for the civilian. For the second part, see Barbasetti, *Ehren-Codex*, 64.

98. Von Spohn, *Ehrenfragen*, 30, 27.

99. Von Hartmann, *Moderne Probleme*, 43.

100. Wilhelm Heydrich, "Eine Ehrenschuld," in *DKJ*, no. 1, 2 January 1912.

101. For example, see Barbasetti, *Ehren-Codex*, 69.

102. See Major von Krafft, *Dienst und Leben des jungen Infanterie-Offiziers* (Berlin, 1914), 243; and von Boguslawski, *Die Ehre*, 83–84.

103. Arthur Schnitzler, *Ritterlichkeit*, ed. Rena R. Schlein (Bonn, 1975), 60.

104. *SPdR*, 72d Session, 20 April 1896, 1810, as paraphrased by August Bebel.

105. *SPdR*, 241st Session, 12 March 1914, 8260, as quoted by von Brockhausen of the Conservatives. In later Reichstag debates on the dueling question, the Social Democrats were constantly having to justify Lassalle's actions in light of their own virulent opposition to what they customarily referred to as a feudal practice.

106. For a detailed account of the affair, see Dr. Adolph Kohut, *Das Buch berühmter Duelle* (Berlin, 1888), 105–26. Von Rakowicz married Helene, then died. Helene extended her reputation as an adventuress and committed suicide in old age.

107. Ristow, *Ehrenkodex*, 118.

108. Act 2, scene 9, as cited in Haider, *Die Ehre* (Munich, 1972), 87.

109. Arthur Schnitzler, *Reigen und andere Dramen: Das dramatische Werk*, vol. 2 (Frankfurt am Main, 1962), 311. Other works by Schnitzler in which the duel and/or honor theme somehow figures are *Der Weg ins Freie* (1908), "Das Tagebuch der Redegonda" (1908), *Fink und Fliederbusch* (1916), "Casanova's Heimfahrt" (1917), and "Spiel im Morgengrauen" (1926).

110. See Fontane, *Effi Briest*, 15.

111. Fontane, *Effi Briest*, quotes in order of appearance: 34, 36, 32, 6, 300.

112. Fontane, *Effi Briest*, chapter 27, 238–41. There was a real Effi Briest whose story Fontane used as his model. Her name was Elisabeth Freiin von Plotho, called "Else," born in 1853 on her parents' Elbian estate. In 1873 at the age of nineteen she married the twenty-four-year-old Hussar officer Armand Leon von Ardenne. The pair settled in Berlin along the Lützowufer near the old Zoological Garden. The drama that concerns us was precipitated in 1886 when Ardenne ran across stored letters in a box from a close friend of his, the judge Emil Hartwich, to his wife, both of whom were planning to abandon their spouses and elope. Ardenne instigated divorce proceedings against Else on the basis of the letters and challenged Hartwich. Hartwich was known as an excellent shot, but Ardenne had already notched up several duels. Experience carried the day, and Hartwich begged forgiveness just before he died. Three and one-half months later Ardenne's marriage was dissolved, with the father retaining wardship of the children. Ardenne was convicted of his crime, but was soon pardoned and went on to forge a brilliant career in the War Ministry. After the divorce, Else devoted her life to care of the sick and needy. She died one year before her hundredth birthday in 1952 in Lindau am Bodensee. See Hans Werner Seiffert with Christel Laufer, "Fontane's *Effi Briest* und Spielhagen's *Zum Zeitvertreib*: Zeugnisse und Materialien," in *Studien zur neueren deutschen Literatur*, ed. Hans Werner Seiffert (East Berlin, 1964), 260–66. As cited in Fontane, *Effi Briest*, 308–12.

113. See Julian Pitt-Rivers, "The Concept of Honor," in *Honour and Shame: The Values of Mediterranean Society*, ed. J. G. Peristiany (Chicago, 1966), 26.

114. See Kaufmann, *The Portable Nietzsche*, "Notes" (1880–81): 73–74.

115. Theodor Fontane, *Cécile* (Munich, 1969), quotes in order of appearance: 170–75, 178. Cécile dies a mysterious death shortly after the duel.

Chapter VI

1. Alfred d'Almbert, *Physiologie du duel* (Brussels, 1853), 16.

2. *SPdR*, 126th Session, 17 November 1896, 3314.

3. *DKJ*, no. 32, 1 February 1893.

4. See Emile Colombey, *Histoire Anecdotique du Duel* (Paris, 1861), 328.

5. See Axel Vorberg, *Der Zweikampf in Frankreich* (Leipzig, 1899), 56.

6. Ibid., 57–58.

7. See Gabriel LeTainturier-Fradin, *Le Duel à travers les Ages, Histoire et Législation, Duels Célèbres—Code du Duel* (Paris, 1892), 191–94; and Dr. Adolph Kohut, *Das Buch berühmter Duelle* (Berlin, 1888), 220–22, for accounts of famous political duels of the time.

8. See LeTainturier-Fradin, *Le Duel*, 67–69.

9. See, for example, the 1845 Beauvallon-Dujarries duel in Kohut, *Das Buch*, 208.

10. This report appeared in the *Revue critique de législation et de jurisprudence, 1858–1859*, as cited in LeTainturier-Fradin, *Le Duel*, 74–75.

11. Ibid., 75.

12. Ibid.

13. See Robert A. Nye, "Fencing, the Duel and Republican Manhood in the Third Republic," in *Journal of Contemporary History* 25 (1990): 371.

14. Don Alfonso von Bourbon und Österreich-Este, *Kurzgefasste Geschichte der Bildung und Entwicklung der Ligen wider den Zweikampf und zum Schutze der Ehre in den verschiedenen Ländern Europas vom Ende November 1900 bis 7. Februar 1908* (Vienna, 1909), 7.

15. Ibid.

16. Gustave Flaubert, *L'Education Sentimentale* (Paris, 1985), 294–95.

17. Grosculade, "Le Duel pour Tous," in *L'Illustration*, 28 July 1888.

18. Libretto by Enrico Golisciani. See *The Simon and Schuster Book of Opera* (New York, 1978), 289.

19. Chatauvillard, *Essai*, "Du Duel à L'Epée," chapter 5, article 16. All this jumping around could lead to a fall, and occasionally duelists did take tumbles. It was a matter of debate whether or not an opponent was justified in continuing his assault under such circumstances, since the fall could be brought about by either his skill or the incompetence of his fallen foe. Sometimes falling was even a play-possum ruse to put another off guard. It goes without saying that Germans deplored such tactics.

20. "Le Duel Pini-San Malato," in *L'Illustration*, 12 March 1904.

21. "Un Duel de Maîtres D'Armes," in *L'Illustration*, 2 February 1901.

22. See *The Times*, 8 September 1890, in *A Complete Bibliography of Fencing and Duelling*, ed. Carl Thimm (London, 1896), 453.

23. "Le Duel du prince de Sagan et de M. Abel Hermant, au parc de Saint-Ouen," in *L'Illustration*, 18 April 1896.

24. See Josef Bartunek, *Die Austragung von Ehrenangelegenheiten: Ein Beitrag zur zeitgemässen Lösung der Satisfaktionsfrage* (Vienna, 1912), 19–20; and Carl von Rüts, *Die Duellgegnerschaft* (Berlin, 1903), 7.

25. "L'Escrime à Paris," in *L'Illustration*, 9 June 1888.

26. Major Ben C. Truman, *The Field of Honor: Being a Complete and Comprehensive History of Duelling in all Countries* (New York, 1884), 26.

27. Robert A. Nye, *Masculinity and Male Codes of Honor in Modern France* (Oxford, 1993), 163–66.

28. "L'Escrime à Paris," in *L'Illustration*, 16 June 1888.

29. Ibid.

30. Guy de Maupassant, *Oeuvres Complètes* (Paris, 1979), 138.

31. Germaine de Staël, *De L'Allemagne* (Paris, 1958), 77.

32. "Le Duel dans les Universités Allemandes," in *L'Illustration*, 30 September 1893.

33. "Les Duels D'Etudiants," in *L'Illustration*, 27 August 1910.

34. See the discussion of Emile André in *DKJ*, no. 271, 1 October 1897.

35. Comte de Duverger de St. Thomas, *Nouveau Code du Duel* (Paris, 1887), 156–57. See Chatauvillard, *Essai*, "Des Témoins: De Leur Devoir en Général," chapter 4, article 6, 20–21: "Le devoir des témoins consiste à régler les choses de manière à ce qu'il y ait le moins de désavantage possible pour celui qu'ils accompagnent; cependant ils doivent toujours êtres justes, équitable et polis les uns envers les autres." This generally translated into making sure that both duelists escaped unhurt.

36. Mark Twain, *A Tramp Abroad* (New York, 1879), 59. In fairness, the French had not always been so milquetoast. In the half decade from 1830 to 1834, when the Parisian pistol duel boomed, there were 129 recorded dueling fatalities—approximately one-third of the estimated total duels ending in death. In contrast, following the duel's authoritative codification by Chatauvillard in 1836 (thus ameliorating abuses) and strong judicial pronouncements by France's Attorney General Dupin in 1837 and 1839 concerning the duel and its deleterious effects, during the five-year span from 1839 to 1843 fatalities sunk dramatically to 29 without any correspondingly appreciative dip in the number of annual duels. See Vorberg, *Der Zweikampf*, 59; Albert von Boguslawski, *Die Ehre und das Duell* (Berlin, 1896), 53–54; and d'Almbert, *Physiologie*, 85–91. It would seem that during the middle years of the century the staged French pistol duel established itself as a means by which to salve the sting of injured honor while yet eluding the grasp of French justice. But as it became generally accepted practice in French jurisprudence to prosecute only those dueling fatalities incurred as a result of irregular procedure, Dupin's requisitions may simply have functioned as an unexpected yet pleasant reprieve that French duelists did not intend to squander, as a sort of welcome excuse among duelists to stem the body count through bogus combat. Anyway, there seem not to have been any candle-lit vigils in Notre Dame over the passing of the real thing.

37. *L'Illustration*, 8 November 1902.

38. Ibid.

39. See V. G. Kiernan, *The Duel in European History: Honour and Reign of the Aristocracy* (Oxford, 1988), 267.

40. "Le Duel André-de Négrier," in *L'Illustration*, 11 August 1906.

41. See *L'Illustration*, "Un Duel de Maîtres D'Armes," 2 February 1901; *L'Illustration*, "Le Duel Pini-San Malato," 12 March 1904; and *L'Illustration*, "Duels D'Escrimeurs," 31 January 1905.

42. Twain, *A Tramp*, 61.

43. From the *Sunday Times*, 21 September 1890, in *A Complete Bibliography*, 458.

44. *DKJ*, no. 320, 19 November 1903.

45. Maupassant, *"Un Lâche,"* in *Oeuvres Complètes*, 916.

46. Quoted in Kohut, *Das Buch*, 173.

47. Nye, *Male Codes of Honor*, 175–76, 187–90.

48. Ibid., 160.

49. Kohut, *Das Buch*, 176.

50. "Le Duel du 3 Septembre," in *L'Illustration*, 9 September 1882.

51. Kohut, *Das Buch*, 226.

52. See Edgar Holt, *The Life of Georges Clemenceau, 1841–1929* (London, 1976), 8n. I, as cited in Kiernan, *The Duel*, 267.

53. See Nye, *Male Codes of Honor*, 194–96.

54. As cited in Duverger de St. Thomas, *Nouveau Code*, 148.

55. From *The Daily News*, 18 May 1891, in *A Complete Bibliography*, 466.

56. See Vorberg, *Der Zweikampf*, 60–61.

57. Chatauvillard gave civilians and retired officers, as well as all officers unfamiliar with the weapon, the right to always reject a saber duel. See *Essai*, "De la Nature des Armes," chapter 2, article 1, 13–14.

58. Flaubert, *L'Education Sentimentale*, 289.

59. From Steinmetz, *The Romance of Duelling in All Times and Countries* (London, 1868), i, vii, as quoted in Kiernan, *The Duel*, 265.

60. See Nye, *Male Codes of Honor*, 197–98.

61. In the first round, Floquet's left calf and Boulanger's left index finger were bloodied, but the bout was not discontinued. At the signal *"Allez!"* commencing the second round, Boulanger dived at the surprised Floquet, who buried the point of his épée in the General's bearded throat. To prevent a fatal hemorrhage, the attending physician stopped-up the gash with his fingers. Perhaps it would have been a more fitting and heroic death-knell to the General and the Boulangist movement had he succumbed to his wound, but he did recover only to fumble away his political gains in January of the next year and commit a pitiful suicide on the grave of his mistress two years after that. Clemenceau, who had served as Floquet's second, proposed the epitaph: "Here lies General Boulanger, who died as he lived—like a second lieutenant." The death of the Boulangist movement unleashed a series of duels among the General's disenchanted apostles in which no one was killed. See "Le Duel Boulanger-Floquet," 21 July 1888, in *L'Illustration*; and LeTainturier-Fradin, *Le Duel*, 202–5.

62. Ambrose Bierce, *The Devil's Dictionary* (New York, 1991), 37. This work was begun as a weekly column in 1881 and continued until 1906. It was published as a complete text originally in 1911.

Conclusion

1. Guy de Maupassant, "Un Duel," in *Boule de Suif, Le Maison Tellier* (Paris, 1973).

2. Jürgen Kocka, "Einleitung," in *Bürger und Bürgerlichkeit im 19. Jahrhundert*, ed. Jürgen Kocka (Göttingen, 1987), 11.

3. See David Blackbourn, *Populists and Patricians: Essays in Modern German History* (London, 1987), "The Discreet Charm of the German Bourgeoisie," 70.

4. If you wish to read "Silver Blaze" for yourself, quite a good story actually, stop here . . . for the "curious incident" alluded to by Holmes was the dog not barking (or enough) when someone the dog knew well entered the stable to abduct a prize race horse it was supposed to be guarding. There is more than just a lesson in detective work here—like Maupassant's *"Un Duel,"* there is something of an historical allegory. See Sir Arthur Conan Doyle, "Silver Blaze," in *The Complete Sherlock Holmes*, vol. 1 (Garden City, New York: 1930), 347.

5. Ute Frevert, *Ehrenmänner: Das Duell in der bürgerlichen Gesellschaft* (Munich, 1991). See also id., "Bürgerlichkeit und Ehre: Zur Geschichte des Duells in England und Deutschland," in *Bürgertum im 19. Jahrhundert: Deutschland im europäischen Vergleich*, vol. 3, ed. Jürgen Kocka (Munich, 1988).

6. Jürgen Kocka affirms the essential affinities between *"frühliberalen"* thinking and *"bürgerliche Kultur."* See Jürgen Kocka, "Bürgertum und bürgerliche Gesellschaft im 19. Jahrhundert: Europäische Entwicklungen und deutsche Eigenarten," in *Bürgertum*, 1:36–37. See also Kocka's foreword to *Liberalismus im 19. Jahrhundert: Deutschland im europäischen Vergleich*, ed. Dieter Langewiesche (Göttingen, 1988), 10; and id., 13: "Liberalism and 'bourgeois society' appear to have formed a symbiosis."

7. For treatments of the *Bildung* thesis, see Frevert, *Ehrenmänner*, 178–96; "Bürgerlichkeit und Ehre"; and "Die Ehre der Bürger im Spiegel ihrer Duelle: Ansichten des 19. Jahrhunderts," in *Historische Zeitschrift* 249 (1989), and for its English version, see id., "Bourgeois Honor: Middle-Class Duellists in Germany From the Late Eighteenth Century to the Early Twentieth Century," in *The German Bourgeoisie: Essays on the Social History of the German Middle Class from the Late Eighteenth to the Early Twentieth Century*, ed. David Blackbourn and Richard J. Evans (London, 1991).

8. Thomas Mann, *Der Zauberberg* (Frankfurt am Main, 1952), 959.

9. V. G. Kiernan, *The Duel in European History: Honour and Reign of the Aristocracy* (Oxford, 1988), 330.

10. See Friedhelm Guttadin, *Das Paradoxe Schicksal der Ehre: Zum Wandel der adligen Ehre und zur Bedeutung von Duell und Ehre für den monarchischen Zentralstaat* (Berlin, 1993), 7–43.

11. Arno J. Mayer, *The Persistence of the Old Regime: Europe to the Great War* (New York, 1981), 13.

12. Ibid., 127. England and France are the occasional exceptions in other respects to Mayer's general argument. Because it is in the light of these two western industrialized countries that a German *Sonderweg* should be primarily discussed, I cannot therefore agree with David Blackbourn's assessment that,

"Work of this kind [Mayer's] has had the effect of making the 'feudalized' German bourgeoisie seem less peculiar after all." Work of this kind rather reinforces the case (and, in my prejudiced view, Mayer's strongest national case) to be made for a deeply "feudalized" German bourgeoisie vis-à-vis comparatively unsullied France and England. Although approving of what he sees as the implications of Mayer's thesis, Blackbourn predictably rejects Mayer's conclusion that the idea of an *embourgeoisement* in nineteenth-century Germany, and the rest of Europe, is a lot of nonsense. Both Blackbourn and Mayer are partially right: the idea of *embourgeoisement* is plainly more nonsensical in the context of some countries than in others. See Blackbourn, "Discreet Charm," 67–68.

13. Kocka, "Bürgertum," 53.

14. Luigi Barbasetti, *Ehren-Codex* (Vienna, 1896), 2.

15. Isabel V. Hull, *The Entourage of Kaiser Wilhelm II, 1888–1918* (Cambridge, 1982), 196.

16. *SPdR*, 235th Session, 13 March 1914, 8091, according to Wendel of the SPD.

17. See *SPdR*, 127th Session, 19 November 1896, 3329, and Lenzmann of the Liberal Union's report of an officer of the First Badenese Guard Regiment asking a soldier, during an instruction class, "Who is the inner enemy?" The soldier shot back the rote answer: "Civilians."

18. See Jonathan Steinberg, "The Kaiser's Navy and German Society," in *Past and Present* 28 (July 1964).

19. See Frevert, *Ehrenmänner*, 123.

20. Friedrich Meinecke, *Erlebtes, 1862–1901* (Leipzig, 1941), 167–68.

21. Fritz Stern, *The Politics of Cultural Despair: A Study in the Rise of Germanic Ideology* (Berkeley, 1961), 98.

22. Eric Bentley, *A Century of Hero-Worship* (Boston, 1957), 200.

23. Henry M. Pachter, *Modern Germany: A Social, Cultural, and Political History* (Boulder, Colo.: 1978), 41.

24. Barbara Tuchman, *The Proud Tower: A Portrait of the World Before the War, 1890–1914* (New York, 1966), 375–76.

25. E. Thesing, *Duell—Ehre—„Ernst"* (Marburg, 1896), 10, as cited in Guttandin, *Paradoxe Schicksal*, 289–90.

26. Mayer, *Persistence*, 306, 290.

27. For these terms, see Hans-Ulrich Wehler, "Deutsches Bildungsbürgertum in vergleichender Perspektive—Elemente eines 'Sonderwegs'?" in *Bildungsbürgertum im 19. Jahrhundert*, ed. Jürgen Kocka (Stuttgart, 1989), 223; and Wehler, "Wie 'bürgerlich' war das Deutsche Kaiserreich?" in *Bürger*, 268.

28. See Detlef Bald, "Zum Kriegsbild der militärischen Führung im Kaiserreich," in *Bereit zum Krieg: Kriegsmentalität im wilhelmischen Deutschland 1890–1914*, ed. Jost Dülffer and Karl Holl (Göttingen, 1986); and Fritz Stern, *Gold and Iron: Bismarck, Bleichröder, and the Building of the German Empire* (New York, 1977), for the mutually profitable alliance between old elites and the new upper bourgeoisie of finance capitalism.

29. Wehler, "Wie 'bürgerlich'?" 271.

30. For much of the above, see Kocka, "Bürgertum," 47–54; and id., "Bürg-

ertum und Bürgerlichkeit als Probleme der deutschen Geschichte vom späten 18. zum frühen 20. Jahrhundert," in *Bürger*, 33–48.

31. Mayer, *Persistence*, 98–99.

32. Wehler, "Deutsches Bildungsbürgertum," 222.

33. Wehler, "Wie 'bürgerlich'?" 258, 272, 273. Wehler opts for the expression *"Sonderbedingungen"* (special conditions) instead of the more daring term of *Sonderweg* in his discussion of German history. See Wehler, "Deutsches Bildungsbürgertum," 236.

34. Wolfram Siemann, *Gesellschaft im Aufbruch: Deutschland, 1849–1871* (Frankfurt am Main, 1990), 222.

35. David Blackbourn and Geoff Eley, *The Peculiarities of German History: Bourgeois Society and Politics in Nineteenth-Century Germany* (Oxford, 1984).

36. Ibid., 235.

37. Blackbourn and Evans, *The German Bourgeoisie*, 14.

38. See Blackbourn, *Peculiarities*, 190–94.

39. David Blackbourn, "Kommentar" [to Hans Ulrich Wehler's "Wie 'bürgerlich' war das Deutsche Kaiserreich?"], in *Bürger*, 283.

40. Blackbourn, *Peculiarities*, 199–205.

41. Guttandin, *Paradoxe Schicksal*, 369, 370.

42. Richard J. Evans, *Rethinking German History: Nineteenth-Century Germany and the Origins of the Third Reich* (London, 1987), 112, 108. For similar "comparative" advice see also Kocka, "Bürgertum und Bürgerlichkeit," 51.

43. Blackbourn, "Discreet Charm," 73.

44. Robert A. Nye, *Masculinity and Male Codes of Honor in Modern France* (Oxford, 1993), 167. *Embourgeoisement* is a word also used by Nye to describe the duel's status in nineteenth-century France (ibid., 133).

45. And the British case in this respect is neither—to quote Geoff Eley— "historically misconceived" nor "ideal-typical." Little or no dueling—or harmless dueling—in a country at the fin de siècle was far and away the European norm. For Eley's humble caveats against the British comparison, see "Liberalism, Europe, and the Bourgeoisie 1860–1914," in *The German Bourgeoisie*, ed. Blackbourn and Evans, 312–13.

46. See Blackbourn, *The German Bourgeoisie*, 14, for his view that "Ute Frevert . . . provides a much-needed corrective on [an] issue often taken as symptomatic of bourgeois feudalization: dueling."

47. Ralf Dahrendorf, *Society and Democracy in Germany* (New York, 1967), 3–16, 28–29.

48. Steven Hughes, "Honor in Modern Italy and the *Codice Cavalleresco* of Iacopo Gelli," in a paper prepared for the American Historical Association Annual Meeting (San Francisco, 6–9 January 1994), 2.

49. Cited by Tyler Marshall, "Saying 'NO' to Nazis in Germany," in *Los Angeles Times*, 5 December 1992.

50. Robert Koehl, "Feudal Aspects of National Socialism," in *The American Political Science Review* 54, no. 4 (December 1960): 921, 929.

51. The "Flag-Bearer" was part of the 1937 "German Art" exhibit held in Munich to contrast such work with the "degenerate art" of Jewish and so-called "modern" artists.

52. Franz von Bolgar, *Die Regeln des Duells* (Vienna, 1891), III; and Gustav Ristow, *Ehrenkodex* (Vienna, 1909), 18.

53. Gustav Hergsell, *Duell-Codex* (Vienna, 1891).

54. Quotes in order of appearance: Ristow, *Ehrenkodex*, 79; ibid., 80; Hergsell, *Duell-Codex*, 87; Ristow, *Ehrenkodex*, 1; Hergsell, *Duell-Codex*, 67; Ristow, *Ehrenkodex*, 13; ibid., 3; Hergsell, *Duell-Codex*, 4; Barbasetti, *Ehren-Codex*, 15; von Bolgar, *Die Regeln* , 8.

55. It was only out of respect for the victims of a mine disaster that the tournament was canceled at the last minute. See Mayer, *Persistence*, 100. The life-style of Friedrich Alfred Krupp, residing since the 1890s at the 300-room Villa Hügel, was in stark contrast to his *Vormärz* grandfather who lodged across the street from his factory. See Kocka, "Bürgertum," 67.

56. Mark Girouard, *The Return of Camelot: Chivalry and the English Gentleman* (New Haven, 1981). The primary difference between the two styles seems to have been the fact that the Englishman tended to reflect more fully chivalry's service component of noblesse oblige, a notion to which German men of honor paid lip service but for the most part regarded as an effete British eccentricity.

57. Karl Dietrich Bracher, *The German Dictatorship* (New York, 1970), 357.

58. See Heinz Höhne, *The Order of the Death's Head: The Story of Hitler's SS*, trans. Richard Barry (New York, 1970), 159.

59. For quotes, see Herbert F. Ziegler, *Nazi Germany's New Aristocracy: The SS Leadership, 1925–1939* (Princeton, 1989), XV; Robert Koehl, *The Black Corps* (Madison, 1983), 226; and Roger Manvell and Heinrich Fraenkel, *Himmler* (New York, 1965), 48.

60. Höhne, *Death's Head*, 152, 149.

61. Peter Padfield, *Himmler* (New York, 1990), 139.

62. Höhne, *Death's Head*, 151–52.

63. Padfield, *Himmler*, 139.

64. For quotes, see Henry V. Dicks, *Licensed Mass Murder: A Socio-Psychological Study of Some SS Killers* (New York, 1972), 49; Höhne, *Death's Head*, 159; and Ziegler, *Germany's New Aristocracy*.

65. Bracher, *German Dictatorship*, 421.

66. Hans Buchheim et al., *Anatomy of the SS State*, trans. Richard Barry, Marian Jackson, and Dorothy Long (New York, 1968), 321, 328.

67. Dahrendorf, *Society and Democracy*, 329.

68. Padfield, *Himmler*, 139.

Bibliography

Manuscript Sources

Bayerisches Hauptstaatsarchiv (Munich), Abteilung IV, Bestand Kriegsminis-
terium, Mkr. 1854M–1855, 11097–11098, 11223–11226, 17640.
Geheimes Staatsarchiv (Berlin), Bestand Justizministerium, Rep. 84a 8034–
8042.
Generallandesarchiv (Karlsruhe), Bestand Kriegsministerium, Bestand 456 F9.
Hauptstaatsarchiv (Stuttgart), Bestand Kriegsministerium, Bestand M 1/7
Bu 35.

Published Documents

Stenographische Protokolle des Reichstags, Sessions from 1886–1914 (as collated
in *GSA*, Rep. 84a 8036 and 8037).

Newspapers

Das Kleine Journal, Berlin (from the Staatsbibliothek Ost-Berlin): 1883–1884,
1892–1907, 1910, 1912–1913.
Illustrierte Zeitung, Leipzig (from the Bildarchiv Berlin): 1895.
L'Illustration, Paris (from the Kunstbibliothek and the Bildarchiv Berlin): 1880–
1911.

Books and Articles Cited in Text

Alighieri, Dante. *The Divine Comedy*. Trans. H. R. Huse. U.S.A., 1954.
Allers, C. W. *Das Deutsche Corpsleben*, with introductory text by Professor Fr.
Moldenhauen. Stuttgart, Berlin, Leipzig, ca. 1902.
Andrews, Donna T. "The code of honor and its critics: the opposition to
duelling in England, 1700–1850." *Social History* 5, no. 3, 1980.
Aschheim, Steven E. "Zarathustra in the Trenches: The Nietzsche Myth and
World War I." *Religion, Ideology and Nationalism in Europe*, Festschrift
Yehoshua Arieli, Jerusalem, 1986.
Balan, C. *Duell und Ehre: Ein Beitrag zur praktischen Lösung der Duellfrage unter
besonderer Berücksichtigung der Verhältnisse des Deutschen Offizierkorps*. Ber-
lin, 1890.
Baldick, Robert. *The Duel*. Great Britain, 1965.
Barbasetti, Luigi. *Ehren-Codex*. Vienna, 1898.
Barber, Richard. *The Knight and Chivalry*. New York, 1970.
Bartunek, Josef. *Die Austragung von Ehrenangelegenheiten: Ein Beitrag zur
zeitgemässen Lösung der Satisfaktionsfrage*. Vienna, 1912.
Below, Georg von. *Das Duell in Deutschland: Geschichte und Gegenwart*. Kassel,
1896.

Below, Georg von. *Das Duell und der germanische Ehrbegriff*. Kassel, 1896.

Bentley, Eric. *A Century of Hero Worship*. Boston, 1957.

Berenson, Edward. "The Affaire Caillaux: Honor, Masculinity, and the Duel in France of the Belle Epoque." *Proceedings of the Western Society for French History*. New Orleans, 1990.

Bierce, Ambrose. *The Devil's Dictionary*. New York, 1991.

Billacois, François. *Le Duel dans la société française des XVIe–XVIIe siècles: Essai de psychologie historique*. Paris, 1986.

Binding, Dr. Karl. *Die Ehre. Der Zweikampf*. Leipzig, 1909.

Blackbourn, David. *Populists and Patricians: Essays in Modern German History*. London, 1987.

Blackbourn, David, and Geoff Eley. *The Peculiarities of German History: Bourgeois Society and Politics in Nineteenth-Century Germany*. Oxford, 1984.

Blackbourn, David, and Richard Evans, eds. *The German Bourgeoisie: Essays on the Social History of the German Middle Class from the Late Eighteenth to the Early Twentieth Century*. London, 1991.

Boguslawski, Albert von. *Die Ehre und das Duell*. Berlin, 1896.

Bolgar, Franz von. *Die Regeln des Duells*. Vienna, 1891.

Bracher, Karl Dietrich. *The German Dictatorship*. New York, 1970.

Breslauer [Rechtsanwalt]. *Duellstrafen: Materialien gesammelt von Breslauer*. Berlin, 1890.

Brunschwig, Henri. *Enlightenment and Romanticism in Eighteenth-Century Prussia*. Trans. Frank Jellinek. Chicago, 1974.

Buchheim, Hans, et al. *Anatomy of the SS State*. Trans. Richard Barry, Marian Jackson, Dorothy Long. New York, 1968.

Bullock, Alan. *Hitler: A Study in Tyranny*. New York, 1971.

Bumke, Joachim, *The Concept of Knighthood in the Middle Ages*. Trans. W.T.H. and Erika Jackson. New York, 1982.

Chatauvillard, Comte de. *Essai sur le Duel*. Paris, 1836.

———. *Duell-Codex*, translated from the French with notations by C.v.L. Karlsruhe, 1888.

Clausewitz, Carl von. *On War*. Ed. Anatol Rapoport. New York, 1968.

Colombey, Emile. *Histoire Anecdotique du Duel*. Paris, 1861.

Coudenhove, Heinrich Graf. *Der Minotaur der „Ehre": Studie zur Antiduellbewegung und Duell-lüge*. Berlin, 1902.

Craig, Gordon. *From Bismarck to Adenauer: Aspects of German Statecraft*. New York, 1965.

———. *Germany, 1866–1914*. New York, 1978.

Croabbon, A. *Le Science du point d'honneur: Commentaire raisonné sur l'offense*. Paris, 1894.

Cysarz, Herbert. "Vom Diesseits und Jenseits der Ehre." *Dichtung und Volkstum* 2, 1942.

Czernin, Rudolf Graf. *Die Duellfrage*. Vienna, 1904.

Dahrendorf, Ralf. *Society and Democracy in Germany*. New York, 1967.

d'Almbert, Alfred. *Physiologie du duel*. Brussels, 1853.

Dangelmaier, Dr. Emil. *Der Kampf um die Ehre*. Vienna, Leipzig, 1896.

Deák, István. "Latter Day Knights: Officer's Honor and Duelling in the Austro-Hungarian Army." *Österreichische Osthefte* 28 (1986).

————. *Beyond Nationalism: A Social and Political History of the Habsburg Officer Corps, 1848–1918.* Oxford, 1990.

Delbrück, Hans. "Politische Korrespondenz." *Preussische Jahrbücher* 84, May 1896.

Demeter, Karl. *Das Deutsche Offizierkorps in Gesellschaft und Staat, 1650–1945.* Frankfurt am Main, 1962.

Dewitz, Hauptmann Ernst von. *Der Zweikampf: Vortrag gehalten am 1.Dezember 1880.* Berlin, 1892.

Dicks, Henry V. *Licensed Mass Murder: A Socio-Psychological Study of Some SS Killers.* New York, 1972.

Dijkstra, Bram. *Idols of Perversity: Fantasies of Feminine Evil in Fin-de-Siècle Culture.* New York, 1986.

Dönhoff, Marion Gräfin. *Kindheit in Ostpreussen.* Berlin, 1990.

Don Alfonso von Bourbon und Österreich-Este. *Kurzgefasste Geschichte der Bildung und Entwicklung der Ligen wider den Zweikampf und zum Schutze der Ehre in den verschiedenen Ländern Europas vom Ende November 1900 bis 7. Februar 1908.* Vienna, 1909.

Doyle, Sir Arthur Conan. *The Complete Sherlock Holmes.* Garden City, New York: 1930.

Duverger de St. Thomas, Comte de. *Nouveau Code du Duel.* Paris, 1887.

Eis, Egon. *Duell.* Munich, 1971.

Evans, Richard J. *Rethinking German History: Nineteenth-Century Germany and the Origins of the Third Reich.* London, 1987.

Fazy, Georges. *Le Duel.* Geneva, 1871.

Flaubert, Gustave. *L'Education Sentimentale.* Paris, 1985.

Fogel, Gerald I., Frederick M. Lane, and Robert S. Liebert, eds. *The Psychology of Men: New Psychoanalytic Perspectives.* New York, 1986.

Fontane, Theodor. *Cécile.* Munich, 1969.

————. *Effie Briest.* Berlin, 1984.

Frevert, Ute. "Bürgerlichkeit und Ehre: Zur Geschichte des Duells in England und Deutschland." *Bürgertum im 19. Jahrhundert: Deutschland im europäischen Vergleich,* vol. 3. Ed. Jürgen Kocka. Munich, 1988.

————. "Die Ehre der Bürger im Spiegel ihrer Duelle: Ansichten des 19. Jahrhunderts." *Historische Zeitschrift* 249, 1989.

————. *Ehrenmänner: Das Duell in der bürgerlichen Gesellschaft.* Munich, 1991.

Fürich, W. von. "Das Duell kritisch beleuchtet." *Frankfurter Zeitgemässe Broschuren,* vol. 7. Ed. Dr. Paul von Haffner. Frankfurt am Main, 1886.

Geyer, Michael. "The Stigma of Violence. Nationalism and War in Twentieth-Century Germany." *German Studies Review: Special Issue—German Identity* 15, no. 4, Winter 1992.

Gies, Frances. *The Knight in History.* New York, 1984.

Girouard, Mark. *The Return to Camelot: Chivalry and the English Gentleman.* New Haven, 1981.

Goethe, Johann Wolfgang von. *Faust.* Stuttgart, 1986.

Goffmann, Erving. *Interaction Rituals: Essays in Face to Face Behavior.* Chicago, 1967.

Greenberg, Joel. "Honor Thy Sister." *The Jerusalem Post Magazine,* 3 January 1992.

Guttandin, Friedhelm. *Das Paradoxe Schicksal der Ehre: Zum Wandel der adligen Ehre und zur Bedeutung von Duell und Ehre für den monarchischen Zentralstaat.* Berlin, 1993.

Haider, Franz. *Die Ehre als menschliches Problem.* Munich, 1972.

Harding, David, ed. *Weapons.* London, 1980.

Hartmann, Eduard von. *Moderne Probleme.* Leipzig, 1886.

———. *Tagesfragen.* Leipzig, 1896.

Harvey, Charles T. *Shooting Muzzle-Loading Hand Guns.* N.p., 1949.

Hell, Hans. *Das Duell: ein Problem.* Berlin, 1904.

Hergsell, Gustav. *Duell-Codex.* Vienna, Pest, Leipzig, 1891.

Hoerner, Herbert. *Die letzte Kugel.* Stuttgart, 1939.

Hohenzollern, Friedrich Wilhelm IV. *Allerhöchste Verordnungen über die Ehren-gerichte und über das Verfahren bei Untersuchungen der zwischen Offizieren vorfallenden Streitigkeiten und Beleidigungen, sowie über die Bestrafung des Zweikampfes unter Offizieren.* Berlin, 1843.

Höhne, Heinz. *The Order of the Death's Head: The Story of Hitler's SS.* Trans. Richard Barry. New York, 1970.

Holt, Edgar. *The Life of Georges Clemenceau, 1841–1929.* London, 1976.

Horowitz, Helen Lefkowitz. *Campus Life: Undergraduate Culture from the End of the Eighteenth Century to the Present.* New York, 1987.

Hughes, Steven. "Honor in Modern Italy and the *Codice Cavalleresco* of Iacopo Gelli." Paper prepared for the American Historical Association Annual Meeting, San Francisco, 6–9 January 1994.

Huhle, Henner, and Helma Brunck. *500 Jahre Fechtmeister in Deutschland: Ältester privilegierter Berufsstand.* Frankfurt am Main, 1987.

Hull, Isabel V. *The Entourage of Kaiser Wilhelm II, 1888–1918.* Cambridge, 1982.

James, Henry. *The American.* New American Library, 1980.

Jarausch, Konrad H. *Deutsche Studenten, 1800–1970.* Frankfurt am Main, 1912.

Jerome, Jerome K. *Three Men on the Bummel.* Leipzig, 1900.

Jeudon, L. *Le Morale de l'honneur.* Paris, 1911.

Kaufmann, Walter, ed. and trans. *The Portable Nietzsche.* New York, 1968.

Keyserling, Hermann Graf. *Erörterungen über das Duell nebst einem Vorschlage.* Dorpat, 1883.

Kiernan, V. G. *The Duel in European History: Honour and Reign of the Aristocracy.* Oxford, 1988.

Kitchen, Martin. *The German Officer Corps.* Oxford, 1968.

Kocka, Jürgen, ed. *Bürger und Bürgerlichkeit im 19. Jahrhundert.* Göttingen, 1987.

———, ed. *Bürgertum im 19. Jahrhundert: Deutschland im europäischen Vergleich,* vol. 1. Munich, 1988.

———, ed. *Bildungsbürgertum im 19. Jahrhundert,* pt. 4. Stuttgart, 1989.

Koehl, Robert. "Feudal Aspects of National Socialism." *The American Political Science Review* 54, no. 4, December 1960.

———. *The Black Corps.* Madison, 1983.

Kohut, Dr. Adolph. *Das Buch berühmter Duelle.* Berlin, 1888.

Krafft, Major von. *Dienst und Leben des jungen Infanterie-Offiziers: Ein Lern- und Lesebuch.* Berlin, 1914.

Krause, Peter. *"O du alte schöne Burschenherrlichkeit": Die Studenten und ihr Brauchtum.* Graz, Vienna, Cologne, 1979.

Lacaze, Pierre. *En Garde: du duel à l'escrime.* Paris, 1991.

Landry, Stuart O. *Duelling in Old New Orleans.* New Orleans, 1950.

Langewiesche, Dieter, ed. *Liberalismus im 19. Jahrhundert: Deutschland im europäischen Vergleich.* Göttingen, 1988.

Lea, Henry Charles. *The Duel and the Oath.* Philadelphia, 1974.

LeTainturier-Fradin, Gabriel. *Le Duel à travers les Ages, Histoires et Législation, Duels Célèbres—Code du Duel.* Nice, 1890.

Liepmann, Dr. M. *Duell und Ehre.* Berlin, 1904.

Luft, David. "Schopenhauer, Austria, and the Generation of 1905." *Journal of Central European History*, March 1982.

Lugs, Jaroslav. *Handfeuerwaffen.* German Democratic Republic, 1976.

Mann, Heinrich. *Der Untertan.* Berlin, 1964.

Mann, Thomas. *Der Zauberberg.* Frankfurt am Main, 1952.

Manvell, Roger, and Heinrich Fraenkel. *Himmler.* New York, 1965.

Marks, Erich. *Bismarcks Jugend.* Berlin, 1915.

Marshall, Tyler. "Saying 'NO' to Nazis in Germany," in *Los Angeles Times*, 5 December 1992.

Maupassant, Guy de. *Contes et Nouvelles.* Paris, 1957.

———. *Boule de suif, La Maison Tellier.* Paris, 1973.

———. *Oeuvres Complètes.* Paris, 1973.

Mayer, Arno J. *The Persistence of the Old Regime: Europe to the Great War.* New York, 1981.

Mayreder, Rosa. *A Survey of the Woman Problem.* New York, 1913.

Meinecke, Friedrich. *Erlebtes, 1862–1901.* Leipzig, 1941.

Meyers, Jeffrey. "The Duel in Fiction." *The North Dakota Quarterly* 51, no. 4, 1983.

Millingen, J. G. *The History of Duelling,* vol. I. London, 1841.

Millington, Barry. *Wagner.* New York, 1984.

Mitchell, Timothy. *Blood Sport: A Social History of Spanish Bullfighting.* Philadelphia, 1991.

Müller, Heinrich. *Gewehre, Pistolen, Revolver.* Leipzig, 1978.

Nietzsche, Friedrich. *Also Sprach Zarathustra: Ein Buch für Alle und Keinen.* Stockholm, 1948.

Nitobe, Inazo. *Bushido: The Warrior's Code.* Santa Clarita, Calif.: 1979.

Nye, Robert A. "Dueling and Republican Manhood in the Third Republic." Unpublished paper, 1989.

———. "Fencing, the Duel and Republican Manhood in the Third Republic." *Journal of Contemporary History* 25, 1990.

———. *Masculinity and Male Codes of Honor in Modern France.* Oxford, 1993.

Oettingen, Alexander von. *Zur Duellfrage.* Dorpat, 1889.

Ostwald, Dr. Wilhelm. *Die zwei Seelen in unserer Brust.* Leipzig, 1908.

Öthalom, Albert von. *Ehre und Ehrenschutz.* Vienna, Leipzig, 1908.

Pachter, Henry M. *Modern Germany: A Social, Cultural, and Political History.* Boulder, Colo.: 1978.

Padfield, Peter. *Himmler.* New York, 1990.

Paulsen, Friedrich. *System der Ethik*. Berlin, 1889.

Peristiany, J. G., ed. *Honour and Shame: The Values of Mediterranean Society*. Chicago, 1966.

Pilbeam, Pamela M. *The Middle Classes in Europe, 1789–1914: France, Germany, Italy, and Russia*. Chicago, 1990.

Prokowsky, Dieter. *Die Geschichte der Duellbekämpfung*. Bonn, 1965.

Pushkin, Alexander. *Erzählungen*. Dessau, 1954.

———. *Eugene Onegin*. Trans. Walter Arndt. New York, 1963.

Raabe, Wilhelm. *Sämtliche Werke*, Series 1. Leipzig, 1925.

Reder, Dr. A. *Der Zweikampf im Deutschen Reichstag, 1896*. Munich, 1896.

Ristow, Gustav. *Ehrenkodex*. Vienna, 1909.

Roberts, Adrian Clive. "Arthur Schnitzler as a Pacifist Writer: The Critique of War and Militarism in Selected Works." Unpublished Ph.D. dissertation, University of California at San Diego: 1986.

Rohte, Carl. *Das Zweikampfdelikt in den geltenden Strafgesetzen der Staaten Europas*. Leipzig, 1908.

Rosenberg, Hans. *Bureaucracy, Aristocracy and Autocracy: The Prussian Experience, 1660–1815*. Cambridge, Mass: 1958.

Rudorff, Raymond. *Knights and the Age of Chivalry*. New York, 1974.

Rumschöttel, Hermann. *Das bayerische Offizierkorps, 1866–1914*. Munich, 1972.

Rüts, Carl von. *Die Duellgegnerschaft*. Berlin, 1903.

Sabine, Lorenzo. *Notes on Duels and Duelling*. Boston, 1855.

Salvisberg, Dr. Paul von. *Das Duell und die Academische Jugend*. Munich, 1896.

Schnitzler, Arthur. *Die Theaterstücke von Arthur Schnitzler*, vol. 1. Berlin, 1912.

———. *Erzählende Schriften von Arthur Schnitzler*, vol. 1. Berlin, 1916.

———. *Reigen und andere Dramen: Das Dramatische Werk*, vol. 2. Frankfurt am Main, 1962.

———. *My Youth in Vienna*. Trans. Catherine Hutter. New York, 1970.

———. *Ritterlichkeit*. Ed. Rena R. Schlein. Bonn, 1975.

———. *Traumnovelle und andere Erzählungen: Das erzählerische Werk*, vol. 6. Frankfurt am Main, 1979.

Schopenhauer, Arthur. *Essays and Aphorisms*. Ed. and trans. R. J. Hollingdale. Middlesex, England: 1970.

Schorske, Carl. *Fin-de-Siècle Vienna*. New York, 1981.

Schramm, Dr. Hugo. *Ein Pereat den Duellen*. Leipzig, 1869.

Schwartz, Warren F., Keith Baxter, and David Ryan. "The Duel: Can These Gentlemen be Acting Efficiently?" *The Journal of Legal Studies* 13, 1984.

Seiffert, Hans Werner, and Christel Laufer. "Fontane's *Effi Briest* und Spielhagen's *Zum Zeitvertreib*: Zeugnisse und Materialien." *Studien zur neueren deutschen Literatur*. Ed. Hans Werner Seiffert. East Berlin, 1964.

Siemann, Wolfram. *Gesellschaft im Aufbruch: Deutschland 1849–1871*. Frankfurt am Main, 1990.

The Simon and Schuster Book of Opera. New York, 1978.

Simplicissimus. Der Student: Kulturbilder aus dem Simplicissimus, vol. 1. Albert Langen Verlag, 1905.

Simpson, Antony E. "Dandelions on the Field of Honor: Dueling, the Middle Classes, and the Law in Nineteenth-Century England." *Criminal Justice History* 9, 1988.

Solzhenitsyn, Alexander. *The Gulag Archipelago*. New York, 1973.

Spitzemberg, Hildegard Baronin. From her diary, *Am Hof Hohenzollern*. Ed. Rudolf Vierhaus. N.p., 1965.

Spohn, Clemens von. *Beurteilung der verschiedensten Ehrenfragen, die zu Ehrenhändeln und Ehrengerichten Anlass geben*. Berlin, 1911.

Staël, Madame de. *De L'Allemagne*, vol. 1. Paris, 1958.

Steinberg, Jonathan. "The Kaiser's Navy and German Society." *Past and Present* 28, July 1964.

Steinmetz. *The Romance of Duelling in All Times and Countries*. London, 1868.

Stern, Fritz, *The Politics of Cultural Despair: A Study in the Rise of Germanic Ideology*. Berkeley, 1961.

———. *Gold and Iron: Bismarck, Bleichröder, and the Building of the German Empire*. New York, 1977.

Stevens, W. O. *Pistols at Ten Paces*. N.p., n.d.

Stolberg-Wernigerode, Otto Graf zu. *Die Unentschiedene Generation*. Munich, Vienna, 1968.

Swartz, Marc J. "Shame, Culture, and Status among the Swahili of Mombasa." *Ethos* 16, no. 1, March 1988.

Tarde, Gabriel. *Etudes pénales et social*, pt. 1. Paris, 1892.

Tavernier Adolph. *L'Art du duel*. Paris, 1885.

Thesing, E. *Duell—Ehre—„Ernst"*. Marburg, 1896.

Thimm, Carl, ed. *A Complete Bibliography of Fencing and Duelling*. London, 1896.

Thümmel, Conrad. *Der gerichtliche Zweikampf und das heutige Duell*. Hamburg, 1887.

Treitschke, Heinrich von. *Deutsche Geschichte im Neunzehnten Jahrhundert*, vol. 5. Berlin, 1894.

———. *Politik: Vorlesungen gehalten an der Universität zu Berlin*, vol. 1. Leipzig, 1918.

———. *Aufsätze, Reden und Briefe*, vol. 1. Ed. Dr. Karl Martin Schiller. Meersburg, 1929.

Trench, Charles. *A History of Marksmanship*. Great Britain, 1972.

Trilling, Lionel. *The Liberal Imagination*. New York, 1978.

Truman, Major Ben C. *The Field of Honor: Being a Complete and Comprehensive History of Duelling in all Countries*. New York, 1884.

Tuchman, Barbara. *The Proud Tower: A Portrait of the World Before the War, 1890–1914*. New York, 1966.

Twain, Mark. *A Tramp Abroad*. New York, 1879.

Universal: Chronik unserer Zeit. Frankfurt am Main, 1832.

Vagts, Alfred. *A History of Militarism*. New York, 1959.

Von einem älteren aktiven Offizier, *Die conventionellen Gebräuche beim Zweikampf, unter besonderer Berücksichtigung des Offizierstandes*. Berlin, 1890.

Von einem Corpsstudenten. *Verfolgte Unschuld?* Erlangen, 1896.

Von einem Praktiker. *Unser Ehren- und Waffen-Comment*. Thorn, 1893.

Vorberg, Axel. *Der Zweikampf in Frankreich*. Leipzig, 1899.

Wallechinsky, David. *The Complete Book of the Olympics*. Boston, 1991.

Webb, James R. "Pistols for Two . . . Coffee for One." *American Heritage* 26, no. 2, February 1975.

Weber, R.G.S. *The German Student Corps in the Third Reich*. London, 1986.

Wehler, Hans-Ulrich. *The German Empire, 1871–1918*. Dover, N.H.: 1985.

Wiesinger, Albert. *Das Duell vor dem Richterstuhle der Religion, der Moral, des Rechtes und der Geschichte*. Graz, 1895.

Wild-Queisner, Robert. *Das Duell: Ein Wort zur Beleuchtung desselben nach Ursprung, Form, Zweck und Nothwendigkeit für den Civil- und Militairstand*. Berlin, 1887.

Woeltz, Richard A. "Sport, Culture, and Society in Late Imperial and Weimar Germany: Some Suggestions for Future Research." *Journal of Sport History* 4, 1977.

Wolf, Jürgen, ed. *Materialien: Heinrich Mann, „Der Untertan."* Stuttgart, 1979.

Wyatt-Brown, B. *Southern Honor: Ethics and Behavior in the Old South*. Oxford, 1982.

Ziegler, Herbert. *Nazi Germany's New Aristocracy: The SS Leadership, 1925–1939*. Princeton, 1989.

Ziegler, Prof. Theobald. *Der deutsche Student*. Berlin, Leipzig, 1912.

———. *Über Universitäten und Universitätsstudium*. Berlin, Leipzig, 1912.

Index